SHIPWRECKS
AT DEATH'S DOOR

SCHOONER MYSTIC WRECK, PILOT ISLAND, WIS.

...Between Washington Island and the tip of the southern peninsula lies the passage named Death Door.... Perhaps a better explanation of the grim name might be found in the disasters which have overtaken mariners since the advent of the first white explorers.... the minds of modern dwellers of this region are filled with tales of shipwreck and disasters which the passing years have witnessed in the waters around Death Door...."

--from the book, *Lake Michigan* (1944), by Milo Quaife.

SHIPWRECKS
AT
DEATH'S DOOR

CRIS KOHL

AND

JOAN FORSBERG

SHIPWRECKS AT DEATH'S DOOR

ISBN-13: 978-0-9679976-8-1

ISBN-10: 0-9679976-8-2

LIBRARY OF CONGRESS CONTROL NUMBER: 2006931673

Published by
SEAWOLF COMMUNICATIONS, INC.
P.O. BOX 66
WEST CHICAGO, IL 60186
USA

Photo credits are shown in terms of the author's source for the photograph rather than a specific photographer who might have taken it, except where the photographer is known and specifically named. Photographs © photographers as indicated (excluding Cris Kohl and Joan Forsberg). Artwork © artists as indicated. Text, maps, drawings and photos by Cris Kohl and/or Joan Forsberg are all © Seawolf Communications, Inc.

Printed in China

FIRST EDITION

10 09 08 07 06   5 4 3 2 1

FRONT COVER ARTWORK: *The Cana Island lighthouse keeper and his assistant rush to the rescue of the crew from the burning ship,* FRANK O'CONNOR, *on October 2, 1919. Read this story on pages 201-218.* SPECIALLY COMMISSIONED OIL PAINTING CREATED BY ROBERT MCGREEVY. See www.mcgreevy.com for more art and information. BACKGROUND UNDERWATER PHOTO of the FRANK O'CONNOR taken by Cris Kohl.

HALF TITLE PAGE COLOR IMAGE: *Detail of a postcard (postmarked June 2, 1907) of the "Schooner* MYSTIC *Wreck, Pilot Island, Wis." at Death's Door Passage. The* MYSTIC *story appears on pages 91-92.* IMAGE COURTESY OF THE DOOR COUNTY HISTORICAL MUSEUM.

FULL TITLE PAGE BLACK-AND-WHITE BACKGROUND PHOTO: *When the two-masted schooner,* OTTER, *stranded in a storm near Death's Door in 1895, the Lifesaving Crew worked hard to try to save the lives of the crew. Turn to pages 157-159 to read this tale.* IMAGE COURTESY OF THE DOOR COUNTY MARITIME MUSEUM AND LIGHTHOUSE PRESERVATION SOCIETY, INC.

BACK COVER IMAGES: Top row: *Lake Michigan map highlighting the Death's Door area* BY CRIS KOHL. *Horseshoe Bay was unkind to the schooner,* IVER LAWSON, *which ended up being photogenically stranded there in 1905 (see pages 169-172).* COURTESY OF THE DOOR COUNTY MARITIME MUSEUM AND LIGHTHOUSE PRESERVATION SOCIETY, INC.. Middle row: *The schooner,* JAMES E. GILMORE, *became a total wreck after stranding at Pilot Island in late 1892 (story on pages 84-91).* COURTESY OF THE DOOR COUNTY HISTORICAL MUSEUM. *Joan Forsberg explores the bowsprit area of the scow-schooner,* OCEAN WAVE, *in 105 feet of water near Death's Door (story on pages 99-110).* PHOTO BY CRIS KOHL. Lower left photo: *Maritime historians Cris Kohl and Joan Forsberg.*

INTRODUCTION

We, like many other people, flee to Door County, a peninsula in northeastern Wisconsin (which includes Death's Door) for escape. And we do it as often as possible. This region is mostly maritime and rural in nature. Its northern European connections and ethnicity also appeal to us, undoubtedly because of our own Teutonic-Scandinavian backgrounds. Living in bustling Chicago, the largest city on the Great Lakes, offers certain appealing characteristics and advantages for us, but a relaxing serenity and a strong appreciation of maritime history are not among them.

Great Lakes maritime history, though exciting and dramatic, is underappreciated or, like the lakes themselves, taken for granted, irresponsibly overlooked or outrightly forgotten. Waterways, once a natural highway providing ready transportation for people and goods, are now viewed as impediments in our mad rush to travel from Point A to Point B in as straight a line and as short a time as possible. This frustration with our inland seas has subconsciously led to a disregard verging on disrespect for the fact that our Great Lakes lands and cities were settled because of the Great Lakes, not in spite of them. Chicago and every Great Lakes town and city exists because of these waterways and ships. Yet today, we are too frantically caught up with life in the fast lane -- interstates, airlines, casinos, internet, television, all sensationalized -- to see that world. We have moved too fast to take Great Lakes maritime history, carved into the granite of the past as it is, along with us. We try to make up for this by "oohing" over Tall Ships when they fleetingly visit.

With this book, we are attempting to help remedy this situation in our own small way. Local historians, artists, writers and long-time residents decry the evolving face and character of Door County -- with seemingly endless changes springing up along waterfronts where quaint harbors once stood -- but hopefully that simple, old-fashioned element which many generations of visitors found so appealing will prevail and will not, as has happened in many parts of the Florida Keys in the past 30 years, disappear forever. Our Great Lakes maritime history is very important and it should be neither ignored nor forgotten. It has been with us for a long time. But tired, too-oft-told nautical tales can be re-researched and rendered in a freshly modern way, just as old sailors' saloons have been revitalized into a new generation of watering holes which are just as popular today as the old establishments were yesterday (30 years from now, these new patrons will be bemoaning all the changes!)

We visit Door County for relaxation in a quaint, maritime setting -- and to explore its exciting shipwrecks! The Death's Door area, inescapable as it is from all the water around it, fortunately touts its maritime heritage proudly. We have tried to gather all the thousands of scattered pieces of information about this area's maritime history, organize them, and present them in a user-friendly format. We hope this book is a positive addition to the landscape of that region's maritime history.

Cris Kohl and Joan Forsberg
High Lake, Illinois
Summer, 2006

ACKNOWLEDGEMENTS

As with everything in life, the writing of a non-fiction book, specifically the compilation of its many facts, becomes easier with assistance. In these troubled economic times, when museums and archives are experiencing financial challenges, several fountainheads of affordable source information fortunately still flow. We owe credit to many.

The authors' sincere *Thank You's* go out to the following individuals and organizations (with their staffs), arranged alphabetically:

Great Lakes maritime historian Henry N. Barkhausen, scuba diver/historian Jim Baye, underwater photographer *par excellence* Kim Brungraber, scuba diver/historian Gary Cihlar, Great Lakes maritime artist Jim Clary, charter boat captain Kathy Engebose, Todd Frisoni of the Door County Ice Cream Factory with the Blossom Family Collection in Sister Bay, WI, Michigan state historian Dr. John Halsey, Lansing, MI, library expert Lara Hernandez Corkrey of West Chicago, IL, Gary Jubin of Titletown Jet Center, Green Bay, WI, Chuck Larsen of Green Bay Scuba, Great Lakes maritime artist Robert McGreevy, Kevin J. O'Connor of Tonawanda, NY, and other members of the remarkable O'Connor family, Chicago researcher Howard Openlander, Great Lakes maritime artist Charles Peterson, researcher/wreck hunter/scuba diver Steve Radovan, Shoreline Charters operator/diver Jim Robinson, the late maritime historian Herman Runge, lighthouse archivist/photographer Wayne Sapulski, Jim and Pat Stayer for sharing their computer expertise and other generous assistance, maritime historian/author/researcher/scuba diver Jon Paul Van Harpen, scuba diver Randy Wallender, and the late maritime historian Dr. Richard Wright, for his ongoing inspiration.

The Center for Archival Collections of Bowling Green State University (OH) (especially the former Institute for Great Lakes Research, which is now one of its components), and in particular Robert Graham and his assistants; the Chicago Public Library; the *Door County Advocate* newspaper, Sturgeon Bay, WI; the Door County Historical Museum (particularly Ann Jinkins and Maggie Weir, the former of whom opened as-yet-unsorted archival treasures to the authors), Sturgeon Bay, WI; the Door County Maritime Museum (especially archivist June Larsen), Sturgeon Bay, WI; the Door County Public Library at Sturgeon Bay, WI, (particularly Nancy Emery), and its branch at Baileys Harbor; the Great Lakes Historical Society, Vermilion, OH; the Great Lakes Marine Collection of the Milwaukee Public Library/Wisconsin Marine Historical Society; the Michigan State Historical Library in Lansing, MI; the National Archives, Great Lakes branch, Chicago (Glen Longacre in particular); the Neptune's Nimrods (the oldest, and perhaps the most active, scuba dive club in Wisconsin); the Historical Society of the Tonawandas, Tonawanda, New York (the resourceful Ned Schimminger in particular); and the main library at Northern Illinois University (NIU) in DeKalb, IL.

Our apologies to anyone we may have inadvertently overlooked.

CONTENTS

DEDICATION:

TO ALL OF THE CHRONICLERS OF

DEATH'S DOOR'S MARITIME HISTORY, ESPECIALLY

THE DOOR COUNTY ADVOCATE,

HJALMAR R. HOLAND,

ARTHUR C. & LUCY F. FREDERICKSON,

WALTER M. & MARY K. HIRTHE,

PAUL J. CREVIERE, JR.,

AND JON PAUL VAN HARPEN

THE MARITIME HISTORY OF DEATH'S DOOR

An understanding of shipwrecks begins with some background nautical knowledge. What far too many people in the Great Lakes are forgetting (indeed, if they ever learned it to begin with in this amnesic modern era) is that nearly every community, great and small, along the freshwater seas -- Chicago, Toronto, Milwaukee, Detroit, Cleveland, Toledo, Buffalo, Duluth, Sault Ste. Marie, Thunder Bay, Oswego, Port Huron, Sarnia, Alpena, Muskegon, Marquette, Munising, Manitowoc, St. Joseph and scores of others -- owes its start and development to ships.

Not roadways. Not railways. Not aircraft. Ships.

In the case of the region which encompasses all of the connecting waterways between Lake Michigan and Green Bay, there exists a rich fabric of maritime history with several interwoven strands: early exploration and harbors, early shipbuilding, lighthouses, lifesaving stations, the Sturgeon Bay Ship Canal, ferries, maritime commerce, modern shipbuilding, and maritime recreation. We will take a brief look at each of these categories.

Early Exploration and Harbors

Long before the first Native Americans arrived in the Death's Door area, forces of nature sculpted the region. The predominant feature is the rocky escarpment which forms the western arm of the horseshoe-

The geological "horseshoe" called the Niagara Escarpment extends from Niagara Falls to Chicago, including Death's Door

This detail of an early French map showing the Death's Door region was printed in 1670. CRIS KOHL COLLECTION

shaped Niagara Escarpment, a unique geological feature left behind when the last Ice Age, which formed the Great Lakes, ended a mere 12,000 years ago. Lake Michigan and Lake Huron are unique in that these similarly-sized bodies of fresh water are the only two of the five Great Lakes which share the same elevation above sea level. Each also has a large bay attached to it, but separated by the Niagara Escarpment: Green Bay is connected to Lake Michigan, and Georgian Bay to Lake Huron.

The Door Peninsula, 80 miles long and 25 miles wide at its base tapering northward to a point, forms the main land mass separating Green Bay from Lake Michigan. A dozen islands form a broken barrier between the Door Peninsula mainland and the upper peninsula of Michigan mainland.

The first Native Americans arrived at the Death's Door area about 11,500 years ago, eventually forming several different tribes, the best known of which are probably the opposing Pottawatamis and Winnebagos. One of their legends relates the story of how Death's Door received its foreboding name. One warring tribe was on the peninsula mainland, the other, on Washington Island. Planning a violent attack, one huge group of several hundred warriors paddled canoes towards their foes.When they reached the middle of the six-mile crossing, a sudden and very violent storm upset most of the canoes, drowning many (estimates range from 100 to over 600 in the truly tall tale versions) of their occupants. Since that time, believed to have taken place in the early 1600's, Native Americans referred to that water passage as "the door of death." French explorers in the mid-1600's translated it into "Porte des Morts," a name which, although it did not appear on maps until about 1840, is still used on navigation charts today. Door County received its name from this "Death's Door" appellation.

French explorers and fur traders regularly visited the Death's Door area from the 1630's onward. By 1670, the Jesuits had established a mission near Green Bay to convert the Native Americans to Christianity. Much archaeological evidence of the French presence in the 1680-1700 era has been found on Rock Island and is exhibited there at Viking Hall.

The most famous of the French visitors to this region was the intrepid explorer, Robert Cavelier de La Salle, who arrived in his vessel, the *Griffon*, the very first sailing ship ever built on the upper Great Lakes. La Salle sent

10

Above: *This scenic cliff on the north side of Rock Island near Death's Door is part of the geologic formation called the Niagara Escarpment, an Ice Age scar which, beginning near Niagara Falls, runs northwest, generally in the shape of a horseshoe, across Manitoulin Island, then west through the Straits of Mackinac and finally southward again into Wisconsin before gradually disappearing near Chicago.* PHOTO BY CRIS KOHL

Below: *During the heyday of sailing ships (1860's to 1880's), Death's Door Passage between Lake Michigan and Green Bay was often crowded.*
ART ("AT DEATH'S DOOR") BY, AND COURTESY OF, CHARLES PETERSON.
CONTACT: C. L. PETERSON STUDIO, BOX 81, EPHRAIM, WI 54211, TEL.: 920-854-4033

the fur-laden *Griffon* back to Niagara with a very small crew of only six men, and the ship tragically went missing on this return leg of its maiden voyage, establishing the oldest and greatest mystery of the Great Lakes. See chapter 2 for more information about the *Griffon*.

The British defeated the French in the Seven Years' War (1756-1763), thus acquiring all French lands on mainland North America, and a troop-carrying schooner named the *Edward Augustus*, under Capt. Balfour, sailed into the mouth of the Fox River and first raised the British ensign at Green Bay on October 12, 1761, near the end of that conflict.

However, these Northwest lands passed into the control of the new country called the United States of America after its successful revolution against the British in the 1770's and 1780's.

After the War of 1812, the final conflict between Britain and the United States, the U.S. flag finally flew securely at Green Bay (then still called Fort Howard, with its population of approximately 250) on July 16, 1816, after the U.S. schooners, *Washington* (under Capt. Grignow), *Mink* (under Capt. Labord), and *Hunter* (under Capt. Chappeau) arrived there. On their way, a storm drove these ships into a harbor on an island near the mouth of Green Bay, where they stayed for four days until fair weather returned. They named that place Washington Harbor, after the largest schooner in their small fleet. It has kept that name for nearly 200 years.

The first steamship to visit the Death's Door area was the famous paddlewheeler, *Walk-in-the-Water*. Built in 1818 on Lake Erie, this ship visited Mackinac in 1819, thus becoming the first vessel to slice through Lake Huron's waters by mechanical means, and Green Bay in August, 1820, extending its claim to fame to become the first steamship on Lake Michigan.

Most of the area's Native Americans, fleeing advancing colonists, migrated west across the Mississippi River by the late 1830's. Early white fur-traders and fishermen lived in scattered, secluded areas of Death's Door by the 1830's; one story is told of two commercial fishermen living on Detroit Island who were attacked by local Indians and driven away in 1834. In 1836, a small fishing community was established on Rock Island (which had previously been called Pottawatamie Island, Pou Island, Louse Island and Kean's Island). Wisconsin's first lighthouse was established on Rock Island that same year, after Congress approved an act establishing the Territory of Wisconsin (statehood came 12 years later, in 1848).

The first town in the area, however, was established in the late 1840's because of a ship. Capt. Justice Bailey's schooner pitched severely in a Lake Michigan storm in 1848, compelling him to seek some sort of a shelter along the inhospitable and largely unknown western shoreline north of Milwaukee harbor. On board, he carried a "cargo" of immigrants from

Door County signs reflect the importance of nautical transportation in this area's rapid development. **Above:** *Baileys Harbor's signs depict the ship which started this community.* **Right:** *Ephraim's signs reflect the importance of its harbor and ships.* **Below:** *Two sailors' taverns near Death's Door offer maritime atmosphere.* PHOTOS BY CRIS KOHL

Buffalo hoping to reach Milwaukee. With the storm worsening and his cargo panicking, Bailey spied an inlet breaking the wild shoreline. Risking many lives and his ship, he gambled on sailing into this uncharted refuge, and breathed easier upon dropping anchor safely, protected from the howling winds. He stayed here several days waiting out the storm, and during this time, he curiously rowed ashore and studied the resources available there. Reaching Milwaukee several days later, he revealed to his employer the presence of this harbor of safety, as well as its timber-studded and limestone-rimmed shoreline. A colony settled there in 1849, establishing the first village site in Door County. The county's first pier was constructed there in 1849.

A pier was a wonderful device which provided the springboard between the only means of transportation and settlement in the region at that time. A pier was necessary to access the practical loading and unloading of a ship's cargo. Most schooners required six to twelve feet of water in order to stay afloat, meaning that usually they could not get closer to shore than a few hundred feet. Without a pier, cargo had to be moved to or from that ship by means of a small rowboat, a painstakingly slow process. Once a pier was constructed, a village quickly grew up around it. Along the shorelines near Death's Door, a pier was mandatory for the establishment of any community.

Close to the time that Baileys Harbor was set up as a village, a pier and a small community called the Irish Village sprang up on the west side of Washington Harbor on Washington Island. By 1899, 500 people, predominantly of Scandinavian descent, lived on the island. Washington Island today claims to have the largest Icelandic population in the USA.

Horseshoe Island in Green Bay has been described as having the finest natural harbor anywhere on Lake Michigan, and for that reason, a pier was constructed here in 1850. It quickly became an ideal refueling stop for steamers, but the island is small, and by 1853, it had run out of wood, and the hopes for a permanent settlement died.

Rowleys Bay was first settled in 1850, and its port and pier specialized in the shipping of cedar.

Hedgehog Harbor was founded in 1856. Fisherman George Lovejoy had wintered his small, home-built sloop there, but the following spring, found the water too low to launch. Even worse, hedgehogs, more commonly known as porcupines, had gnawed holes in his hull. Hence the early name of this bay. It eventually became a lumbering and fishing port renamed Gills Rock (after lumberman Elias Gill) in the early 1870's.

In 1853, a pier was constructed at the fishing community (and former Indian village) called Fish Creek, opening its door to the lumber trade.

The town of Ephraim was founded in 1853 by the Norwegian Reverend Andreas Iverson and his Moravian followers who hoped to make it a true utopian society. Neighboring communities sometimes referred to the religious-minded and tavernless community as "God's little pocket." Limestone quarry production in the late 1800's helped spur its economy.

The year 1855 saw the first pier built at Egg Harbor when lumber shipping began there. This community received its unique name either from a) the large number of duck eggs found there by Increase Claflin, a pioneer who settled at nearby Fish Creek in 1844, or b) from a reputed 1825 egg fight which took place between crewmembers and picnickers who stopped there on a boating trip from Green Bay.

In the late 1850's and throughout the 1860's, Chambers Island was active in lumbering and shipbuilding.

The first pier at Jacksonport was built in 1858. The town received its name in 1868, honoring one of its founding businessmen. Its three piers saw much traffic throughout the late 1800's.

The lively community of Little Sturgeon Bay served as the county seat in the 1860's and 1870's, thriving on the shipbuilding, lumber, lime and ice industries. However, two events negatively impacted the community during the 1870's: the disastrous October, 1871, fire which destroyed most of the town, and the construction and success of the Sturgeon Bay Ship Canal which established a safe connection between Lake Michigan and Green Bay. Gradually Little Sturgeon Bay's commerce was siphoned off by Sturgeon Bay, which also eventually usurped the title of county seat.

The town of Sturgeon Bay officially received that name in 1860, forever relinquishing its earlier names of Otumba, Graham and Tehema. Menominee Native Americans actually gave the region the Sturgeon Bay name because they saw the bay as being shaped like the head of a sturgeon fish. The construction and increasing usage of the Sturgeon Bay Ship Canal in the late 1870's and early 1880's molded the town into an important port, a position which it has held for over 125 years and which it holds to this day.

In 1866, John Eliason built a pier at what was to become Ellison Bay (an error by an immigration clerk had changed "Eliason" to "Ellison").

Sister Bay, gradually settled by Europeans, mostly Norwegians, from 1857 to 1868 and named after the Sister Islands lying just offshore, built its first pier in 1869 and quickly established itself as a lumber shipping point.

A lumbering community called Newport, just northeast of Rowleys Bay, built its first pier in 1879, but was a ghost town 20 years later.

North Bay, busy as a port in the 1880's and 1890's, never realized its ambitious dream of becoming a major business center.

St. Martin Island, in the 1830's, attracted roving fishing families, mainly from the Mackinac region, because of its excellent fishing grounds. At first, these families island-hopped depending upon where the best fishing appeared to be each season, but eventually, many settled here permanently. Coopers became busy on the island building barrels. A dock was constructed, and schooners stopped to trade necessities of life (such as flour, salt, sugar, tea, coffee, pork and cooking utensils) for barrels of salted fish which they, in turn, transported to large centers such as Milwaukee and Chicago. The era of greatest growth for St. Martin Island occurred between 1860 and 1880. A community called Sac Bay developed on the southwest side of the island. The 1870 census showed 102 people living on the island, but that number fluctuated with the fishing season. Big lake trout -- and reports indicate that 60 and 70 pounders were caught -- were used by the islanders for special Thanksgiving meals in place of turkeys. In 1883, 150 people used St. Martin Island as their base during fishing season, but only 10 families lived there year-round. The island's school, which had seen 60 students at a time in the 1860's, taught only 15 by 1883. In April, 1883, the wealthy Chicago fish dealer, A. Booth, purchased two-thirds of the island, built a pier on the northeast side, and bought almost every fish caught in northern Lake Michigan. However, by the late 1880's, fish had become less plentiful, and the island families began moving to the mainland. By 1890, most of the residents were gone, and by 1900, the homes stood vacant, the school was silent, the docks were boatless and the forest began covering the cemetery and trails. Although almost completely owned by private parties, the island has no permanent human residents.

Summer Island, in the summer of 1848, had eight families living on it, all involved in commercial fishing. These were roving families, residing here only in the summer to take advantage of the nearby fishing grounds. For many, Summer Island became their favorite summer home, and for that reason, the island received that name.

Poverty Island was given its name by the first people who explored its small, rocky, generally inhospitable surface -- they concluded that whoever settled there would be destined for a life of poverty. Its name and daunting physical features kept away permanent settlers.

Reportedly there were more than 60 piers along the 256-mile-long shoreline of Door County by the early 1880's, providing the means of loading the many workhorse schooners with cargoes of lumber (planking, posts, shingles, railroad ties and cordwood), fish, grain, limestone and ice.

Before there were any roads, people relied upon ships to provide for most of their transportation needs. Ships required one main venue: water, and the more of it, the better. Fortunately, this region was blessed with the natural, fluid highway of water which included Lake Michigan and Green Bay. Unfortunately, the connecting waterways included Death's Door.

Early Shipbuilding

The Death's Door region consists of islands and peninsulas, which, by their natures, have considerable water around, or nearly around, them. It comes as no surprise that water conveyances were constructed with vigor.

Reportedly the first person to build a ship larger than a small fishing craft in the Death's Door area was a Rock Island settler named George Lovejoy. He constructed an unnamed freighting vessel in about 1850.

In the late 1850's the Laurie brothers, Robert and Alexander, built several schooners named the *Peninsula,* the *Belle Laurie* and the *Katie Laurie.*

Probably the most colorful early shipbuilder was Capt. David Clow, who had settled on Chambers Island in 1850. He constructed a number of schooners, among them the *Pocahontas* and the 120-foot-long, 285-ton *Sarah Clow,* the latter of which, when it was built in 1862, was the largest ship ever launched in Door County. Surprisingly, the *Sarah Clow* was constructed by only two people -- Capt. David Clow and his wife Sarah. This strong woman could pull and push on a whip-saw as well as any man, and together, the husband-and-wife team felled many of the oak trees on Chambers Island, whipped them into boards and planks, and used wooden "trunnels" (treenails) as fasteners because the iron ones were too expensive. Not satisfied to rest on past laurels, Clow built the 155-foot-long schooner *Lewis Day* in 1868, then one of the largest ships on the Great Lakes.

Several fine, early vessels were constructed at the community named Little Sturgeon Bay. Chicago business magnate F. B. Gardner owned, among other companies, a large sawmill there, and after the Civil War, he hired Thomas Spear, an expert ship carpenter from Maine. With about 200 men, Gardner and Spear (along with Spear's two sons, George and Marshall) built a number of fine ships between 1866 and 1874. These sturdy vessels included the steam tug, *John Spry* (92' x 15' x 5', built in 1866), and the schooners *James G. Blaine* (177' x 33'7" x 12'8", launched as the 579-ton bark *Pensaukee* in 1867, the first large vessel built in Little Sturgeon Bay), the 332-ton *Lake Forest* (146'7" x 29' x 11'1", launched in 1869), the three-masted, 496-ton *Halsted* (171'1" x 33'4" x 12'4", launched in 1873), the large, 545-ton *Ellen Spry* (172'9" x 33' x 13'1", built in 1873), and the largest of them all, the massive, 617-ton *J. W. Doane* (183'6" x 33'3" x 13'6", launched in 1874).

Freeland Berring Gardner (1817-1883) had established a lumber yard in Chicago in 1851, and he had a company ship, a brig which he named the *F. B. Gardner* (138'7" x 31'6" x 11'7" when launched), built in Sheboygan, Wisconsin, in 1855. At his shipyard in Little Sturgeon Bay in 1866, Gardner had this vessel lenghened by 40 feet and converted into a bark. Already old by the time its namesake died in 1883, the *F. B. Gardner* outlived him by

Two of the fine ships which were built at Little Sturgeon Bay before Sturgeon Bay gained shipbuilding dominance: **Above,** *The 177-foot-long schooner,* Pensaukee, *later renamed the* James G. Blaine, *constructed in 1867, stranded and broke up at Oswego, New York, on July 8, 1908.* **Below,** *The 146-foot-long schooner,* Lake Forest, *built in 1869 and abandoned in about 1910 due to age and condition.* Cris Kohl Collection

Large black-and-white prints of "Bird's Eye View" renditions of America's towns were very popular in the latter half of the 19th century. The town of Sturgeon Bay was honored, not once, but twice, with such detailed art, the first time in 1880 (above) and the second occasion in 1893 (below). Besides a slight increase in the size of the community, the 1893 print shows landmarks which did not yet exist in 1880, notably the first railroad bridge across the bay and the Dunlap Reef Lights. Shipping traffic in both scenes appears to be brisk. Sturgeon Bay grew dramatically in maritime importance with the construction of the Sturgeon Bay Ship Canal in the 1870's. CRIS KOHL COLLECTION

August Rieboldt (1849-1921) and Joseph Wolter (1857-1929; mayor of Sturgeon Bay, 1904-1912) (above, Cris Kohl Collection) in 1896 moved their shipbuilding business, which they had started in 1885, from Sheboygan to Sturgeon Bay, built a drydock and employed 200 men mainly in the repair of wooden ships. The firm of Rieboldt & Wolter also constructed many fine, new vessels at its Sturgeon Bay shipyard (below, Door County Maritime Museum and Lighthouse Restoration Society, Inc.) These included the passenger steamer J. Bonner (83'3" x 19'5" x 5'2", launched in 1901, renamed Bath City in 1914, and abandoned in 1922 in Lake Superior), tug Peter Reiss (76' x 22' x 11', built in 1906, dismantled in 1934), and in 1918 the unusual, experimental, and unsuccessful 250-foot-long wooden steamer named the Sturgeon Bay (which sank outside Cleveland in 1934 and was dynamited). Rieboldt and Wolter Shipbuilding Corp. became the Universal Shipyard, which, in 1926, was succeeded by the Sturgeon Bay Shipbuilding and Drydock Co.

more than two decades, burning and sinking a few miles off Port Sanilac, Michigan, on Lake Huron, on September 15, 1904. This sturdy ship was then nearly 50 years old!

Several other wooden ships were rebuilt at Little Sturgeon Bay, but the community's "Golden Age" began to tarnish in 1871, when the destructive fires which plagued the Great Lakes in October took their toll upon this town. Once repaired, Little Sturgeon Bay was knocked down a second time when a fire in 1877 burned down the sawmill, compelling Gardner to close his shipyard. The perimeter of Green Bay had also run out of timber. Lastly, the effects of the construction and the opening of the Sturgeon Bay Ship Canal hammered the final nails into that town's coffin, but paved the way for Sturgeon Bay's golden future.

Serious shipbuilding at Sturgeon Bay began after the success of the canal in the early 1880's inundated the town and harbor with maritime traffic. Symbolic of the changing times, the Spear family shipbuilders of Little Sturgeon Bay moved their talents to Sturgeon Bay, and to take advantage of the new canal's needs, they constructed mainly tugboats. This was, however, but the vanguard of much greater shipbuilding activity.

Many ships were launched at Sturgeon Bay in the late 1800's, including the unrigged barge, MIKE DOHERTY, which was pulled down this simple ramp in 1899. This vessel sank in 1919 after loading at Cedar River, Michigan, and was deemed not worth salvaging.
DOOR COUNTY MARITIME MUSEUM AND LIGHTHOUSE RESTORATION SOCIETY, INC.

Lighthouses

It is a highly-publicized statement that Door County, Wisconsin, has more lighthouses than any other county in the United States. Add the two on Michigan islands which also separate Lake Michigan from Green Bay and the total is twelve lighthouses which stand in the area of Death's Door.

Why were so many lighthouses constructed in this small area? Its geography -- many miles of curving and indented rocky shoreline, dozens of islands and shoals, narrow passageways from one body of water to another -- lends itself easily to the creation of shipwrecks. So lighthouses were constructed at strategic locations designed to warn the sailor, especially at night, of encroaching danger in hopes that the navigator could avoid them.

The very first lighthouse in the state of Wisconsin was constructed on a bluff on the northwest corner of Rock Island in 1836, 12 years before Wisconsin actually attained official statehood. The **Pottawatomi Lighthouse** could be seen by the vast majority of ships sailing between the city of Green Bay and eastern Great Lakes ports. Completely rebuilt in 1858 due to crumbling construction, the light was automated in the early 1980's and was restored in the 1990's-early 2000's. In 1858, a nine-sided cast-iron lantern and a 4th Order Fresnel lens replaced the original 11 oil lamps and 11 parabolic reflectors. It is a one-mile hike from the ferry landing to the lighthouse.

The first **Plum Island Lighthouse** was built in 1848 and was known as the Porte des Morts Lighthouse. Perhaps the same person who so poorly built the lighthouse at Rock Island constructed this one; by 1857, this lighthouse was in such serious disrepair that in 1858, its equipment was dismantled and transported to nearby "Port du Mort Island" (renamed Pilot Island in 1875) and used there in the newly constructed lighthouse. Reportedly the old man who acted as the first Plum Island Lighthouse keeper more often than not drank the alcohol which was delivered to him for lighting purposes, and, when inebriated, boasted of piracy and other wild, unconventional behaviour. The ruins of this old lighthouse lie overgrown in the interior of Plum Island.

Milwaukee businessman Alanson Sweet, who owned the ship which Capt. Justice Bailey had sailed in 1848 into the protected bay which became Baileys Harbor, invested heavily in establishing this community. Seeing a future in the timber and building stone resources of the area, Sweet persuaded the federal government to erect a lighthouse. In 1851, they built the **Baileys Harbor Lighthouse** on a small island at the harbor entrance, the first such structure to serve a harbor community in Door County. This old lighthouse, replaced by the Baileys Harbor Range Lights in 1869, serves as a secluded, private residence today.

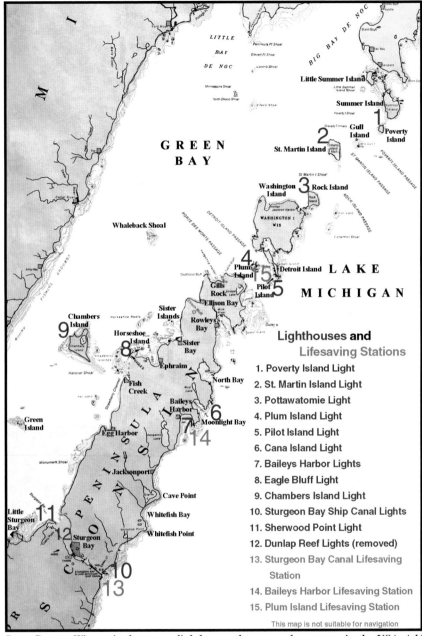

Door County, Wisconsin, has more lighthouses than any other county in the USA. Add the two lighthouses in Michigan at the map's northern part, and one can see the extent and influence of maritime activity in the area where Lake Michigan meets Green Bay. Of the three original Lifesaving Stations, the Baileys Harbor one combined with the one on Plum Island to run seasonally out of Washington Island, with the main Coast Guard station still operating year-round at the Sturgeon Bay Ship Canal. MAP BY CRIS KOHL

23

The **Pilot Island Lighthouse**, built in 1858 and furnished with the first Plum Island Lighthouse's equipment, probably led the most colorful existence of all the lighthouses in this area because of the many shipwrecks and near-shipwrecks which occurred at this tiny (3.7 acres) spot. From 1858 until 1897, a significant transitional time period when sailing ships declined while steam-powered vessels increased, the Pilot Island Lighthouse was the only aid to navigation for mariners heading through Death's Door. For some people who stayed at this remote, isolated island, the profound solitude felt like a prison, but for others, it was a welcomed taste of heaven on earth. The lighthouse was automated in 1962.

Eagle Bluff Lighthouse, located in Peninsula State Park, became operational in the autumn of 1868, guiding ships as they navigated the Strawberry Channel in Green Bay. This lighthouse, automated since 1926 and now open to the public, has been restored and is maintained and managed by the Door County Historical Society.

The **Chambers Island Lighthouse,** built in 1868 at a cost of $9,000, sits on the northwest corner of the island, on 40 acres of land purchased from Lewis Williams, who became the first lighthouse keeper, serving in that position for 21 years. The distinctive brick light tower is square on the bottom half and octagonal in the top half.

The **Baileys Harbor Range Lights** were constructed of wood (compared to the brick or stone of nearly all the other lighthouses) in 1869 at a cost of only $6,000 to offer ships better guidance into the harbor. The front light was a wooden tower, while the rear light 950 feet away consisted of a light tower atop a one-and-a-half story light keeper's residence which more closely resembled an old schoolhouse than a lighthouse. The lights have been inactive since 1969, replaced by a steel light tower which stands nearby.

The famous **Cana Island Lighthouse**, with its 88-foot-tall tower, was built in 1869. By 1902, the tower's tan-colored bricks were deteriorating due to weather, particularly violent fall and winter storms, so the tower was encased in steel sheeting and painted white. The 3rd Order Fresnel lens has a range of 17 miles. The fully automated lighthouse has been restored and is operated as a museum by the Door County Maritime Museum and Lighthouse Preservation Society, Inc.

The **Poverty Island Lighthouse**, with its 75-foot-tall tower made of red bricks, was built in 1875. Since its automation in 1957, with no one living here to maintain the buildings, this remote site is in pitiful disrepair.

The **Dunlap Reef Lighthouse**, built in 1881, is covered on page 28.

The bright red **Sturgeon Bay North Pierhead Light**, constructed in 1881-1882, juts out into Lake Michigan from a breakwall at the entrance to the Sturgeon Bay Ship Canal.

Above: *The Pottawatomie Light, built on Rock Island's north shore between 1836 and 1838 from rock taken out of the island's famous cliff face, is the oldest lighthouse in Wisconsin.* PHOTO BY CRIS KOHL

Below: *Another early Death's Door region lighthouse, built in 1858, is the old light at Baileys Harbor, one of three in the country which had a "birdcage" style lantern perched at the top. Today this inactive lighthouse, which is located on a small island in the harbor, is a private, rather secluded residence, and another light marks a safe water passage into Baileys Harbor.* PHOTO BY CRIS KOHL

This early photo shows the Cana Island lighthouse in 1883, 14 years after it was built. Located on an island which receives the full force of almost every lake storm, the light tower was encased in protective steel sheets in 1902. A low, gravel causeway, built during World War One, connects the island to the mainland.

NATIONAL ARCHIVES PHOTO

The **Sherwood Point Lighthouse** was built in 1883 at a cost of $12,000. Its 4th Order Fresnel lens has a range of 15 miles. Fully automated for its centennial in 1983, this was the last manned lighthouse on the U.S. side of the Great Lakes. Today, the Coast Guard maintains this light and leases this property as a private residence.

Built during the final five months of 1896 at a cost of $21,000, the **Plum Island Range Lights** consist of a 4th Order Fresnel lens in the rear light, and a 6th Order Fresnel lens in the front light. These lights were automated in 1969 by a commercial cable running underwater from Northport to Plum Island, a distance of 8,750 feet (or 1.5 miles).

Situated on the mainland at the Lake Michigan entrance to the Ship Canal, the **Sturgeon Bay Ship Canal Lighthouse** was built in 1898-1899 at a cost of $20,000. The tower height of 98 feet and the 3rd Order Fresnel lens gives this light a range of 17 miles. The Coast Guard now maintains and operates both lights at the entrance to the Ship Canal.

The site for the **St. Martin Island Lighthouse** was purchased by the federal government from the Booth Packing Company on November 10, 1899. The six-sided, 85-foot-tall, kerosene lamp light tower and its fog signal were established on April 15, 1905. With time, a brick living quarters building, a generator room and a wood garage were constructed. The light was automated in 1980.

The annual Door County Lighthouse Walk is usually held on the third weekend in May, offering visits to nearly every lighthouse and a number of boat tours of Door County waters and lights. This is organized by the Door County Maritime Museum and Lighthouse Restoration Society, Inc.

Above: *Today, the Cana Island lighthouse is open from May to October as a museum, part of the Door County Maritime Museum and Lighthouse Preservation Society, Inc. Many a ship has been saved by this light.*

Below, left: *Eagle Bluff Lighthouse, constructed in 1868, is located in Peninsula State Park, between Ephraim and Fish Creek. The anchor on display is from the* OAK LEAF.

Below, right: *The Sturgeon Bay North Pierhead Light, built originally in 1882, was part of the protective breakwall system at the Sturgeon Bay Ship Canal.* PHOTOS BY CRIS KOHL

Dunlap Reef Lights

The Lighthouse Which Isn't There Any More

In the center of Sturgeon Bay, a 700-foot-long rocky spine of limestone shoal, called Dunlap Reef, lies submerged just barely below the water's surface parallel to the shipping channel, posing a serious navigational hazard to ships plying these waters. When the Sturgeon Bay Ship Canal opened and shipping traffic in the bay increased dramatically, more and more strandings occurred.

Constructed in 1881, the Dunlap Reef Range Light consisted of an actual wooden lighthouse, nearly perfectly square at 23 feet by 25 feet, sitting on a stone-filled timber crib foundation. Attached to the back was a large boathouse. The front range light, 707 feet ahead of the lighthouse, was little more than a shed topped by a lantern which the lighthouse keeper had to keep fueled.

Modern improvements in the channel and to beacons caused the lighthouse to be deactivated in 1924. In 1925, the lighthouse structure was sold, minus its beacon tower containing the lantern house and its plate-glass windows, to Ruben Dickenson, who carefully dismantled the house, moved all the materials to 411 South 4th Avenue in Sturgeon Bay, and painstakingly reconstructed the building there, where it still stands, although remodelled, as a private residence today.

(Above: CRIS KOHL COLLECTION. Below: DOOR COUNTY HISTORICAL MUSEUM)

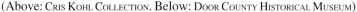

Above: *Sherwood Point, named after fur-trapper-turned-barrel-maker Peter Sherwood, who settled here in about 1850, is a narrow peninsula jutting into Green Bay about six miles west of the city of Sturgeon Bay. Built in 1883, this lighthouse was the very last manned lighthouse on the U.S. side of the Great Lakes, finally being automated in its centennial year, 1983. The red bricks came from the federal lighthouse depot in Detroit; other lighthouses near here were built of materials from Milwaukee. The pyramidal fog signal building was added in 1892.*

Right: *Sherwood Point Light-house keeper William Cochems, who held that position from 1895 to 1934, built this stone birdbath in memory of his loving wife, Minnie, who was his assistant lighthouse keeper from 1898 until she died suddenly of a heart attack in 1928.* PHOTOS BY CRIS KOHL

29

Above: *The Plum Island Range Lights replaced a lighthouse which had been cheaply built on the island in 1848, but which crumbled soon, so its equipment was dismantled and moved to Pilot Island in Death's Door Passage in 1858. The several ferry boats between Northport and Washington Island pass this lighthouse daily.* Photo by Cris Kohl

Below: *The St. Martin Island (Michigan) Light, just north of Death's Door, was established in 1905 to mark another of the lake-to-bay passages. The large house, fog signal building and oil storage building are all crumbling. By the time this lighthouse was constructed, most of the full-time residents of this once-impressively-populated island had moved to the mainland.* Photo by Cris Kohl

Lifesaving Stations

The idea of setting up Life-Saving Stations in shipwreck-prone areas became a reality in 1878 when the government organized volunteers in New England and established stations. The idea almost immediately took hold in the Great Lakes. Canada soon followed suit on its side of the freshwater seas and its other shorelines. Patrick Etheridge of the Cape Hatteras Life-Saving Station in North Carolina is credited with giving this organization of brave men who often risked their lives its unofficial motto:

> The Blue Book says we've got to go out and it doesn't say a damn thing about having to come back.

Initial expectations in the Death's Door region ran high:

> It is probable that life-saving stations will be established at Baileys Harbor and Washington Island next season.
> --*Chicago Inter Ocean*, May 15, 1882.

In 1878, the new U. S. Life-Saving Service purchased land at Baileys Harbor for a station. At that time, Baileys Harbor was the only indentation along this shoreline where a ship could find reliable refuge. With the opening of the Sturgeon Bay Ship Canal in 1882, attention turned to its protected entranceway, and a Life-Saving Station was built there in 1886. The one at Baileys Harbor had to wait until 1896, nearly 20 years after the land there was acquired. The Sturgeon Bay Canal Life-Saving Station (above), designed by government architect Albert Bibb, who created a number of Life-Saving Station plans, cost only $4,560 to build. The most distinctive features of the one-and-a-half-story station were its twin rescue boat bays, its walkway along the roof peak and its lookout cupola. A new Coast Guard station replaced this building long ago. Door County Historical Museum

Cork lifejackets, or vests, were standard equipment on ships and for Life-Saving crews, called "surfmen." Standing at the bow is Carl Anderson, the fourth keeper of the Sturgeon Bay Canal Life-Saving Station (see p. 158). He had started at that location as one of the original surfmen in 1886 and worked his way up. Keepers were retained year-round, but surfmen worked only during the navigation season. <small>DOOR COUNTY HISTORICAL MUSEUM</small>

Tuesdays were mandated as boat drill days for members of the Life-Saving Service (the Coast Guard after 1915). This 1919 photograph shows the surfmen at the Sturgeon Bay Canal Coast Guard Station purposely rolling their boat and righting it again. Reportedly some of these men became so skilled at this manoeuvre that they ended up on the overturned hull nearly dry. <small>DOOR COUNTY MARITIME MUSEUM AND LIGHTHOUSE PRESERVATION SOCIETY, INC.</small>

Launching the Life Boat.

Going off to a wreck.

Above: *Life-Saving crews sprang into action as quickly as firefighters.* CRIS KOHL COLLECTION. **Right:** *Another view of Life-Savers going to the rescue of a stranded crew.* CRIS KOHL COLLECTION. **Below:** *This zealous Coast Guard crew spent December 31 practicing rescue work at the Sturgeon Bay Ship Canal.* PHOTO BY CRIS KOHL

Of the three Life-Saving Stations eventually constructed in the Death's Door area, the first was set up at the eastern, or Lake Michigan, end of the Sturgeon Bay Ship Canal in 1886, four years after the canal officially opened. The huge volume of maritime traffic which this new canal created prompted the construction of this station.

The establishment of the second (Plum Island) and third stations (Baileys Harbor) took longer because of the existence of the one at the Sturgeon Bay Ship Canal. Originally planned as the first one for this area, the land for the Baileys Harbor Station was acquired in 1878, but the station, with its four-story lookout tower, was not constructed until many years later:

> Contractor Olson reports the Plum Island lifesaving station
> nearly completed, and the work on the station at Baileys Harbor
> well advanced. Both stations are to be ready November 1.
> --*Detroit Free Press*, September 16, 1895.

Contractor C. J. Olson of Marinette, Wisconsin, built the stations at Plum Island and Baileys Harbor using the same design for a total of $9,000.

In the twentieth century, the federal government streamlined its nautical services. In 1915, the Revenue Cutter Service, which was also known as the Revenue Marine (established in 1790) and the Life-Saving Service (begun in 1878) merged to form a military branch of the armed forces called the Coast Guard. In 1939, the Lighthouse Service (which had been formed in 1789) also merged into the Coast Guard. Two other government agencies, the Steamboat Inspection Service (established in 1852) and the Bureau of Navigation (which had been founded in 1884) had united in 1932, but in 1946, immediately after World War II, they combined with the Coast Guard.

The Coast Guard was part of the Department of the Treasury, but in 1967, it was transferred to the new Department of Transportation until 2003, when it became part of the new Department of Homeland Security.

From 1915, the Coast Guard operated the three Life-Saving Stations in the Death's Door area. The main station, operating year-round, has always been, and continues to be, the one at the Sturgeon Bay Ship Canal. Thanks to modern technology, that canal station can protect a much larger area than in the past. The Baileys Harbor Station saw less and less use, with all but two surfmen transferred to other stations in 1933. Finally, in 1948, that station was abandoned. The isolation at, and the continuing deterioration of, the Plum Island Station forced its abandonment in 1990, when the Coast Guard set up a seasonal station on Washington Island.

The brave men and women of the Life-Saving Service/Coast Guard have proven instrumental in saving many lives and much property in the Death's Door area for well over a century.

The Sturgeon Bay Ship Canal

Joseph Harris, Sr., founder of the area's first and major newspaper, the *Door County Advocate*, with its first issue appearing on March 22, 1862, was more proud of another achievement. In the early 1860's, he framed the legislation for a proposed Sturgeon Bay-to-Lake Michigan ship canal, which would not only save ships many hours of sailing time to reach Green Bay from the southern approach on Lake Michigan (and vice versa), but would also provide a route by which vessels would avoid the dangerous Death's Door Passage. For years, Harris raised funds and lobbied the state and federal governments for land grants to ensure the completion of this canal.

Between the lake and the bay, over a period of hundreds of years, Native Americans had worn a clear path which they used to portage their canoes.

The idea of constructing a canal to connect Green Bay with Lake Michigan at Sturgeon Bay had first been suggested by government surveyors in 1835. In 1856-1857, Green Bay lumber businessmen had a survey made of the old portage trail. The Wisconsin legislature granted a charter to build the canal, but a financial recession stalled the plans, and the charter expired.

Joseph Harris firmly believed that a canal was vital for the development of Sturgeon Bay as a commercial and maritime center. In 1861, he traveled to Washington, D.C. to request a federal land grant of 200,000 acres to finance the building of this canal. This land would include a segment through which the canal itself would be dug, as well as considerable land on both sides of it, but also land throughout the Door County-Green Bay area which would be sold to finance the canal's construction. The Senate approved his plan, but the House of Representatives rejected it by a two-vote margin.

Harris' regular use of his newspaper's editorial column kept the proposed canal project in the forefront of public attention. In 1864, Harris won election to the Wisconsin State Senate, where he rallied the state to support the canal. Through one of the ongoing editorials in the *Door County Advocate*, he wrote this on November 17, 1864, detailing the "Reasons Why Congress Should Grant Lands To Aid In Its [the canal's] Construction." Note the repeated references to shipwrecks at Death's Door:

> 1st. The proposed ship canal will shorten the voyages from Green Bay to Chicago on each round trip about two hundred miles, or one fifth of the entire distance.
>
> 2d. It will avoid the present dangerous channels through the Islands at the north end of the peninsula called "Porte du Mort," or "Death's Door," where many valuable vessels and their cargoes are annually lost.
>
> 3d. It will, by means of the breakwater, to be built on the Lake

shore, give to the entire shipping traversing Lake Michigan, a safe harbor on the west shore of the Lake, much needed at that point, enabling vessels, with the assistance of powerful steam tugs, to be constructed for that purpose, to run into Sturgeon Bay, proverbial for being the most commodious and the finest harbor on the upper Lakes, it being eight miles long, with an average width of more than one mile, and thus adding a new harbor on the Lake shore without Congress appropriating one dollar in money for constructing the same.

4th. The length of the proposed canal is one and a half miles, to be built not less than one hundred feet wide nor less than fifteen feet deep.

5th. The quantity of lumber that would annually pass through the canal is estimated at 150,000,000 feet.

6th. The quantity of cord wood, tan bark, staves, cedar posts, railroad ties, telegraph poles, shingles and shingle bolts annually passing through the canal, estimated in cord bulk, would be 50,000 cords.

7th. This immense quantity of freight is carried by about seventy to one hundred vessels, and would make over three thousand passages annually through the canal.

8th. The development of the Lake Superior region, now rapidly progressing, and the system of railroads now being constructed, designed to bring the mineral ores to Green Bay for shipment, will soon largely increase the number of vessels seeking an outlet from Green Bay into the Lake, and not only the present but the future enormous traffic of that region requires the opening of this new channel into the Lake as a link in the great chain of new routes and lines of communications demanded by the opening up of the inexhaustible lumber and mineral resources of northeastern Wisconsin and Lake Superior.

9th. The estimated cost of constructing the canal and breakwater is $500,000.

10th. The average number of vessels lost annually on the Islands, at the channel of "Death's Door," is estimated at ten, and the value of the same and their cargoes at $150,000.

11th. Many grain-laden vessels, on their passage from Chicago (and other grain ports) down the lake, are lost at "Death's Door," in trying to take shelter under the Islands in stormy weather.

12th. There is a strong current setting through "Death's Door," dangerous to vessels navigating it, many vessels having been lost in consequence thereof even in moderate weather, by being drifted onto the shores, which, being rock-bound, is certain destruction to the craft going ashore.

13th. The official map of survey made by the United States Government, a copy from which is now in the hands of the Committee on Public Lands, shows the location of Sturgeon Bay, with soundings, &c., and profile of the dividing ridge and of the point of rocks putting out into the Lake, on which is proposed to build the breakwater, (and the light-house for which Congress made an appropriation a few years ago, but which will be of no practical use on that part of the coast until the ship canal is completed.) The map of the survey, &c., shows the canal to be a perfectly feasible project.

14th. The Bill now before Congress provides that the donation of lands asked for shall be made to the State of Wisconsin; limits the time for the commencement and completion of the work, and embodies carefully guarded provisions to regulate the grant, and protect the public domain and treasury of the nation in the event of failure on the part of the State to complete the work.

15th. It is an important public work, involving but a small grant of public land to consummate a great public improvement, which, when completed, will be hailed with joy and satisfaction, not only by the great lumber interests of Green Bay, but by thousands of shippers, captains, seamen, and shipowners of the upper Lakes.

16th. To show more fully the dangerous navigation of the "Death's Door" channel, it is only necessary to state that within the last few years the Government has been under the necessity of removing the light-house from Plum Island to Pilot Island, and only last fall added to the present light house a "fog-horn," worked by caloric power, to warn vessels trying to make the passage. These wise precautions are commendable; but the true remedy is for Congress to give to the mariner, and the large and increasing interests concerned, a safe channel that looks as though Nature intended should at some day be made through the portage at Sturgeon Bay.

Harris' claim that an average of ten ships and their cargoes were lost each year at Death's Door was an exaggeration, one which he would certainly have been aware of from information printed in his own newspaper. But such political license in order to achieve a goal was commonplace.

In 1866, Harris returned to Washington, D. C., to lobby full-time for his canal project. This time he succeeded. The federal government first agreed to fund the surveys for the canal, and to pay for the work which was to be done at the eastern entrance of the canal, and the state dispensed a federal government grant of 200,000 acres of timberland, to be alloted one-quarter at a time after each quarter of the work was completed.

In 1870 and 1871, problems with the granted land, beyond politics, befell the canal project organizers. Trespassers illegally cut down vast tracts of timber and removed them. An estimated $75,000 worth of pine was cut and stolen during that time, prompting the *Door County Advocate* to write, "This drain upon the means to build the Canal must be stopped at once."

Two weeks later, the great Peshtigo Fire of October, 1871, destroyed much more timber from these canal grant lands. It was estimated that one-quarter of the 200,000 acres of timber lands granted by Congress for the canal project were "rendered worthless by the fires and by trespass." Fortunately, the remaining pine lands were deemed to be of sufficient value to cover the costs of constructing the canal.

The digging of the canal began on July 8, 1872. By the end of 1873, the first quarter of the project was deemed completed so that the first 50,000 acres of land became available to sell, raising revenues to finance the next quarter of the construction. Unfortunately, because of the depression of 1872, these 50,000 acres of land were not of much value. By 1874, sales had faltered, then stopped. The canal project languished for several years.

One good thing to come out of this delay was the engineering development of hydraulic, steam-powered, barge-mounted pumps, which reduced the cost of excavating one cubic yard of material from 33 cents to 20 cents, ultimately realizing a saving of over $100,000 on the canal's costs.

A harbor of refuge is a relatively protected body of water where vessels

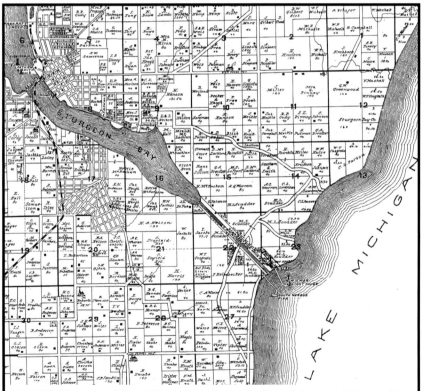

*The 1899 **Illustrated Atlas of Door County** clearly showed the straight lines of the Sturgeon Bay Ship Canal connecting open Lake Michigan with the protected waters of Sturgeon Bay.* COURTESY OF JON PAUL VAN HARPEN

The Canal, Stugeon Bay, Wis.

Above: *In this colorized postcard, circa 1907, an excursion steamer heads towards the open waters of Lake Michigan after having transited the Sturgeon Bay Ship Canal from Green Bay. The ship is likely one of the Goodrich excursion steamers.*

Below: *In the early 1900's, during the heyday of passenger excursion travel on the Great Lakes, large ships, most frequently of the Goodrich and Hart Lines, carrying hundreds of passengers from Chicago, Milwaukee and elsewhere, hopped from port to port in Green Bay. Sometimes these vessels would enter the canal after dark and offer their passengers a moonlight cruise into Sturgeon Bay.*

BOTH IMAGES: DOOR COUNTY MARITIME MUSEUM AND LIGHTHOUSE PRESERVATION SOCIETY, INC.

4572. MOONLIGHT AT CANAL ENTRANCE. STURGEON BAY. DOOR COUNTY. WISCONSIN.

could retreat and find shelter during bad storms. In anticipation of future use, a protective set of breakwalls had been built by the government by late 1875 at the point where the proposed canal would enter Lake Michigan.

When economic times improved, the project was resumed, but the economy in the 1870's wavered radically. In the spring of 1878, 9,000 acres of grant lands were offered for sale by the canal organizers to raise money for the continued dredging of the canal, but only 1,500 acres were sold, and those went for an average of only $3.50 an acre.

Work was speeded up so that a preliminary canal, usable by small commercial ships, was ready by the summer of 1878. On the afternoon of Saturday, June 29, 1878, between five and six o'clock, two dredges worked towards each other from opposite directions. Capt. George H. Sager, the canal superintendent, took a shovel and manually removed the final, small barrier of earth, allowing the two bodies of water to mingle. Capt. W. T. Casgrain, the canal engineer, and another man quickly jumped into a skiff and made their way through the narrow channel, becoming the first people to pass through the cut. The schooner, *Kate Laurie,* was the first sail vessel through the new canal -- on Saturday, July 6, 1878. In 1879, the first sizable ship passed through the canal. The steamer, *Welcome,* carried an excursion party to Ahnapee from Sturgeon Bay on Sunday, July 20, 1879.

The *Chicago Times*, in summarizing the completion of the Sturgeon Bay Ship Canal, reported in late November, 1881:

> ...Over 1,100,000 cubic yards of earth were excavated, about 100,000 cubic yards more than the estimated allowed for. The highest point was thirty-six feet above the level of Lake Michigan, but from one end to the other very little rock was encountered. The work was commenced in 1872, but the most of it has been done since 1877. It has cost first and last, including the revenue derived from the sale of three-fourths of the land-grant, money advanced by stockholders, and interest thereon, not far from $700,000. The Government, realizing the importance of the improvement, has spent about $125,000 in constructing a harbor at the eastern terminus of the canal, and building 1,600 feet of piers guarding the approaches. Other appropriations have been made for lighthouses at the entrance of the canal and on the promontory which marks the entrance to Sturgeon Bay from the west. The harbor was intended as a haven of refuge for vessels driven from the lake, but, the idea has been conceived of making a ship harbor of Sturgeon Bay. The owners of the canal will ask the Government to take it off their hands and pay them what it has cost, and make it free. They hold that it is a great public improvement, and that it should be exempt from tax. Under their

charter they are empowered to levy toll on all vessels passing through the ditch until the money used in its construction shall be made up. This is, in effect, a perpetual lease on the property. The income from the canal may pay a handsome interest on the capital invested, but the surplus, if there should be any, could be put into repairs and solid improvements. Plausible arguments are advanced to show why the canal should be made free, and to prove that it cannot be free until the Government buys it. It is probable that the Wisconsin delegation in Congress will heartily endorse the scheme.

Newspaper accounts in mid-December, 1881, gave the final report on the canal prepared by Capt. Nader, the Wisconsin State Engineer:

> ...the total number of vessels that passed through the canal in 1880, while it was yet in an unfinished condition, was 533.
>
> ...there is still the difficulty about canal tolls which would only be settled by an act of congress. It would, in my opinion, be for the interest of commerce if the United States should assume control of this important work as early as possible. No doubt it will have to come to this sooner or later and the sooner the better. This canal is destined to be a great commercial highway, and when once in the control of the general government, the tolls

The tug, GEORGE STONE, *towed several sailing ships at once through the Sturgeon Bay Ship Canal. Usage fees were unavoidable pre-1893, but group tows saved vessel masters some money.* DOOR COUNTY MARITIME MUSEUM AND LIGHTHOUSE PRESERVATION SOCIETY, INC.

can be removed from vessels seeking refuge and a suitable safe-harbor can be constructed at the head of Sturgeon Bay at a very moderate cost....

The number of vessels which passed through the new, unfinished canal during the 1881 season was 1,480, paying a total of $20,222.10 in tolls.

State officials accepted the Sturgeon Bay Canal as a safe route to Green Bay from Lake Michigan and declared it officially completed in early December, 1881. However, the canal was privately owned, a situation which allowed the owning company to charge a fee of each ship using the canal. That and the towing fee which needed to be paid to a tugboat for moving a sailing vessel through the canal sometimes brought the cost of using the Ship Canal so high that vessel captains decided to run the long way around through Death's Door Passage instead of parting with that much money.

After Capt. Nader's report, the final quarter of the land grant was patent-ed to the company which owned the canal. However, the federal government was slow to take the advice in the report, and it was another dozen years ("the sooner the better" notwithstanding) before it followed the recommend-ation and purchased the canal.

The company offered to sell the canal to the federal government for the sum of $187,000. The government countered with the fact that the company still had property from the land grant to sell. A compromise price was reached. As reported by the *Detroit Free Press* on April 4, 1892:

> Senator Vilas, of Missouri, has introduced a bill providing for an appropriation of $81,833 for the purchase of the Sturgeon Bay canal from the private corporation which has always controlled it. This purchase, if made, will exempt a large Lake Michigan vessel interest from the payment of burdensome tolls.

On December 9, 1892, the formal transfer of the Sturgeon Bay Ship Canal to the federal government took place.

Sturgeon Bay, which had been incorporated as a village in 1874, was granted a city charter in 1883, largely due to the increase in maritime traffic and its resulting expansion of commerce because of the new Ship Canal.

Ultimately Joseph Harris' son, grandson and great-grandson all served as editors of the *Door County Advocate*, but Harris himself always felt that his crowning achievement was the construction of the Ship Canal

The Joseph Harris, Sr. Memorial, located in Otumba Park in Sturgeon Bay, commemorates the man who is called "The Father of the Canal," honoring his numerous accomplishments, particularly his untiring work to steer the Sturgeon Bay-Lake Michigan Ship Canal project to completion.

Above: *And you thought that only Chicago wreaked havoc upon its natural waterways! The Sturgeon Bay Ship Canal, constructed between 1872 and 1881, converted the northern two-thirds of the Door Peninsula into a large island. The angled breakwaters reach out 1,000 feet into the lake. The 7,400-foot-long, 100-feet-wide canal has saved vessels a distance of 100 miles of travel, as well as avoiding the dangerous Death's Door Passage at the northern tip of the peninsula.* PHOTO BY CRIS KOHL

Below: *The Sturgeon Bay Ship Canal Coast Guard Station was originally built as a Life-Saving Station in 1886 at the Lake Michigan entrance to the canal, with a full-time keeper and seven seasonal crewmembers called "surfmen" residing there.* PHOTO BY CRIS KOHL

Above: *History comes to life when Tall Ships visit the Great Lakes and transit the Sturgeon Bay Ship Canal, evoking scenes of what it was like over 100 years ago.* PHOTO BY CRIS KOHL

Below: *A noble Tall Ship from the east coast, the* PRIDE OF BALTIMORE **II**, *passes the Coast Guard Station at the Lake Michigan entrance to the ship canal.* PHOTO BY CRIS KOHL

Above: *Built originally in 1882, the Sturgeon Bay Ship Canal North Pierhead Light deteriorated rapidly and was replaced in 1903 with this red structure.* Photo by Cris Kohl

Below: *Wisconsin's official Tall Ship, the three-masted Great Lakes schooner,* Dennis Sullivan, *from Milwaukee, glides gallantly out of the ship canal, about to pass the North Pierhead Light on its way into Lake Michigan's open waters.* Photo by Cris Kohl

Ferries

Ferry vessels filled a transportation need in the Death's Door area. Officially, the first ferry was chartered in 1859 at Sturgeon Bay, when the county board approved of one which crossed Sturgeon Bay. In 1860, E. S. Fuller operated two ferries there, one for passengers and another for teams of horses and wagons. These early Sturgeon Bay ferries were propelled by oars, with passengers being expected to help row. In the late 1860's, a rope was stretched across the bay and horses on both sides pulled the ferry back and forth. In the early 1870's, with an increase in traffic, the county board invited tenders for a steam-powered ferry. Robert Noble (see next page) was given a ten-year charter in 1873, and on board his self-built steamer, *Ark*, he charged 5¢ for each passenger and 20¢ for a team and wagon (about one-half of what the prices had been previously!) However, two enterprising lumbermen named John Leathem and Tom Smith built a toll bridge across the bay. It opened in 1887, instantly putting the ferry out of business.

The only other ferries in use in the Death's Door area have been the ships which actually cross the water passage called Death's Door from Gills Rock or Northport to Washington Island.

In the 1920's, automobile "touring" gradually replaced boat "excursioning." People were drawn to the freedom and thrills of exploring different parts of the country by self-driven autos on roads of varying and often questionable quality. The magnet of Washington Island during the initial years of the motor car's popularity, plus the residents' yearning for regularly scheduled mainland connections, compelled enterprising boatmen to establish a ferry to the island. In 1923, Capt. William Jepson's steamer, the *Wisconsin*, began carrying a maximum of four automobiles and 40 people across the waters of Death's Door. The vehicles were driven on board the ferry over thick, wooden planks temporarily placed on the railing. Once on board, the autos were lashed to the railing. In 1929, a larger steamer, the *Welcome*, capable of transporting ten autos and 100 passengers at once, went into service replacing the smaller vessel.

The ferry, however, would operate only when the passage was free of ice, and during cold winters, islanders, frustrated by isolation, risked driving their cars on the ice to the mainland. One such event turned disastrous. On March 9, 1935, five young men, returning to Washington Island from a basketball game at Ellison Bay in which they had participated, were offered a ride in a 1930 Model A Ford two-door sedan. The car broke through the ice and all six drowned. The bodies were recovered, four of them still inside the automobile. This tragedy hardened the determination of Arni Richter, the captain of the *Welcome* since 1931, to provide regular winter ferry service, which he started and continued for years with stronger, steel ships.

Capt. Robert Noble.
CRIS KOHL COLLECTION

The Iron Ferryman of Death's Door

The first ferry operator in the Door County area was an ambitious, strong-willed individual named Robert Noble who had tragically lost the ends of his fingers and his legs as a result of a dramatic fight for survival in Death's Door.

Robert Noble had spent the Christmas of 1863 with friends at Washington Island and decided to return to the mainland, about five miles away, in his small, flatbottomed skiff on December 31st. However, when he was abreast of Plum Island, the bitter cold and the ice stopped him. He came ashore, alone and with no food or shelter. He survived the night in the old lighthouse ruins, and decided to return to Washington Island on January 1, 1864 (the coldest day on record in several decades!) by walking across the ice. Several times he fell into the freezing water, but always managed to crawl out again. Finally he reached Detroit Island, but he failed to find any shelter until his third day of trekking through the wilderness. When he reached Detroit Harbor, a commercial fisherman took him in, but Robert Noble's hands and feet had become frostbitten. Immersing them in kerosene (a neighbor's suggestion) only made them worse. He remained at Detroit Harbor for the next five months, attempting to recuperate with no professional help. His rotting fingers fell off and pieces of his lower legs came off in putrid chunks. Finally, in June of 1864, Noble was taken by sailboat to his home in Sturgeon Bay. A visiting doctor from Kenosha operated on him with rough tools, removing both legs just below the knees. Later, artificial legs which he carved himself helped Noble go on with his life. He built a dock and a small sidewheel steamer which he named the *Ark*, and ferried people and goods across Sturgeon Bay. By the early 1880's, needing a larger boat, he and his business partner built the 74-foot-long steamer which they named the *Robert Noble*. Capt. Robert Noble told his story in a 1904 interview in the *Door County Advocate*. Unfortunately, he lived in destitution, dying in 1929 at age 92.

Right: *The steambarge* ROBERT NOBLE, *built by R. Noble and J. Johnston in 1883, and operated by them, carried passengers across Sturgeon Bay in her first years. Converted in 1887 to a freight carrier by new owners A. W. Lawrence and George C. Spear of Sturgeon Bay, the ship traveled between Green Bay ports. This vessel caught on fire and burned to a total loss just off Menominee, Michigan, on November 7, 1888.* CRIS KOHL COLLECTION

Above: *The passenger-and-auto ferry,* Washington, *crosses Death's Door Passage between Northport and Washington Island. Built by Peterson Builders of Sturgeon Bay in 1989, the 100-foot-long, 97-ton* Washington *uses her twin 500-horsepower Cummins engines to transport 22+ cars and 250 passengers. Two Gills Rock ferries, the* Yankee Clipper *(built in 1970) and the* Island Clipper *(1988) also service the island. On April 23, 2003, the newest and largest of the ferries, the 104-foot* Arni J. Richter, *with greater icebreaking capability, was launched by Bay Shipbuilding in Sturgeon Bay.*

Below: *When Death's Door Passage lies becalmed, the* Washington's *wheel is easily handled, even by a shipwreck diver.* Photos by Cris Kohl

Above: *Another of the Washington Island ferries is the 90-foot-long* ROBERT NOBLE, *named after an early ferryman (see page 47). Constructed by Peterson Builders of Sturgeon Bay in 1979, it can carry 20+ automobiles and 175 passengers. Since World War II, several increasingly larger ferries have been built to service this route: the 65-foot-long* GRIFFIN, *launched in 1946, could carry nine automobiles and 100 passengers, as could the C. G.* RICHTER, *built in 1950. The 1960* VOYAGEUR *could take 14 cars and 100 people, while the 1970, 87-foot* EYRARBAKKI *can handle 18 cars and 100 people.*　　PHOTO BY CRIS KOHL

Below: *The small passengers-only ferry named the* KARFI, *built in Escanaba in 1967, carries visitors between Washington Island and nearby Rock Island.* PHOTO BY CRIS KOHL

Maritime Commerce

From the first visit by French explorers in 1634, and for 200 years after that, the predominant interest in this area for the white man was the all-important fur trade. Declining fur quantities spurred the development of a new economic interest in the 1800's: commercial fishing

Commercial fishermen from Mackinac first moved west to the islands -- Rock, St. Martin, Summer and Little Summer -- in the 1830's, living on these islands seasonally while they wintered at a mainland location. Countless keels from their many small fishing boats ground upon the stone and sand beaches, or tied off to new piers, to bring ashore their catches for the salting process. This business became the main reason for the Michigan-Wisconsin boundary dispute of the 1920's and '30's. However, unlike the fur trade, the fishing industry continues to exist to this day in this region.

In the 1850's, the lumber milling and stone quarrying businesses began initially at Baileys Harbor (although layered Rock Island stone from its exposed northwest cliff face had been quarried specifically for the construction of the lighthouse there in 1836). The first sawmill at the town of Sturgeon Bay was built in 1853. Ships were vital for the transportation of the millions

A "Big Tow" on Sturgeon Bay. Prior to 1892 when the Sturgeon Bay Ship Canal was purchased by the federal government and made toll-free, canal and towing fees proved prohibitively costly for many vessel owners. To save money, several sailing ships would pool their finances to hire one powerful tow vessel. Two, three and four towed sailing vessels were common. People took notice when a tugboat had FIVE vessels in tow, as in the above photograph. The tug is the GEORGE NELSON, *and the barges, in towing order, are the* CHARLES E. WYMAN, *the* LYMAN M. DAVIS, *the* IVER LAWSON, *the* OSCAR NEWHOUSE, *and the* AUGUSTUS. *In particularly busy times, even SIX ships were towed by a single tug.*
DOOR COUNTY MARITIME MUSEUM AND LIGHTHOUSE RESTORATION SOCIETY, INC.

Above: *In 1893, a few miles west of the town of Sturgeon Bay, John Leathem and Thomas Smith established a limestone quarry which, at its peak, employed 100 men. The open face of this quarry can be seen today across the road from the waterfront park.*

Left: *The loading of tons of stone onto the company ships was slow and difficult work.*

Below: *Stone crushing mills were conveniently located at dockside where ships (in this case, the* HENNEPIN*) could be quickly loaded.*
ALL PHOTOS: DOOR COUNTY MARITIME MUSEUM AND LIGHTHOUSE RESTORATION SOCIETY, INC.

Above: *The famous "Christmas Tree" schooner,* ROUSE SIMMONS, *seen here on Sturgeon Bay in a rare photograph, often carried local lumber.* DOOR COUNTY HISTORICAL MUSEUM

Below: *Some schooners, like this one at Ephraim, showed holiday cheer with a Christmas tree attached atop their main mast.* ART ("JULE TIDEN") COURTESY OF ARTIST CHARLES PETERSON

141 EXCURSION STEAMER PASSING THROUGH THE CANAL AT STURGEON BAY, DOOR COUNTY, WISCONSIN

Above: *The steamer,* CAROLINA, *took many excursionists to various ports in the vicinity of Death's Door between March 28, 1906, when the Goodrich Line bought this 14-year-old ship to replace their burned steamer,* ATLANTA, *and May 10, 1933, when the* CAROLINA *was sold at public auction in Chicago and laid up at Sturgeon Bay for several years before finally being scrapped there in 1942.*   POSTCARD COURTESY OF THE JIM BAYE COLLECTION

Below: *Anderson's Dock in Ephraim always buzzed with activity when a ship arrived. The steamer,* BON AMI *(later renamed the* NORTH SHORE*), was one of several vessels which regularly carried passengers as well as freight to towns like Sturgeon Bay, Egg Harbor, Fish Creek and Ephraim.*   ART ("THE BON AMI AT ANDERSON DOCK") COURTESY OF ARTIST CHARLES PETERSON. CONTACT: **C. L. PETERSON STUDIO, BOX 81, EPHRAIM, WI 54211, TEL.: 920-854-4033**

Goodrich

lake Vacations

MACKINAC

CRUISE—*via* Green Bay

S. S. CAROLINA

Round Trip	
$33.00 Meals and Berth Included	A 3-day outing—along Wisconsin's Coast—in beautiful Green Bay—across the upper lake—through the straits to Mackinac. See historic Mackinac Island. See Sturgeon Bay, Fish Creek, Ephraim, Sister Bay, Washington Island, Escanaba.
$17.00 One Way	Lv. Chicago, Tuesday, 2 P.M. Back Friday, 4:30 P.M.

2 Green Bay Trips

Via Sturgeon Bay Ship Canal and Beautiful Green Bay

S. S. ARIZONA

Round Trip	
$24.50 Meals and Berth Included	Lv. Chicago, Monday, 2 P. M. Back Thursday, 4:30 P. M. Stopping at Milwaukee, Manitowoc, Sturgeon Bay, Fish Creek, Ephraim, Sister Bay, Washington Island.
	Lv. Chicago, Friday, 2 P. M. Back Monday, 7 A. M. Stops at Milwaukee, Manitowoc, Sturgeon Bay, Marinette and Menominee. **Tickets Sold to All Points.**

All schedules **Daylight Saving Time**
For vacation guides to Michigan and Wisconsin summer resorts, call, write, or phone Randolph 4076

Goodrich Transit Company
CITY OFFICE—104 SOUTH CLARK STREET
DOCK: SOUTH END MICHIGAN AVE. BRIDGE, CHICAGO

GOODRICH STEAMSHIP LINES

Left: *Chicago's Goodrich Line and Green Bay's Hart Line of passenger-and-freight-carrying ships were the two largest excursion operations effecting the beginning of tourism in the region around Death's Door in the late 1800's. This 1924 newspaper advertisement from the* Chicago Herald-Examiner *gave routes and prices of two vessels. The 245-foot-long, steel-hulled* Carolina, *which enjoyed the greatest popularity of all the excursion steamers servicing this area, was launched as the* Hartford *at Philadelphia in 1892, and came to the Great Lakes after running guns for Cuban rebels during the Spanish-American War. The 220-foot-long* Arizona, *built as the* City of Racine *in 1889, was abandoned at Toledo, Ohio, in 1938. Other Goodrich Line vessels cruising this area were the* Chicago, *the* Sheboygan, *the* Alabama *and the* Georgia. Cris Kohl Collection

Below: *The* Bon Ami *was one of the popular excursion vessels in the Hart Line which, along with the* Sailor Boy *and the* Thistle, *served the summer trade from 1906 to 1920 along both sides of Green Bay, including Sturgeon Bay, Marinette, Menominee and Escanaba.* Door County Maritime Museum and Lighthouse Preservation Society, Inc.

of board feet of milled lumber and thousands of tons of crushed stone which left the Death's Door area, carried to many destinations on Lake Michigan and beyond for use in docks, buildings and roads, as described in this article:

> There has been a large amount of stone shipped this season from Washington Island to Manistee, Mich., and other east shore ports, where it is used for harbor piers and building purposes. F. C. Reynolds & Co., Manistee, own a quarry on the island, and they have shipped over a thousand cords since last June. The stone is freighted on the barge *Milwaukee*, which carries seventy cords a trip, and makes a round run every two days. Wing & Morgan, also of Manistee, are shipping stone from the island. The shipping of stone from this peninsula will grow into a great industry before many years. The demand for this material is constantly increasing, and there is an inexhaustible supply in the big bluffs that line the shores in many places of Door County.
>
> --*Chicago Inter Ocean*, November 3, 1881.

Numerous stone quarries were operating near the town of Sturgeon Bay in the early 1900's, and the Leathem and Smith quarry at the mouth of the bay was destined to become the largest stone-crushing operation in Wisconsin. But fish, lumber and stone were not the only commerce.

Maritime tourism, a branch of the resort trade, began slowly after the Civil War, reaching its golden age between 1890 and 1920. The Goodrich Company's (1855-1930) fleet of ships commenced operations in 1855, but no vessels ventured to ports near Death's Door until the year after the Civil War ended. Within two decades, the Goodrich ships had taken so many visitors to Door County harbor towns that a Chicago newspaper in 1888 wrote:

> A more delightful and enchanting place for the pleasure seeker, or those wanting a short respite from business, cannot be found than the points on Green Bay touched by the Goodrich Line. It is not only the paradise of the fashionable world but the angler's mecca of inexhaustible resources, the huntsman's bonanza, the invalid's acme of sanitary perfection; in short the complete utopia of the tourist and pleasure seeker.

Other popular excursion steamer companies were the Hart Line (1878-1920), which operated ships such as the *Welcome*, the *C. W. Moore*, the *Fannie C. Hart*, the *Eugene C. Hart*, the *Harriet A. Hart*, the *Sailor Boy*, the *Thistle* and the *Bon Ami*, and the Hill Steamboat Line (1886-1926), which ran the steamers *Eva M. Hill*, the *Cecilia Hill*, the *Flora M. Hill*, the *Maywood* and the *City of Marquette*.

A combination of the convenience of the automobile (and the price of a new Model T Ford had dropped from $950 in 1913 to $365 in 1917 due to mass production improvements), road development, and the ill effects of the Great Depression starting in late 1929 ended excursion vessel traffic by the early 1930's--not only in Green Bay-Door County, but nearly nationwide.

The Michigan-Wisconsin Boundary War

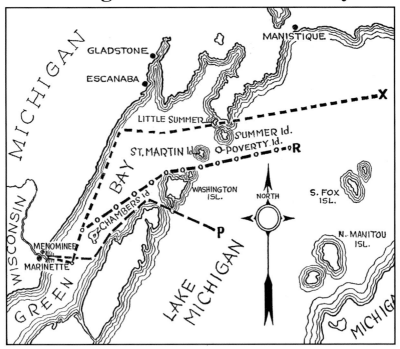

Valuable fishing rights and the possession of certain islands appeared as tempting prizes in a century-long struggle between the states of Michigan and Wisconsin to establish a boundary line in the Death's Door area.

The line which extends as the letter "P" was referred to as the summer ship channel which, until 1926, the state of Michigan contended should be the boundary. The Supreme Court denied that line, and intended to substitute the line marked "R". However, an error in the court description made line "X" the boundary, clearly giving Wisconsin more land (including Michigan's St. Martin Island, Poverty Island and Summer Island) and more water. This error reopened the old conflict, with not only Michigan reclaiming its islands and the surrounding waters, but with Wisconsin arguing that the state boundary should run along the center of Green Bay, which it ultimately did when the final settlement was reached. But there was one more attempt to blur the two states' jurisdictions.

In 1976, Wisconsin Senator Gaylord Nelson proposed that 15 islands (eight in Wisconsin and seven in Michigan, referred to collectively as the Grand Traverse Islands) be incorporated into an interstate or national park. These islands and their acreages are, in Wisconsin: Detroit (649), Fish (1.5), Fisherman Shoal (1), Hog (1.87), Pilot (3.70), Plum (265.9), Rock (906), and a 134-acre parcel at Boyer Bluff on Washington Island; in Michigan: Gravelly (3), Gull (13.5), Little Gull (5.25), Little Summer (490.5), Poverty (192), Rocky (9.7) and St. Martin (1,292). However, nothing developed from this proposal.

Above: *Equipment from fishtugs dries at the Gills Rock docks. Commercial fishing remains an active profession in the Death's Door area, with respectable catches of whitefish and perch still occurring. Sturgeon, so plentiful in the early days that two bays and towns were named after it, mysteriously disappeared from this area after the construction of the Sturgeon Bay Ship Canal in the late 1870's. Many shipwrecks have been located by commercial fishermen who spend so much time working in these local waters.*

Below: *Commercial tugboats, like the (left to right)* SUSAN L., *the* WILLIAM C. SELVICK, *and the* JIMMY L., *still line the docks at Sturgeon Bay, where they are used mainly for hauling barges and moving larger commercial vessels.* PHOTOS BY CRIS KOHL

Modern Shipbuilding

In the late 1800's, the wharf life of Sturgeon Bay was busy with a large variety of ships (schooners, steamers, tugs and barges) hauling mainly lumber, stone and ice. As the city developed, the commercial waterfront area gradually became devoted to vessel repair work and shipbuilding.

Rieboldt and Wolter's firm was purchased by outside interests and renamed several times: the Universal Shipyard in 1911, the Sturgeon Bay Shipbuilding Company in 1920, and the Sturgeon Bay Shipbuilding and Drydock Company in 1926. In 1934, it was sold to Capt. John Roen (who found fame in 1944 as the man who raised the 600-foot *George M. Humphrey* from the Straits of Mackinac in the largest salvage operation in Great Lakes history) and William Wolter, Joseph's son.

Peterson Boat Works was established in Sturgeon Bay in 1907, building smaller vessels such as powerboats, sailing yachts, fish tugs and canoes. A 1918 fire shut down the business, but the owner's son reopened it in 1933.

Two old friends named John Leathem and Thomas H. Smith partnered in shipbuilding and other businesses starting in 1890. By the time Smith died in 1914, John Leathem had retired, so Mrs. Smith took over as president of the Leathem and Smith Towing and Wrecking Company, with assistance from her son, Leathem (whom his parents had named after their friend and eventual business partner). In 1921, 37-year-old Leathem took over and renamed the business the Leathem D. Smith Shipbuilding Company.

The inventive Leathem D. Smith designed an innovative self-unloading device which revolutionized the shipping industry. This new bulk materials self-unloading equipment saved the ship and cargo owner time and money, and could be installed in old or new vessels. In the 1920's and '30's, 30 ships were thus equipped.

Leathem D. Smith, as president of the Leathem D. Smith Shipbuilding Company of Sturgeon Bay, ran the business very well, its profits being respectable but not spectacular. World War II changed all that. In 1941, the monthly payroll of the company was $7,000 for its 40 employees; by January 1, 1944, it had escalated to $1,250,000 for 5,200 employees. In 1943, the Smith Shipbuilding yard, using Henry Ford's successful assembly line process where each worker learned and performed only one specific job, produced an average of one completed ship a week, including subchasers for the US Navy and anti-submarine Corvettes for Canada.

The first self-unloading apparatus invented by Leathem D. Smith was installed on the wooden steamer, HENNEPIN, *shown at the Leathem Smith Stone Company (another of L. D. Smith's companies) dock in Sturgeon Bay. Smith also invented the first shipping containers.* DOOR COUNTY MARITIME MUSEUM AND LIGHTHOUSE PRESERVATION SOCIETY, INC.

58

Above: *The steel, powered barge called the* MATERIAL SER-VICE *was built by the Leathem Smith Company at Sturgeon Bay in 1929.* DOOR COUNTY MARITIME MUSEUM AND LIGHTHOUSE PRESERVATION SOCIETY, INC.

Middle right: *Most of the* MAT-ERIAL SERVICE'S *short life was spent hauling bulk cargoes through the canal system of Chicago, or not too far beyond in Lake Michigan.*
CRIS KOHL COLLECTION

Right, lower: *When the* MAT-ERIAL SERVICE *sank off the Cal-umet River in Lake Michigan one night in summer, 1936, with great loss of life, Door County felt the pain, not just for the four victims from there, but for all those who lost their lives, as well as the victims' families. It also hit home because this ship was viewed as "one of their own."* CRIS KOHL COLLECTION

By 1944, at the peak of wartime shipping construction, Sturgeon Bay was booming. As many as 7,000 men and women worked in Sturgeon Bay's shipyards, taxing the city's housing, transportation and schools. Local residents (of which there were 6,500 when the war started) were encouraged to rent out rooms to accommodate the influx of workers, while many shipyard employees managed to get into the dozens of "government defense homes" which were quickly and cheaply built, lacked insulation and were nicknamed "Chicken Coops." Most of these structures were torn down after the war or relocated to college campuses. With gasoline rationing and automobile shortages, the new Sturgeon Bay Transit Company used miniature buses in 1943 to transport the defense workers. Armed members of the U. S. Coast Guard protected the shipyards and their materials during World War II.

A total of 258 ships were constructed by the four shipyards at Sturgeon Bay during World War II for the navy, army and foreign contractors:

> Leathem D. Smith Shipbuilding Company built 93 ships, the largest vessels to come out of Sturgeon Bay. They included 25 cargo freighters, 38 subchasers which were 174 feet long each, and 10 tankers.
>
> Sturgeon Bay Shipbuilding and Drydock Company built 85 vessels which included 15 cargo ships each 99 feet long, and 17 retrieval vessels.
>
> Sturgeon Bay Boat Works constructed 43 ships for the war effort, about half of which were 45-foot-long aircraft rescue boats.
>
> Peterson Boat Works launched 37 boats, all made of wood, ranging from 40-foot-long motor launches to 110-foot subchasers, mine sweepers and personnel boats.

During World War II, a ship was launched on average every five days at Sturgeon Bay, an amazing production record.

After the war, tragedy struck. Leathem Smith was one of four people who drowned on June 23, 1946 when his racing sloop, the 38-foot-long *Half Moon*, capsized in a squall five miles off Sturgeon Bay while returning from Menominee. Of the five people on board, only his 18-year-old daughter, Patricia, survived. None of the five was wearing a lifejacket, and after the ship overturned, the only life preserver found was given by Leathem to his daughter and her college friend, 18-year-old Mary Loomis from Winnetka, IL, to share. After shaking her father's

On Labor Day, 1942, four ships were launched for the war effort at the Leathem Smith Shipyard at Sturgeon Bay. That day also happened to be Mr. Leathem Smith's birthday, and there was no better way to celebrate than to patriotically launch so many war ships! DOOR COUNTY MARITIME MUSEUM AND LIGHTHOUSE PRESERVATION SOCIETY, INC.

hand, Patricia and her friend began swimming towards shore, awkwardly clutching that life preserver between them. Near shore several hours later, an exhausted Mary slipped from the preserver and drowned. Patricia was in the water for a total of six hours before reaching shore and reporting the tragedy. All of the bodies were recovered, and the *Half Moon*, previously owned by James Roosevelt, son of the recently deceased President Roosevelt, was found and raised. After Leathem Smith died, his shipyard was sold to the Christy Corporation.

Ship construction continued in full swing after the war. In 1956, Sturgeon Bay Boat Works was renamed Palmer Johnson Boats, Inc. Pat Haggerty purchased the company in 1961 and began the production of luxury yachts and prestigious cruisers for private use, including the $35,000,000 195-foot-long, all-aluminum yacht, *La Baronessa*, in 1998. Peterson Boat Works became Peterson Builders, Inc., and constructed many vessels for the government. Defense contracts dwindled in the 1990's with the end of the Cold War, and the company closed in 1996. Sturgeon Bay Shipbuilding and Dry Dock Company became part of Bay Shipbuilding Company in 1967, and in 1970, it merged with the Christy Corporation.

Six of the Great Lakes' twelve "Thousand Footers" were built at Sturgeon Bay: *Belle River* in 1977 (renamed the *Walter J. McCarthy, Jr.* in 1990), *Lewis*

Left: *The launch of the car-and-passenger ferry ship* BADGER *at Sturgeon Bay in 1953 created a tidal wave that dislodged railroad cars which had been welded to tracks opposite the launch site to act as a buffer for that dock.* DOOR COUNTY MARITIME MUSEUM AND LIGHTHOUSE PRESERVATION SOCIETY, INC.

Below left: *The 410-foot-long* BADGER *operates between Manitowoc and Ludington.* **Below:** *The* SPARTAN, *the* BADGER'S *sister ship, was built at Sturgeon Bay in 1952.* PHOTOS BY CRIS KOHL

The BADGER *at Manitowoc, Wisconsin*

The SPARTAN, *laid up at Ludington, Michigan, as seen from the deck of the* BADGER.

Wilson Foy in 1978 (renamed the *Oglebay Norton* in 1991), *Edwin H. Gott* in 1979, *Indiana Harbor* in 1979, *Burns Harbor* in 1980 and *Columbia Star* in 1981. These ships, each 1,000 feet in length, are landlocked giants, forced by their size to remain on the upper Great Lakes because the locks of the Welland Canal are too small for them to transit and leave.

Today, mostly repairs and maintenance work are done at Sturgeon Bay.

Ships built in Sturgeon Bay sail in many parts of the world. The 1945 *Passaic*, 168 feet long, was sold to the Dominican Republic Navy in 1976. Since 1960, the government of Haiti has leased the 168-foot-long *Tonawanda*, built in 1945. The 1962, 191-foot-long *Charles H. Davis* has been operating in New Zealand as the *Tui* since 1970. The 92-foot-long, 1949 fire tug, *Victor L. Schlaeger,* still works in Chicago. The 213-foot-long, steel-hulled *Aurora* has sailed Alaskan waters since 1977. The 1963 *Beaver Islander* still operates as a Lake Michigan ferry. The 1955 *Emerald Isle* is now the *Diamond Jack,* running tours at Detroit. The 1953, 384-foot-long Navy Ship, *LST-1167*, was transferred to the Turkish Navy in 1974 and renamed *Serdar*. The 1975, 158-foot-long *Oceanus*, is a research vessel for the National Science Foundation at Woods Hole, MA. The 1978, 152-foot-long *MSC-322* (*HMS Addriyah*) is a coastal minesweeper for the government of Saudi Arabia. The 1979 fire tug, *Curtis Randolph,* operates in Detroit. The 110-foot-long submarine chasers, *SC-0643, SC-0538* and *SC-1031*, built in 1942 and 1943, were transferred to Russia under a lend-lease program in 1945 and were never returned to the US Navy. The 173-foot-long *PC-1176*, a patrol craft, participated in the Normandy invasion on June 6, 1944, patrolled the coast of occupied Germany for a year, and was sold in 1960 to the Venezuelan Navy and renamed the *Petrel*. The *PC-1569*, built in 1945, was transferred to South Viet Nam on Nov. 23, 1960.

Ships built in Sturgeon Bay have also become shipwrecks in various parts of the world. The 323-foot-long *Coastal Guide*, launched in 1945, burned and sank in the Pacific Ocean a mile offshore at Everett, Washington, on October 20, 1982 after having been renamed *Al Ind Esk A Sea*. The 1943 *William Howland*, 250 feet long, was renamed the *Cocal* in 1953 and stranded on the coast of Uruguay on March 4, 1969, becaming a total loss. The 250-foot-long *Solidarity*, launched in 1943 as the *Ashbel Hubbard*, was owned in Britain when it "foundered at sea" on March 5, 1951. The tug, *John Hunsader,* built in 1910, was sold to Canadian owners, renamed the *Puckasaw*, was scuttled off Thunder Bay, Ontario, in Lake Superior, in 1934, and is a popular scuba dive site today. The 250-foot-long *Freeman Hatch*, built in 1943 and renamed the *Houston* in 1955, was sunk during the ill-fated "Castro" invasion on April 17, 1961 in the Bay of Cochinos on the south coast of Cuba. The 1972, 234-foot-long *Margaret L.* caught on fire and sank in the Pacific Ocean in March, 1978. The 1943, 110-foot-long submarine chaser, *SC-1032*, renamed *Sheila* in 1952, stranded off Glendon Beach, Oregon, on March 8, 1963, a complete loss. The 60-foot tug, *Welcome*, burned at Windsor, Ontario, on the Detroit River, on September 23, 1958, and was scrapped. The 173-foot-long patrol craft, *PC-1261*, was sunk by shore gunfire off France during the Normandy invasion on June 6, 1944. The 173-foot-long *PC-1563*, built in 1944, was sunk by a typhoon at Guam in the Pacific Ocean in November, 1962. The 285-foot-long *Peoria,* built in 1944, was transferred to the Cuban Navy on June 16, 1947, and, under Castro, sunk as target practice in 1975. The *T-008*, built in 1942 and renamed the *Hodge* in 1950, foundered 3.5 miles off Santa Barbara, CA, on January 10, 1976. The *T-009*, renamed *Galtex* in 1947, stranded 2,000 yards west of the lighthouse at Galveston, Texas, on April 19, 1949, and became a total loss. The 165-foot-long tanker, *YW-127,* built in 1945, was scuttled on the Shark River Artificial Reef, 16 miles off Pt. Pleasant, NJ, on July 16, 1998. The 1945, 323-foot-long *Tulare*, renamed *Tong Hong* in 1963, left Japan on October 25, 1967, bound for Singapore with a cargo of fertilizer, and tragically disappeared with her entire crew of 38.

Right: *Built by Peterson Builders, Inc. of Sturgeon Bay in 1982, this ship, the RS50 (also named* SAFE-GUARD*) is stationed in Hawaii and used in salvage operations. Four ships of the same type and design were constructed by Peterson Builders at the same time.* DOOR COUNTY MARITIME MUSEUM AND LIGHTHOUSE PRESERVATION SOCIETY, INC.

Pat Stayer and Joan Forsberg watch a thousand-footer, the WALTER J. MCCARTHY, JR., *which was the first of six ships this size constructed at Sturgeon Bay between 1977 and 1981, glide past them amazingly quiet as they relax on a much smaller boat, tied off to a shipwreck many miles off Alpena, Michigan, on Lake Huron.* PHOTO BY CRIS KOHL

Maritime Recreation

Today, the waters in and around Death's Door are used mainly for recreation: boating, beachcombing, swimming, fishing and scuba diving.

Since 1970, the number of marinas which have been built or enlarged in Door County has grown dramatically, with sometimes startling numbers of pleasure craft found on the waters of Green Bay and Lake Michigan on weather-friendly weekends during boating season.

To assist the large number of pleasure craft owners since World War II, the Marine Travelift, a large, steel frame on wheels which places a sling under a pleasure craft in order to move it from storage into the water, or vice versa, was invented in 1946 in Sturgeon Bay. This invention is still manufactured in Sturgeon Bay today.

At least five maritime,or maritime-related, museums can be found in the Death's Door region, and they provide visitors with a wealth of information about the ships, shipping and shipwrecks in this area. Several lighthouses have been restored and are open to the public for tours, while boat tours and rentals are available. The waters of Death's Door today are an irresistible attraction to anyone with even a slight interest in water.

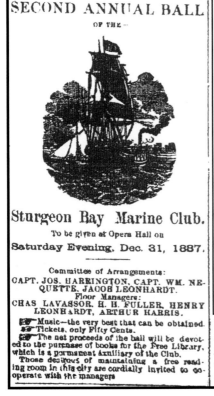

SECOND ANNUAL BALL

OF THE --

Sturgeon Bay Marine Club.

To be given at Opera Hall on

Saturday Evening, Dec. 31, 1887.

Committee of Arrangements:
CAPT. JOS. HARRINGTON, CAPT. WM. NE-QUETTE, JACOB LEONHARDT.
Floor Managers:
CHAS LAVASSOR, H. H. FULLER, HENRY LEONHARDT, ARTHUR HARRIS.

☞ Music—the very best that can be obtained.
☞ Tickets, only Fifty Cents.
☞ The net proceeds of the ball will be devoted to the purchase of books for the Free Library, which is a permanent Auxiliary of the Club. Those desirous of maintaining a free reading room in this city are cordially invited to co-operate with the managers

It holds you SAFE in Life's Storms.

While you have a position and are in good health and sailing along smoothly you are apt to forget that the sea of life is very wide and before you cross it that you are almost sure to run into many storms of adversity.

While you are MAKING money be SAVING money. Then you can weather the financial storms that will come into your life.

We will welcome your account.

BANK OF STURGEON BAY
MEMBER FEDERAL RESERVE BANK

Left: *The Sturgeon Bay Marine Club, started in the 1880's, appears to have been a very sociable group.* Above: *Even banks in 1923 advertised with a nautical motif. Both items are from the* DOOR COUNTY ADVOCATE. CRIS KOHL COLLECTION

Above: *Many marinas, like this one at Egg Harbor, have been built near Death's Door in recent years.* Right: *In the early 1900's, pleasure boating on sailboats was called "yachting."* Cris Kohl Collection. Below: *Sister Bay pleasure craft get decorated for special events.*
Photos by Cris Kohl

In 1969, commercial fishermen founded the Door County Maritime Museum at Gill's Rock, which, since 1971, has operated the Cana Island Lighthouse. A small maritime museum opened at Sturgeon Bay in 1977, replaced 20 years later by an impressive 20,000-square-foot facility. Today, that museum operates the historic Chicago fire tug, FRED A. BUSSE (above) for harbor tours. In 2002, the organization expanded its name to The Door County Maritime Museum and Lighthouse Preservation Society. The maritime museum at Sturgeon Bay (below) is open year-round (tel. 920-743-5958). PHOTOS BY CRIS KOHL

Right: *The Gills Rock branch of the Door County Maritime Museum features many sights and much information about commercial fishing and shipwrecks, such as this display of a scuba diver hovering above shipwreck parts and artifacts. This museum is open from May to October. (12724 Wisconsin Bay Road, telephone 920-854-1844).* PHOTO BY CRIS KOHL

The Door County Historical Museum in downtown Sturgeon Bay also offers many items of interest to maritime history buffs, at 18 N. Fourth Ave., tel. 920-743-5809.

On Washington Island, the log cabin Jacobsen Museum has considerable interesting material about local ships and shipwrecks. May to October.

Below: *On the northeast side of Washington Island, the Jackson Harbor Fishing Museum offers outdoor exhibits as well as indoor displays and much historical maritime information in several buildings on the site. They, too, have information about shipwrecks. This museum is open from May to October. Check days and hours.* PHOTO BY CRIS KOHL

Above: *Historic Rock Island, today a remote state park requiring two ferry rides to reach from the mainland, offers one of the most unusual and unexpected structures in the Death's Door area -- Viking Hall, built by an Icelandic-American electric components businessman from Chicago, Chester Hjortur Thordarson (1867-1946), in the 1920's as an impressive and moving tribute to his Scandinavian heritage. Thordarson had purchased most (over 660 acres) of Rock Island in the early 1900's.*

Below: *Viking Hall's grand boathouse exhibits unique nautical grandeur; inside the hall, the fireplace is large enough to fit half a dozen standing men.* PHOTOS BY CRIS KOHL

68

Above: *The famous Door County "Fish Boil," which reportedly originated in 1961, is a maritime dish of boiled local whitefish with potatoes, white onions and lemon wedges.*

Below: *Scuba diving on shipwrecks is an increasingly popular and adventurous activity. Few people in the Great Lakes know that the cold, fresh waters of our unique inland seas hold the best preserved shipwrecks in the world which can be explored by sport scuba divers. Proper scuba training can be obtained through most scuba dive shops, many YMCA's, and private instructors. More and more people have taken up this exciting activity in recent years. Dive charter boats take divers to shipwrecks in the Death's Door area.*

PHOTOS BY CRIS KOHL

Shipwreck Locations

(corresponding to chapter numbers)

2. *Griffon* (?)   3. Death's Door wrecks
4. *Pilot Island shipwrecks*
5. *Plum Island shipwrecks*
6. *Ocean Wave*   7. *Carrington*
8. *Meridian*   9. The Big Blow of 1880
10. *D. A. Van Valkenburg*   11. *Jennibell*
12. *Lake Erie*   13. *F. J. King*
14. *Fleetwing*   15. *Erastus Corning*
16. *Windsor* and *E. P. Royce*
17. *E. R. Williams*   18. *Otter*
19. *Australasia*
20. *Erie L. Hackley*   21. *Horseshoes*
22. *R. J. Hackett*   23. *C. C. Hand*
24. The Great Storm Shipwrecks
25. *City of Glasgow*
26. *Frank O'Connor*   27. *Lakeland*
28. *Michael J. Bartelme*
29. The Treasure of Poverty Island (?)
30. The Boneyard Ships

This map is not suitable for navigation

Because maritime recreation in the Death's Door region today includes scuba diving, and because shipwrecks are the mainstay of sport scuba diving in the Great Lakes, we offer this map giving the general locations of frequently visited Death's Door shipwrecks, and the approximate locations of undiscovered ones. The site numbers correspond with the chapter numbers in this book. This brief introductory chapter about the area's maritime history has now officially ended. Let the shipwreck tales begin! MAP BY CRIS KOHL

THE WRECK OF THE *GRIFFON*
(SEPTEMBER, 1679)

Griffon! For Great Lakes historians, archaeologists, and many knowledgable boat watchers and scuba divers, that word stimulates the imagination more than the name of any other shipwreck. It was one of the smallest of the commercial ships ever to ply Great Lakes waters, but over time, it has developed the largest reputation of them all.

Basically, the story goes that a French explorer named La Salle had his men construct a wooden vessel in the first few months of the year 1679 in the wilderness which is today that stretch of prime real estate along the Niagara River between the cities of Buffalo and Niagara Falls, New York. La Salle had accumulated heavy debts to the financial backers of his expeditions in the town of Montréal, and their exorbitantly high interest rates pressed La Salle to pay them off as quickly as possible. He had sent a crew of men -- hardy *coureurs de bois* and fur trappers -- ahead to the far side of Lake Michigan to gather valuable beaver pelts, both as trappers and as traders with the indigenous natives. The *Griffon* was built to carry the thousands of pounds of furs back to Niagara, from where they could be quickly conveyed to Montreal in order to keep the financial wolves at bay.

The *Griffon*, the first ship on the upper Great Lakes (west of Niagara Falls), sailed haphazardly from Niagara, across Lake Erie, up the Detroit River, across Lake St. Clair, up the St. Clair River (where the strong current forced the men to get out and pull the ship with ropes along the shoreline), up Lake Huron, and, after a brief stop at the Indian village and the French Jesuit missionary at St. Ignace, through the Straits of Mackinac and across Lake Michigan to the islands separating the lake and Green Bay. La Salle's collection party having been successful, the *Griffon* was soon loaded with

71

Réné Robert Cavelier, Sieur de La Salle (1644-1687), famous French explorer, built and sailed the first ship across the upper Great Lakes and claimed the Mississippi River for France -- before his men murdered him. PUBLIC ARCHIVES OF CANADA

furs--the hope of La Salle--and the commander sent his fortune back on the *Griffon* with a skeleton crew of five men under the command of an untrustworthy pilot.

La Salle never saw his men, his ship or his furs again. Shortly after the *Griffon* left either Washington Island or Rock Island (historians are divided as to which place La Salle used to load his furs) heading for the Straits of Mackinac, a serious storm suddenly sprang up and lasted several days. Native Americans claimed to have seen the ship sink somewhere close to shore in northern Lake Michigan, but La Salle deemed these reports unreliable, suspecting that the natives may have killed his crew, destroyed his ship and stolen his furs. La Salle eventually went on to discover the mouth of the Mississippi River and claim all of the lands between the Great

Mrs. Arthur Wickman of Washington Island painted her vision of what La Salle's ship, the GRIFFON, *could have looked like when it visited Washington Island to take on a cargo of valuable furs. It sailed away and simply disappeared.* DOOR COUNTY HISTORICAL MUSEUM

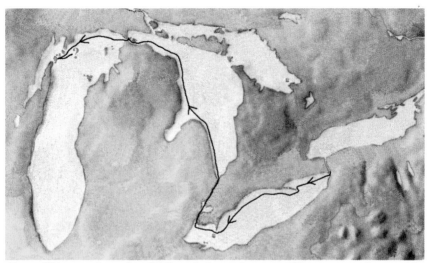

Above: *This map shows the wild Great Lakes as they were 300 years ago, when no cities existed and no politicians had yet placed imaginary lines representing the colossal barriers we have today. The* GRIFFON, *the first ship on the upper Great Lakes, also became the upper lakes' first shipwreck when it disappeared with all hands on the return leg of its maiden voyage in September, 1679. The ship's tragic loss helped lead to explorer La Salle's murder at the hands of mutinous crewmembers. What happened to this sailing vessel has become the Great Lakes' greatest mystery, and the* GRIFFON *has become the holy grail of freshwater shipwrecks. This story, plus the many* GRIFFON *discovery claims which have been made in the past 150 years, form the detailed 68-page flagship chapter of Cris Kohl's book,* **Shipwreck Tales of the Great Lakes.** MAP BY CRIS KOHL*

Below: *That the French spent time in this area in the late 1600's has been archaeologically proven on Rock Island near the Death's Door Passage.* PHOTO BY CRIS KOHL

Lakes and the Gulf of Mexico adjacent to that river for the French crown. Not long afterwards, his crew, long unpaid and doubting La Salle's ability and competence, shot him to death in Texas on March 19, 1687. He was 43.

Numerous expeditions have been launched to locate this fabled and elusive historic shipwreck in hopes of solving the greatest mystery of the inland seas. Famous Great Lakes shipwreck hunters John Steele, Dick Race and David Trotter each took a stab at finding this wreck in recent years, with no luck. Novelist and experienced NUMA shipwreck hunter Clive Cussler looked into the possibility of searching for the *Griffon*, but decided that it would be like looking for a needle in a haystack.

Numerous claims have been made in the past 150 years, at least 16 of them, none of which has, as yet, been proven conclusively to be the wreck of the *Griffon*. Two small books have been written exclusively about the *Griffon*, but the wreck site which they favored was recently proven to be the remains of an 1840's fishing boat. Three museums on Manitoulin Island in northern Lake Huron house pieces of a mysterious shipwreck which could have been the *Griffon*, but too much archaeological evidence picked up there since the late 1800's has been either lost or disturbed.

Since anything is possible, perhaps the *Griffon* retreated into Green Bay during that storm. In the 1930's and 1940's, a shipwreck which appeared to be quite ancient was often discussed locally, efforts being made to identify this mystery vessel which lay along the shoreline in front of the residence of John Blossom just north of Sister Bay in Door County. Its construction suggested a style known in Europe several centuries earlier, and which perhaps was brought to this area by European immigrants in the 1800's. The possibility of it actually being the long-lost *Griffon* was voiced. The mystery floated until 1953, when careful studies concluded that it could not be the *Griffon*, and in early 1954, the retreating winter ice carried out with it every piece of this shipwreck, dooming any further investigation.

In 2001, wreck hunter Steve Libert found a site off Poverty Island and claimed that it is the remains of the *Griffon*. The attentions of the Michigan and French goverments have been grabbed, but positive proof -- one of the two cannons known to have been on board, say, or the wooden figurehead of a griffon in identifiable condition, remains elusive. For all we know right now, the missing *Griffon* may even be one of the shipwrecks at Death's Door!

SHIPWRECKS IN
DEATH'S DOOR PASSAGE

N umerous rock-rimmed and cliff-barricaded islands sit silently, extended in a bespeckled north-south chain, dangerous dotted lines designating the border between Lake Michigan and Green Bay. They pose enormous hazards to navigation: storms, fogs, rocky reefs, craggy shorelines, winds and currents at odds with one another, and collisions with other ships in these narrow waterways. But the most dangerous of all these waterways is the Porte des Morts Passage -- Death's Door itself.

It is difficult to determine exactly what geographic boundaries should be taken into consideration to ascertain the shipwrecks of the Death's Door Passage and only the Death's Door Passage, as many vessels were lost at Pilot Island, which lies at the entrance to Death's Door and has been given its own chapter in this book, and Plum Island, which runs along part of the northeastern edge of the passage and the shipwrecks there have also been given their own chapter. Hence it may appear that there were actually very few ships lost in the Porte des Morts Passage, which would be an incorrect conclusion. Far more vessels were lost by striking rocks along a shoreline of the passage than were lost by blatantly sinking in the open waters in the middle of that passage, so those stranded shipwrecks are described in the chapters which represent those particular geographic shorelines.

The *Chicago Tribune* of Monday, May 27, 1889, wrote this about the passage and its relationship with shipping traffic:

> No spot on the great lakes is better named than Death's Door, the entrance from Lake Michigan into Green Bay. The vessels wrecked at that point since there was a lake marine would make a large fleet, and boats continue to go on with a regularity alarming to owners and underwriters....

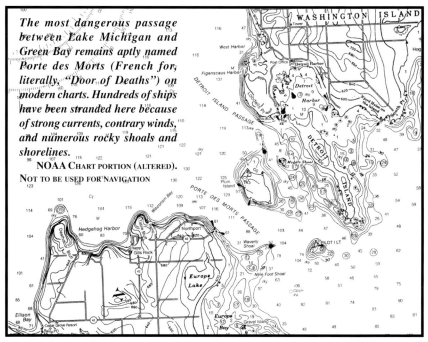

The most dangerous passage between Lake Michigan and Green Bay remains aptly named Porte des Morts (French for, literally, "Door of Deaths") on modern charts. Hundreds of ships have been stranded here because of strong currents, contrary winds, and numerous rocky shoals and shorelines.

NOAA CHART PORTION (ALTERED).
NOT TO BE USED FOR NAVIGATION

An issue of the *Marine Review* from the summer of 1891 wrote this about Death's Door Passage (original spelling and punctuation retained):

> Another vessel, the schooner *Thomas Howland*,... was ashore at "Death's Door," the entrance to Green bay. She went on the rocks while passing into the bay in thick weather. The vessel owners have been pleading with congress for a light...at this point, or the substitution of light-ships for the permanent structure project, which has as yet secured an appropriation of but $60,000. Unless this appropriation is increased by the next congress the lightships should be ordered from the money already appropriated.

The following shipwrecks represent the vessels lost "at Death's Door" butr not at a specific Death's Door location covered in a subsequent chapter:

Margaret Allen (late November, 1847)

This two-masted, 80-foot-long schooner, built only three years earlier at Chicago, was caught in a storm and went, as Mansfield succinctly wrote in his massive 1899, two-volume *History of the Great Lakes*, "ashore and wrecked near Death's Door."

Windham (early December, 1855)

This 112-foot-long, twin-masted schooner was built at Ashtabula, Ohio, in 1843, and was carrying a cargo of lumber bound for Chicago when she dragged her anchor while trying to ride out a storm and stranded on a rocky reef. A day later, the terrified crew was removed from their wrecked ship by the passing brig, *Geneva*.

Maria Hilliard (October, 1856)

Another two-masted schooner, the 112-foot-long *Maria Hilliard*, stranded on a rocky bar and broke apart in Death's Door Passage. No lives were lost. The vessel had been built by James Averill at Chicago in 1844.

Columbia (June 7, 1859)

In 1842 at Sandusky, Ohio, a man named Daniel Dibble built a two-masted brigantine named the *Columbia*, unaware of the important roles this ship would play several years later. On August 17, 1855, the ship passed through the locks of the Soo Canal carrying the very first cargo of iron ore to come out of the Lake Superior district, specifically from Marquette, Michigan, bound for Cleveland. With this one passage, the massive iron ore trade in North America began. In 1857, this small vessel carried the first railroad locomotive (named "Sevastopol") to Marquette, Michigan, on her open deck, the first iron horse brought to upper Michigan.

The *Columbia*, with Capt. Jacob Hansen in charge, reportedly stranded and wrecked on the shoreline of a small bight, or bay, between Hedgehog Harbor and Door Bluff, on June 7, 1859. The ship was carrying a cargo of general merchandise bound from Chicago to Sturgeon Bay. No lives were lost, since the crew escaped by climbing a mast and walking along the yardarm into some trees atop a shoreline bluff. Coincidentally the *Columbia* at the time of her loss was owned by Joseph Harris (in his pre-Sturgeon Bay Canal and pre-*Door County Advocate* days) and another man from Sturgeon Bay named Jesse Birmingham. The latter had been on board the

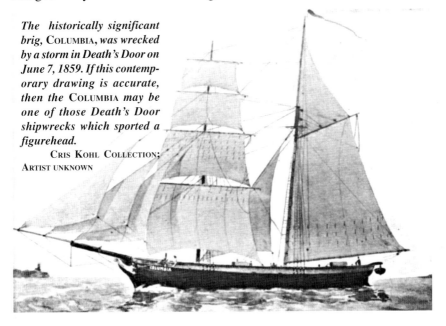

*The historically significant brig, C*OLUMBIA, *was wrecked by a storm in Death's Door on June 7, 1859. If this contemporary drawing is accurate, then the C*OLUMBIA *may be one of those Death's Door shipwrecks which sported a figurehead.*
CRIS KOHL COLLECTION; ARTIST UNKNOWN

ship when she stranded, and he went for assistance, but when he returned four days later, the bad weather had broken up his ship (although the crew had managed to recover most of the cargo). The 176.83-ton *Columbia* measured 91 feet, five inches in length and 24 feet, four inches in beam.

Cairo (October 18, 1863)

The 355-ton schooner, *Cairo*, built at Buffalo in 1853, was stranded on a Death's Door shore by a storm and broke up within hours. No lives were lost, but the cargo of salt and containers of acid were not saved. The ship's rigging was reportedly recovered by the bark, *Newsboy*.

Hampton (September 20, 1873)

This 173.63-ton, 115-foot-long, two-masted brig, launched on May 4, 1845 at Three Mile Bay, New York, was carrying a cargo of lumber when she became waterlogged and broke up during a storm. Capt. Theodore Lane and his crew drifted on a raft for 12 hours before being rescued. Years later, the *Door County Advocate* of November 24, 1888, referred to the *Hampton* as "...another old tub that was well known here...."

Denmark (November 1, 1873)

Built in 1846 at Cleveland by Sanford & Moses, this two-masted, 169.37-ton schooner was driven ashore at Hedgehog Harbor near Death's Door by severe gales. The crewmembers were saved, but the ship was broken to pieces, a total loss. She hailed from Chicago.

Ella Doak (August 5, 1875) -- See chapter 31, pages 254 to 255.

Ardent (October 12, 1880)

This 57-ton schooner stranded at Hedgehog Harbor after her anchor chain broke. The ship, carrying wood and bark, was stripped and abandoned.

Maria (November 5, 1883)

This 104-ton schooner (95' x 23' x 7', official #50612), owned in Milwaukee but built at Port Huron in 1866, was lumber-laden when she blew onto the rocks at Hedgehog Harbor in a storm and went to pieces.

Japan (October 19, 1885)

Built in 1853 at Milan, Ohio, this 192-ton, two-masted schooner (113' x 24' x 10') was loading cordwood at Garret Bay (the western part of Hedgehog Harbor) when a sudden gale drove her ashore, wrecking her.

Fleetwing (September 26, 1888) -- See chapter 14, pages 139 to 144.

Sardinia (July 6, 1900)

Built in 1856 at Penetanguishene, Canada West (which became the province of Ontario in 1867), this 150-ton schooner (105' x 25' x 9'), valued at $800, stranded with a wood cargo at Gills Rock and became a total loss.

THE PILOT ISLAND SHIPWRECKS

A 1980's publication about the ships lost off Door County, hoping to attract scuba divers to this area, focused on the many shipwrecks at Pilot Island, stating that,

> Underwater Pilot Island is proof of the epic of early Great Lakes shipping and disaster. Remains of wooden sailing ships *Nelson, Gilmore, Forrest* [sic], *Norton, Wisconsin, Nichols, Kanter* and *Detroit* lie in piles of wreckage strewn about the bottom. In one place the wreckage is 3 tiers high, one wreck on top of the next.

Although Pilot Island occupies a mere three and one-half acres of hard, layered land, it is like an iceberg -- much more of it is hidden beneath the waves surrounding the island, and that part is even more menacing. Jagged rocks and dangerous ledges lurk just under the surface and have claimed many a vessel. Pilot Island is an immovable object, splitting the already narrow gap through which waters can flow and ships can sail. This hardnosed dot of rugged land exacts attention from concerned mariners in whose course it lies.

The Pilot Island Lighthouse in about 1883. Keepers have called this island a "prison" as well as "a dream of ideality." NATIONAL ARCHIVES

In the 1880's, the *Chicago Tribune* wrote this about the island's reputation:

> ....Pilot Island, the point where they [ships] come to grief, is about 600 feet in diameter and has a flash light. It is seldom without a wrecked vessel resting upon it somewhere....

Remote, dangerous and isolated, Pilot Island has been tough on ships and men (one lighthouse keeper cut his throat there in June, 1880!) Many ships were lucky -- they stranded on Pilot Island but were recovered and returned to service. Here are newspaper reports (with spelling, grammar and punctuation intact) about a few of those near-shipwrecks on Pilot Island:

> As soon as the weather will permit the steambarge *Emma E. Thompson* will leave Chicago for Pilot Island to rescue the schooner *Mary L. Higgie*, ashore on the rocks at that point. On Friday evening she took on a necessary quantity of coal, and Saturday morning she took on one of Atkins & Beckwith's large sized steam pumps. Captain J. L. Higgie, owner of the unfortunate craft, has heard no particulars regarding the stranding further than already published, nor has he learned anything additional with reference to the vessel's condition. She is supposed to be in rather bad shape.
>
> *--- Cleveland Herald*, **Tuesday, May 16, 1882**

> Captain Boyce, master of the schooner *Angus Smith*, reports that he saw a schooner under full sail go ashore on Pilot Island last night at 9:15 o'clock. He thinks it was the *Christina Neilson*. Wind south, light....
>
> ...The schooner *Homer*, light, from Chicago, went ashore at Pilot Island last night. Her bow is out two feet and the stern is afloat. She was not leaking when the captain left this morning. A tug, derrick and a steam pump has gone to her assistance. The captain has been ordered to cut spars ready for the derrick. Wind light, water smooth.
>
> *--- Chicago Inter Ocean*, **Saturday, May 20, 1882**

> The *Mary L. Higgie*, recently on at Pilot Island, will need some new planking on her starboard side, forward, part new keel, part new forefoot and recalking. The expense of rescuing her is also a large item.
>
> *--- Chicago Inter Ocean*, **Monday, May 22, 1882**

> The schooner *Riverside* ran ashore on Pilot Island Saturday night. Her stern is in two and one-half feet of water. Her bottom is all gone. She will be a total wreck. She was bound light from Sheboygan to Escanaba. The captain and part of the crew arrived in safety at Escanaba Sunday in the yawl.
>
> *--- Marquette Daily Mining Journal*, **Wednesday, October 19, 1887**

> The Green Bay *Gazette* of Saturday says: "Capt. Thrall has arrived from Pilot Island where he has been the past two weeks, endeavoring to get off the *Riverside*. He had the boat partly blocked up and was nearly ready to get her off, when a storm arose and did considerable damage to the boat, besides undoing the work that had already been executed. Capt. Thrall intends to take a couple of scows to the island and sink

them on each side of the boat and lift and float her to a dry dock.
--- *Door County Advocate*, **Saturday, June 16, 1888**

The schooner *Riverside* is again afloat, having been released from Pilot Island Reef Wednesday night. The vessel was towed to Green Bay yesterday. The *Riverside* went ashore on Pilot Island over a year ago, and was last spring purchased from the underwriters by Captain P. F. Thrall and others, of Green Bay, for $2,000. She is reported as being in fine condition.
--- *Chicago Inter Ocean*, **Friday, October 19, 1888**

Capt. McLeod leaves the barge *Dan Rodgers* at Port Huron and goes to Lake Michigan to look after the stranded schooner *Northwest*. She is in a bad place, Pilot Island, and it is predicted that she will winter there....
--- *Detroit Free Press*, **Friday, November 16, 1888**

No effort will be made to release the schooner *Northwest* this season. In fact nothing can be done in that direction until June next, when the weather will have become sufficiently settled. She is being stripped of canvas, running gear and everything else likely to be sought after by "pirates."
--- *Detroit Free Press*, **Thursday, November 22, 1888**

The tug *Nelson*, with Thos. H. Smith and Capt. John Walker on board, went to Pilot Island last Saturday to inspect the schooner *Northwest*, ashore at that point. The schooner is lying in an exposed condition on the spit that makes out into the lake from the southern part of the island, and it is questionable whether she can hold together until spring. There are about nine feet of water aft while there are only about five feet forward, the hull resting on a rock about midships. She is full of water and there must be a big hole in the bottom. The *Northwest* is a big vessel, being about 200 feet long, 40 feet breadth of beam and 16 feet deep. She carries four masts and is said to be insured for $35,000.
--- *Door County Advocate*, **Saturday, December 1, 1888**

George McCloud, wreck master for the underwriters, is kicking himself for having said that the *Northwest* was not worth wrecking [salvaging], and Smith & Davis are kicking themselves for having acted on his opinion. [Note: The expensive *Northwest* was successfully recovered, but was sunk by ice in the Straits of Mackinac on April 6, 1898.]
--- *Escanaba Iron Port*, **Saturday, May 18, 1889**

The schooner *C. C. Barnes* is ashore on Pilot Island. The tug *Monarch* has gone to her relief with a steam pump.
Another schooner, name unknown, is also ashore at the same place.
--- *Chicago Inter Ocean*, **Saturday, May 18, 1889**

The recent stranding of the big steamer *Alva* on Pilot Island, at Death's Door entrance to Green bay, but adds to the general belief of superstition among mariners that there is such a thing as bad luck, which pursues vessels from the day they are launched....
--- *Detroit Free Press*, **Thursday, October 7, 1897**

81

Here are the vessels which were permanently wrecked at Pilot Island:

Dolphin (October 17, 1841)

According to Mansfield (1899), the schooner, *Dolphin*, commanded by Capt. Morgan, went ashore and was a total wreck at Death's Door. Fortunately, the crew was rescued by the passing ship, *Yankee*.

Wisconsin (September, 1847)

Again citing Mansfield (1899), the schooner, *Wisconsin,* reportedly the first vessel built at Green Bay in 1834, was totally wrecked at Death's Door near Pilot Island in September, 1847.

Henry Norton (October, 1863)

The lumber cargo was lost, but the crew was saved when the 151-ton schooner, *Henry Norton*, stranded on Pilot Island while enroute from Green Bay to Chicago in October, 1863. This 84-foot long, 12-foot-wide, twin-masted vessel was quite old, reportedly built in 1834 at Richmond, Ohio.

Daniel Slauson (October 22, 1863)

Enroute from Chicago to Buffalo with a cargo of wheat, the 273-ton schooner, *Daniel Slauson*, stranded at Pilot Island. The crew managed to return to the ship's home port of Racine, Wisconsin, but the vessel, valued at $17,500 and insured for $10,000, and the cargo, appraised at $35,000 and insured for $15,000, were total losses.

Maple Leaf (November 1, 1867)

After stranding on Pilot Island, the cargoless, 299-ton schooner, *Maple Leaf*, was stripped and abandoned. This ship, built in 1854 at Buffalo, New York, was registered at Chicago at the time of loss. No lives were lost.

Lydia Case (late September, 1872)

The 326-ton, Racine-built schooner, *Lydia Case*, carrying coal, stranded during a severe storm at Pilot Island in late September, 1872, and became a total loss. No lives were lost. Her coal cargo was salvaged a year later.

Cleveland (June 13, 1875)

The 380-ton barkentine, *Cleveland*, was 29 years old and valued at $8,000 when she went ashore at Pilot Island on June 13, 1875, and became a total loss. The ship had been hauling lumber from Menominee to Chicago. The Menominee tug, *Escanaba*, failed to pull her off the rocks, so the *Cleveland* was stripped of any useful rigging and abandoned.

E. M. Davidson (October 18, 1879)

After the schooner, *E. M. Davidson*, stranded on Pilot Island on October 18, 1879, Capt. William Morris and his crew managed to reach Escanaba and summon tugboat assistance, but several failed attempts prompted the owners to strip the sailing vessel and leave the hull in place over the winter. The *Door County Advocate* warned in mid-November, 1879, that, "Should the stranded craft be rescued it is thought that the expense of wreckage will consume all she is worth." A final, desperate attempt at recovery in late November, 1879, before winter set in, raised the vessel using "jack screws and ways placed under her," but then bad weather quickly put an end to that project. The following spring found the *E. M. Davidson* with serious hull damage, as well as lawsuits for the crew's wages and from one tugboat owner for services rendered (unsuccessfully) the previous autumn.

One year after the *E. M. Davidson* stranded, the *Chicago Inter Ocean* of October 22, 1880, just after the "Big Blow of 1880," reported:

> The late gale has doubtless "finished" most of the vessels that found the beach or the rocks earlier in the season. Among these is the schooner, *J.* [sic] *M. Davidson*, on Pilot Island, Death's Door. When the schooner *Oak Leaf* entered the bay, there the *Davidson* was, thumping away; when the *Oak Leaf* came out of the bay she had entirely disappeared from view. Wolf & Davidson, of Milwaukee, owned the wreck [purchased from the underwriters], and the *Leviathan* spent a great deal of time during the season endeavoring to rescue it, and would have succeeded if she had been favored with any sort of weather. When she left the *Davidson* the last time she had got her entirely winded. The *Davidson* measured 281 tons, was built by Gibson, at Bay City, Mich., in 1871, and at the time of her stranding was owned in Chicago, and was about the last of an unfortunate gentleman's large fortune, most of which was wiped out by the great fire.

The schooner, *E. M. Davidson*, is likely the shipwreck which scuba divers in the 1960's misidentified as the schooner, *Riverside*. Although initial contemporary newspaper reports publicized the fact that the *Riverside* had been abandoned as a complete loss after stranding at Pilot Island on October 15, 1887, she was recovered and returned to service, only to sink in Lake Erie in October, 1893. Ohio scuba divers were actively searching for the wreck of the *Riverside* as this book went to press. Shipwreck artifacts recovered by early scuba divers at Pilot Island spent years on exhibit in local museums incorrectly labeled as coming from the wreck of the *Riverside*.

This shipwreck site was described, several years ago, as sitting on a rough, rocky bottom, becoming silt-covered in the deeper area, lying

> 1,000 yards south of Pilot Island in Porte Des Mortes passage.... While swimming over the inverted hull of this old schooner, you will be impresed at the expanse and sturdiness of the hull bottom. Moving on deeper to the bow, the keel and stem loom up, proudly standing 15 ft. above the strewn wreckage below. Then, you will be abled to swim underneath the capsized hull to explore the inside of the ship's hold.... Stern is [in] 45 ft., bow is [in] 65 ft., wreckage scattered at 60 to 70 ft., slope continues to 100 ft.

The scuba diver describing this shipwreck site concluded with, "This wreck is in open water, and is difficult to locate...."

Forest (October 28, 1891)

The 87-foot-long, 102-ton scow schooner, *Forest,* built in 1857 at Newport (later Marine City), Michigan, by David Lester, was rebuilt and lengthened to 115 feet in 1879-1880, and changed from two masts to three. In 1866, the *Forest* became a Lake Michigan ship for the remainder of her days. The 34-year-old *Forest* stranded on the west end of Pilot Island on October 28, 1891, and was abandoned.

Some published events occurred in the long history of the *Forest.* On April 7, 1874, a sailor on the *Forest* named George Scholz leaped overboard as the ship neared Racine, and his suicide was supposedly caused by "temporary insanity," but a later news report stated that he was "laboring under an attack of delirium tremens at the time." He was buried at Racine.

In 1881, the *Forest* was nearly lost when a storm forced the ship ashore at Newport near Rowleys Bay. The vessel spent the winter stranded there and, after the owner failed to sell his unfortunate vessel for his asking price of $1,000, the ship was abandoned and her enrollment was surrendered at Milwaukee on July 1, 1882. However, the *Forest* was recovered in August and returned to service by October, to sail for another nine years.

Two of the Pilot Island shipwrecks are obvious. Broadside on the left is the twin-masted schooner, James E. Gilmore, *while the tilted, three-masted* A. P. Nichols *sits facing the camera on the right. However, lying between the* Gilmore *and the dock is the nearly submerged* Forest, *which had been lodged there for over a year.* Cris Kohl Collection

H. W. Scove (December 5, 1891)

The 305-ton, 130-foot-long schooner, *H. W. Scove*, built at Manitowoc in 1873, was Milwaukee-bound with a cargo of lumber from Pine Lake when the ship stranded between Pilot Island and Detroit Island in a strong gale and stayed there for the winter. In June, 1892, plunderers trying to steal the ship's stove and cargo were caught on the site (they were sleeping on board their scow), but tugs could still not budge the settled *Scove*. By early 1893, salvage attempts ceased, but the wreck was still considered a hazard to navigation. In late September, 1919, the steamer, *City of Marquette*, had to be towed into Sturgeon Bay because the ship had snagged its propeller around the braided steel rigging from the *Scove* which had been removed by fishermen and dropped in Detroit Harbor, where it was forgotten.

James E. Gilmore (October 16, 1892)

This two-masted schooner (137'7" x 25'4" x11'), launched in March, 1867 at Three Mile Bay, New York, stranded on Pilot Island due to a sudden wind change, and her keel was crushed. The ship, valued at $19,000 in 1871, was appraised at only $3,500 when it stranded 21 years later. The cabins were safe with plentiful provisions, so the crew remained on board

The three-masted schooner, A. P. NICHOLS, *carried a figure-head, as indicated by each of its nine Enrollment Certificates. Unfortunately, only the word "figurehead" appears, not revealing what style or design of figurehead it was.*
ARTIST UNKNOWN. CRIS KOHL COLLECTION

A detail of the above drawing reveals more about this ship. If this artist's rendition of the A.P. NICHOLS *is accurate, then the figurehead mounted beneath the bowsprit was in the shape of some creature with gaping jaws, possibly a serpent. It is not known if the figurehead was still on the wreck when the vessel broke up.*

ARTIST UNKNOWN. CRIS KOHL COLLECTION

overnight. A breeches buoy was set up by lighthouse keeper Martin Knudsen in case of an emergency. The crew came ashore the next day but could not leave the island for nearly two weeks due to bad weather.

A. P. Nichols (October 28, 1892)

This bark, launched at Madison Dock, Ohio, in May, 1861, was converted into a three-masted, 299.67-ton schooner at Chicago in the summer of 1878 with the measurements 145'2" x 30'2" x 11'9".

When the ship dragged its anchors and stranded on Pilot Island, on board was the aged, 320-pound Capt. David Clow -- a long-time shipbuilder and former Chambers Island resident. On the island, he and his wife had built the *Sarah Clow* in 1862, and also the *Lewis Day* in 1868, a vessel which stranded and wrecked at Plum Island on October 16, 1881, when Martin Knudsen was light keeper at Pilot Island. Clow and his sons had purchased the *A.P. Nichols* in 1877. After Knudsen, with difficulty, got the corpulent, 71-year-old captain safely ashore from the stranded *Nichols*, the gallant keeper and the venerable captain remembered each other from the *Lewis Day* loss 12 years earlier. Clow's tired, aged eyes filled with tears at the realization that his sons would have to master his ships from now on.

Under the heading, "PILOT ISLAND. Its Lighthouse Keeper Deserves a Gold Medal," a newspaper printed these words from Capt. David Clow:

This detail of the A. P. NICHOLS stranded on Pilot Island suggests the ease with which its rigging, and any figurehead it might have carried at that time, could have been removed.
CRIS KOHL COLLECTION

"We were bound Chicago to Escanaba, light, and were driven on Pilot island. We had both anchors out, but they failed to hold us and the schooner went on the rocks. As soon as she struck, the seas went over from stem to stern, and it seemed as if none of us could escape. The boat was on a reef of rock with shoals all around. Knutzen [sic] came down from the lighthouse, and although it was 8 o'clock at night and intensely dark, he picked his way through the surf along a ledge of rocks which came nearly to the surface and got quite near to us. He made himself

Journal of Shipwrecks in the Vicinity of Pilot Island

Lighthouse keepers were required to maintain an updated journal giving details about shipwrecks (partial and total lossses) in their area and any assistance they rendered. Here are the entries from the keeper of the Pilot Island Lighthouse for the wrecks of the *Forest*, the *James E. Gilmore* and the *A. P. Nichols* (the "Pilot Island Wrecks"), with original spelling, grammar and punctuation intact:

October, 1891, 28th -- The Scow *Forest* of Chicago stranded on the outer end of reef extending S.W. from this Island at 9.40 P.M. Cause. Was the vessel making more leeway, being close on the wind than was expected. Wind S.S.W. fresh and moderate gale to fresh breeze at time of stranding. Cloudy and dark, and a high sea running. The Light seen by all at the time and before. Vessel was seen by us immediately, the only assistance rendered by us was in making a landing here using our boat next day, and in giving them board and lodging till Nov. 15th. Tonnage 107 $^{78}/_{100}$ tons. Owner A. J. Johnson of Chicago. Vessel was dismantled and the outfit stored here on Nov. 2nd and 3rd. The Scow is a total loss, being all broken up.

1892, October 17 -- The Schooner *James E. Gilmore* stranded on the reef at S.W. end of Pilot Island at about 11 P.M. The cause being the wind striking a head when near the reef and, having only the head sails on and the fore-sail split she could not tack nor clear, therefore drifted on. She was coming to the anchorage for shelter. Hazy and rainy weather. S. and S.W. and Westerly gale varying. Being light could not carry sufficient sail to maneuvre as she should when the wind came ahead and moreover did not have time to put it on before striking. Tonnage 276 tons. Owner John Gerlach of Cleveland. Assistance was rendered from the Light in putting the Master in a way to telegraph to owners and board to Master and crew for a while. No other assistance used.

1892, October 28 -- The said Schooner [*A. P. Nichols*] stranded on N.W. side of Pilot Island at 8 P.M. near the landing. The accident was caused by the dragging of her anchor. She was anchored at the usual anchorage near Plum Island to a 1,400 lb. anchor having lost or sliped the larger anchor to prevent stranding on Southerly side of Plum Island in missing stays when trying to tack through the passage during the afternoon, the fore-boom and main-gaff was broken, and the mizzen topsail and raffe carried away before going to the anchorage; over 100 fathoms chain was run out to anchor to prevent dragging, but failed. Wind was Westerly to N.W. gale to nearly a hurricane at time of accident. Cloudy and Showery weather, but clear. The Light was in plain view and seen by all on board. Assistance was rendered from the light to get ashore and lodging after landing, and for the Master to obtain passage on Stmr. *J. H. Outhwaite* to Escanaba for assistance for release. Tonnage 285 tons. Owners David Clow & Son of Crystal Lake and Chicago, Ill.

Pilot Island and its lighthouse form an appropriately historic backdrop for any scuba divers who are about to explore the Pilot Island shipwrecks, three schooners which stranded at this location in the early 1890's. Inset: This aerial view of the old, long-abandoned Pilot Island Lighthouse shows its need for restoration. PHOTOS BY CRIS KOHL

Although the three schooners, the FOREST, *the* JAMES E. GILMORE *and the* A. P. NICHOLS *stranded and broke up into many pieces, those pieces are large and quite interesting at this shallow (20 to 50 feet deep) site. Inset: Many scuba divers make the plunge each year to explore the underwater delights of the Pilot Island wrecks.* PHOTOS BY CRIS KOHL

Above: *This postcard of a Pilot Island shipwreck sold very well when the "golden age" of postcards began in the first few years of the 1900's. This started as a black-and-white photograph taken in late 1892 -- the vessel has been identified by maritime historian Jon Paul Van Harpen as the schooner* JAMES E. GILMORE *which stranded at that time-- and it was colorized, or tinted, by hand, since color photography did not yet exist. Color printing, however, did exist, so the colorized black-and-white photograph could be mass produced. The colorized postcard was likely printed in Germany by an enterprising company in Door County which recognized that such a dramatic subject would spur sales among visitors to this nautically picturesque part of Wisconsin.* DOOR COUNTY HISTORICAL MUSEUM

Below: *The flattened slabs of the schooner's hull lie in shallow water.* PHOTO BY CRIS KOHL

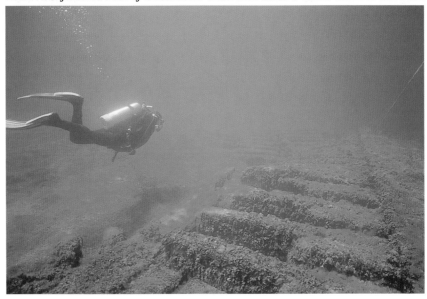

Above: *Joan Forsberg examines bent bolts joining massive wooden timbers of the Pilot Island shipwrecks -- proof of the power of winds, waves and rocks.*   PHOTO BY CRIS KOHL

Below: *This postcard is of the wreck of the old schooner,* MYSTIC, *which stranded on Pilot Island on October 15, 1895, and eventually broke up. In the black-and-white photograph forming the center of this color-framed postcard, the vessel appears to be in good shape and possibly salvageable, but in reality, the stern was seriously damaged. This was verified by reports from Capt. Herman Schuenemann, the man who had chartered the* MYSTIC *to pick up and deliver Christmas trees to Chicago. Seventeen years later, he disappeared with his entire crew on the old schooner* ROUSE SIMMONS *off Two Rivers, Wisconsin -- while delivering Christmas trees to Chicago!* DOOR COUNTY HISTORICAL MUSEUM

91

> heard above the storm, and told me to jump overboard. I did so and went
> in far over my head. As I came up he reached out for me from the shelves
> of rock where he stood and pulled me up near him."

Martin Knudsen did receive recognition in the form of not one, but two medals. The first, made of gold, arrived early in 1893 from the Life Saving Benevolent Association of New York, with these words inscribed (spelling and punctuation intact): "Presented to Martin Knudsen Light House Keeper of Pilot Island Lake Michigan in recognition of his courage and humanity in rescuing at great personal peril the Crews of wrecked Schooners *J. R. Gillmore* and *A. P. Nichols* October, 1892." The second came in early spring, 1893, a silver medal reading "United States of America. Act of Congress June 29, 1874" with the inscription, "To Martin Knudsen Keeper Port Des Morts U. S. Light Station For Service in Saving Life at Wreck of Schooner *A. P. Nichols* October 28, 1892." Martin Knudsen, born in 1854, lived to the age of 86; Capt. David Clow died at age 74 on March 19, 1896.

Mystic (October 15, 1895)

Built at Milan, Ohio, in 1866, the 112.5-foot-long, 25.7-foot-wide schooner, *Mystic*, headed for Little Bay de Noc to take on a cargo of Christmas trees for the Chicago market when it stranded on Pilot Island and became a total loss. Lighthouse personnel helped the crew off the ship and boarded them for two weeks before a steamer returned them to Chicago.

O. M. Nelson (June 4, 1899)

Heading for Detroit with a lumber cargo, this 107.7-foot-long schooner stranded in dense fog off the southwest side of Pilot Island. The five-man, one-woman crew became the guests of lighthouse keeper Martin Knudsen. Anything valuable was stripped from the schooner, and unsuccessful attempts were made to free the hull, all summer long. The ship broke up that winter. The 167-ton *Nelson* was built in 1882 at Suttons Bay, Michigan.

Seaman (November 15, 1908)

Launched at Cleveland, Ohio, in 1848, and measuring 88'6" x 20'4" x 8'4", the three-masted schooner, *Seaman*, was later rebuilt to 120' x 25'6" x 8'7". This 60-year-old ship stranded on Pilot Island with 3,000 bushels of potatoes. The crew was rescued by the Plum Island Life-Saving Station crew, but the ship and cargo were a total loss.

Leila C. (October 3, 1928)

The new, 40-foot-long fish tug, *Leila C.*, was struck by the 396-foot-long ore freighter, *S. B. Coolidge* (launched as the *Australia* at Chicago in 1897), and the much smaller vessel sank within 15 minutes two miles southeast of Pilot Island in 150 feet of water. The two men on board were rescued by the *Coolidge*. The $8,000 fish tug carried no insurance.

5

THE PLUM ISLAND SHIPWRECKS

S hips which ran the navigational gauntlet through Death's Door Passage from Lake Michigan to Green Bay, once they successfully passed between Pilot Island and Nine Foot Shoal, had to ensure that they did not swing too far east and end up stranding on Plum Island. With sudden wind changes, adverse water currents, fogs, storms and shipping traffic in this narrow waterway, the possibility of not making it through was strong. Knowing exactly when to stay on a northern track and when to make a slight turn towards the west made navigation here truly challenging.

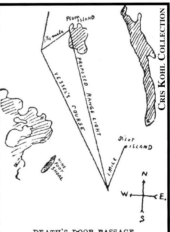

The following article and map of Plum Island and the navigation of Death's Door appeared in the **Chicago Tribune** *on Monday, May 27, 1889:*

A MARINE PUZZLE SOLVED.
DEATH'S DOOR CAN BE ROBBED OF
ITS TERROR BY RANGE LIGHTS

...A way to make Death's Door as safe as any passage on the lakes is now suggested by Capt. Nicholson of the Peshtigo line of barges. Capt. Nicholson has been sailing from Chicago to Green Bay twice a week for a quarter of a century. He says that if a range light and foghorn were placed on Plum Island no Captain could ever mistake the way. The trouble now is that boats going into the passage from Lake Michigan are kept too far to the northward for fear of running on Nine Foot Shoal....With a range light as shown,... vesselmen would know when they had gone just far enough toward Pilot Island, and all uncertainty would be ended.... A number of old-time mariners who were shown Capt. Nicholson's plan most earnestly agreed that he had solved the perpetual puzzle Captains had to solve at Death's Door....

DEATH'S DOOR PASSAGE.

It would be another seven years before the government agreed and built those Plum Island range lights.

93

There were temporary strandings on Plum Island, and even the occasional shipwreck hoax (original spelling and punctuation retained):

> The schooner *Colonel Cook*, coal loaded, is ashore and sunk, on Plum Island. The tug *John Gregory* goes to her from Manitowoc.
>
> **--- *Chicago Inter Ocean*, October 23, 1880**
>
> [Authors' note: The schooner *Colonel Cook* was formerly named the *Augusta*, and as such, she collided with the steamer *Lady Elgin* on September 7, 1860, resulting in about 300 deaths from among those on board the steamship. Possibly the most hated ship ever to sail the Great Lakes, the *Augusta's* name was changed in 1861 to *Colonel Cook* and the ship was painted a different color in a disguising effort to start life anew. The *Colonel Cook* came close to ending her career at Death's Door. The ship was permanently wrecked near Lorain, Ohio, in Lake Erie on September 23, 1894.]

> A postal card, dated Marinette, Wisconsin, November 29th, signed Captain I. Everts, states that a schooner, supposed to be the *Kate Gillette*, 260 tons burden, owned here by T. W. Harvey, laden with 300,000 feet of lumber, is ashore at Plum Island, and that all hands are supposed to be lost. Her crew consisted of John Sims, captain, and nine men. The owners discredit the report; at least that part of it regarding the loss of life. The vessel was considered seaworthy.
>
> **--- *Cleveland Herald*, Thursday, December 1, 1881**

> An evening paper last night stated that a vessel supposed to be the *Kate Gillet* was ashore at Plum Island, and all hands supposed to be lost. Mr. F. W. Harvey, the owner of the vessel, to satisfy the wife of Captain Simms, made telegraphic inquiry and ascertained that the *Gillette* did not leave Marinette until Tuesday morning, so that she could not have been the one wrecked at Plumb Island. Meantime, there will

The Plum Island Life-Saving Station, established in 1896, closed in 1990. The island received its name because it lies "plumb" in the center of Death's Door (spelling notwithstanding). THE DOOR COUNTY MARITIME MUSEUM AND LIGHTHOUSE PRESERVATION SOCIETY, INC.

be some curiosity to know what the name of the fated vessel is.
        --- Chicago Inter Ocean, **Thursday, December 1, 1881**

The schooner *Kate Gillette*, said to be ashore at Plum Island, arrived at Chicago on Thursday from Marinette, in good shape. The report regarding her condition was purely a cruel hoax.
        --- Cleveland Herald, **Tuesday, December 6, 1881**
[Authors' note: The three-masted, 259-ton 129-foot-long schooner, *Kate Gillett*, constructed in 1867 as a twin-master in Conneaut, Ohio, had her name changed to *Horace H. Badger* in 1882. The ship and its cargo of coal stranded on the Cleveland breakwater during a storm on June 11, 1903, with the crew of seven being rescued by the Life-Saving Service. The old vessel was abandoned in place.]

The rocky shoreline of Plum Island's 265.9 acres made the following ships permanent victims:

Grapeshot (November 1, 1867)

The twin-masted, 268-ton schooner, *Grapeshot* (131' x 28' x 10'), built by B. B. Jones in 1855 at Buffalo, NY, stranded in a storm on the north end of Plum Island on Nov. 1, 1867 while hauling lumber to her home port of Chicago. The stern lay sunk to the deck while the bow pointed four feet out of the water. The tug, *Leviathan*, and later the steamer *George Dunbar*, could not pull the ship off, so the *Grapeshot* was stripped and abandoned.

Lewis Day (October 16, 1881)

Built by Capt. David Clow and launched at Chambers Island on Thursday, July 23, 1868, the bark, *Lewis Day* (146'8" x 31' x 11'6" and named after a Green Bay merchant and shipbuilder) was huge for a home-built vessel reportedly constructed in only two years. The 381-ton ship was held together by wooden pegs and fasteners which were much less expensive

The official **Wreck Report** *for the schooner,* LEWIS DAY, *features the handwriting and signature of the "Master + Owner," none other than the man who built the 381-ton ship in 1868, Capt. David Clow.*

NATIONAL ARCHIVES

than their metal counterparts. In his younger days, Capt. Clow had difficulty accumulating enough money to build the ships he had in mind, so he cut financial corners in whatever way he could. Unfortunately, held together by trenails, short for wooden "tree nails," his ships could never rate better than "B1" with insurance companies, which meant that they were virtually uninsurable. So Capt. Clow often sailed his ships by the seat of his pants.

In November, 1869, during one of the worst storms ever to strike the Great Lakes, the *Lewis Day*, with great difficulty, rode it out at anchor in Lake Erie 30 miles from Point Pelee. Unfortunately, the schooner, *Sarah Clow*, which the captain and his wife had built in 1862 and which they had sold three years earlier, sank while attempting to ride out that same storm near Manistee in Lake Michigan.

In one memorably bad run in June, 1876, the *Lewis Day* stranded twice on Plum Island, first while outbound to Chicago and later while returning. Capt. Clow was able to free his ship himself each time, but his luck at self-releasing from Plum Island did not hold out five years later.

The bad luck began on Friday night, October 14, 1881, when the *Lewis Day*, heavily loaded with cedar posts for Chicago (and yes, in defiance of sailors' superstition, left a port on a Friday), ran aground at Cedar River Point on the west side of Green Bay. The vessel was finally released on Saturday morning after jettisoning her deckload of posts. Underway in Green Bay, the *Day* began to leak, but not badly enough for Capt. Clow to run back to port. While beating out of the bay through Death's Door, the *Day* "missed a stay" and went aground on a submerged rocky ledge off the east side of Plum Island at about 10 PM on Sunday, October 16, 1881. The next day, the wind changed and blew strong out of the east, pounding the vulnerable *Lewis Day* on the rocks and filling her with water. Capt. Clow raised a distress signal, and that afternoon, the schooner, *G. D. Norris*, removed the captain and seven sailors. The *Day* soon broke beyond repair, a total loss, particularly since she carried no insurance. Capt. Clow valued his ship at $10,000 and the 200 tons of cedar posts and telegraph poles at $1,000. The *Door County Advocate* of Oct. 27, 1881, reported that

> "Capt. Clow...proposes to build another vessel the coming winter to take the place of the lost craft.... Capt. Clow is himself a ship-builder and his four sons, who sail with him, are all expert ship carpenters.... Luckily, Captain Clow is pretty well 'heeled,' hence the loss [of the *Lewis Day*] is of but little inconvenience to him."

A Chicago paper responded with the hope "that the next vessel built by Capt. David Clow won't be a duplicate of Noah's ark, like the wrecked *Lewis Day*." Capt. Clow had moved to the Chicago area, so he was managing his economic success better than when he worked hard on Chambers Island in the 1860's. Still, old habits of frugality die hard, and he salvaged as much as he could of the *Lewis Day*. He removed all of the sails and rigging, and, after Eli P. Royce, the Escanaba businessman who owned the cargo, had it removed by his schooner, the *Oak Leaf*, Clow made one more unsuccessful attempt to have the *Day* pulled off the rocks, accomplishing only a $400 bill from the tug *Leviathan* for services rendered. On November 10, 1881, Capt. Clow burned the ship, "so as to save the Iron," as he wrote in the official Wreck Report. As the *Lewis Day* was held together by wooden pegs, there would have been very little "iron" to salvage from this shipwreck.

Berwyn (November 23, 1908)

Launched as the *R. C. Crawford* at Algonac, Michigan, in 1866, this sleek ship experienced two name changes, the first on July 24, 1884 at Grand Haven, Michigan, to *Capt. George W. Naghtin*, the second on June 14, 1901 at Chicago to *Berwyn*. The final measurements of this 269-ton, three-masted schooner were 132'2" x 29'2" x 10'. When she met her end, this ship was totally under the control of the steamer which was towing her, the *Walter Vail*. Both ships were bound for Nahma, Michigan, at the top of Big Bay de Noc, to pick up iron ore cargoes when they both stranded on

Plum Island while picking their way through a dense fog in Death's Door. The steamer had the strength to free herself, but her tow would not budge. When the wind suddenly changed to the southeast, the side of the *Berwyn's* hull was pounded to pieces. The ship's rigging and hardware were stripped and conveyed to Chicago, and the vessel was abandoned.

Several years ago, this shipwreck site, reportedly badly broken up and sitting on a rock bottom in about ten feet of water, was described as "lying 180 yards north from the Red Nun Buoy #2 in Detroit Island Passage,... partially buried in its own cargo of high grade iron ore...." This must have been the remains of another ship, because the Berwyn was carrying no cargo when she became a victim of Death's Door.

The schooner, Berwyn, *seen here passing through the locks at Sault Ste. Marie in 1904, was being towed in fog by a steamer on November 23, 1908, when she stranded on Plum Island.* Cris Kohl Collection

97

The 293-ton, three-masted schooner, RESUMPTION, *(143'4" x 29' x 10'3") sailed the lakes for 35 years and was a duplicate of her sister ship,* FORD RIVER.   CRIS KOHL COLLECTION

Resumption (November 7, 1914)

The schooner, *Resumption,* stranded on Plum Island on November 7, 1914, blown there by a severe gale, and became a total loss, despite the efforts of five steamers to pull her off. She carried no cargo (the ship was heading from Chicago to Wells, Michigan, to pick up one) and none of the seven lives on board was lost. Launched at Milwaukee on April 5, 1879, the ship's name bears explaining. In April, 1861, when the Civil War began, the U.S. government suspended specie payment, and it was not until January, 1879, that the "resumption" of specie payment put the government back on a gold basis, much to the nation's enthusiasm. The *Resumption's* figurehead was reportedly decorated with facsimile gold coins.

The rigging and deck hardware from the stranded schooner, RESUMPTION, *were salvaged at Plum Island in late 1914 and 1915. What became of this ship's decorated figurehead is not known.*

COURTESY OF TODD FRISONI OF THE DOOR COUNTY ICE CREAM FACTORY, FROM THE BLOSSOM FAMILY COLLECTION

98

THE *OCEAN WAVE*
(SEPTEMBER 23, 1869)

M any of the thousands of ships which were launched into the fresh waters of the inland seas called the Great Lakes in the past 330 years were given distinctly saltwater names, often suggesting foreign and exotic places -- five vessels were named *Australia*, two were named *Sweden*, three *Asia*'s were launched and three *India*'s slid down the ways. There was a *City of Genoa*, a *City of Glasgow*, a *City of Naples*, a *City of Venice* and three *City of London*'s. Five ships were named *Atlantic*, while twelve carried nameboards reading *Pacific*. There was an *Athens*, three *Sparta*'s, eight *Troy*'s, three *Grecian*'s and four *Egyptian*'s. Twelve ships were launched as *Ocean*, and four sailed the often turbulent waters of the Great Lakes under the name *Ocean Wave*. In the 1800's, a Great Lakes ship watcher could take a virtual tour around the world just by reading the names of the vessels passing any given point.

Of the four *Ocean Waves*, the first was a sidewheel steamer built in 1852 and lost with disastrous effect (28 of the 57 people on board perished) when it burned on Lake Ontario the following spring. That wreck lies upside-down in 153 feet of water three miles off Point Traverse, Ontario, near the town of Picton. The others were schooners of varying types and dimensions, the largest being the three-masted, 129-foot-long *Ocean Wave* built in 1853 at Cleveland, Ohio, and lost with a cargo of corn in the storm-tossed waters of Lake Huron at Hammond Bay on November 19, 1869. The second-largest was the 81-foot-long *Ocean Wave* constructed at Picton, Ontario, on the shores of Lake Ontario, in 1868, and which capsized and foundered with the loss of all hands in that lake on November 9, 1890.

Under sail, rectangular scow schooners were easily handled by a small crew. Here, the CHAMPION *carried a load of sand on Lake Erie at the turn of the last century.*
CRIS KOHL COLLECTION

Scow schooners could be quickly and easily built by unskilled labor, drew shallow drafts, had a cargo carrying capacity larger than other vessel types of similar length due to their box-like shape, most often carried two masts (although a few three-masters existed), and were usually as speedy as their competition despite their blunt bows pushing rather than parting the waters through which they sailed. CRIS KOHL COLLECTION

This is the story of the fourth one, the smallest and most humble of the Great Lakes ships named the *Ocean Wave*.

In late 2003, scuba dive boat captain Jim Robinson of Gills Rock, Wisconsin, received information about an obstruction, possibly a shipwreck, in about 100 feet of water off Whitefish Bay, Wisconsin. Commercial fishermen Mark Weborg and Jim Laughlin, of the fish tug *Robin B.* from Ellison Bay, had snagged their fishing nets and marked that site on their charts to avoid it. This was on the Lake Michigan side of the Door County Peninsula at its southern end between the Sturgeon Bay Ship Canal to the south and Death's Door Passage to the north.

Since this was somewhat distant for Jim to take his boat to investigate, he gave the site information to enthusiastic local shipwreck diver Randy Wallender, who headed his trailerable dive boat to the general location and began searching, picked up something on his depth sounder, did a dive to the bottom of the lake and became the first person to explore this small shipwreck lying at a depth of 105 feet of Lake Michigan water.

The bow portion of this small sailing vessel, which is a scow schooner by design, remains upright and considerably intact, resting tilted slightly to starboard (see underwater photographs, pages 105-107). The stern portion of the ship is badly damaged, apparently from that part of the vessel hitting the lake bottom first, and it appears that the ship broke its back when it hit bottom. A large portion of the ship's cargo of stone lies in a debris field off the port quarter. Snagged commercial fishnets, mostly of the early vintage cotton twine type with a bit of the more modern monofilament ones, lie flat over portions of this shipwreck. The bowsprit surprisingly remains upright in place, defying gravity by lancing out its length of 30 feet over the ship's bow and hovering several feet above the lake bottom on the same horizontal angle it had when the vessel was originally built. Two small anchors rest off the bow, and a bilge pump remains upright on a portion of decking. The unusually long forward cargo hatch is broken in half and obstructed by three deck beams and the centerboard trunk, which lies flat on the lake bottom. A low-rising deck cabin remains in place, and deck beams are viewable beneath the cabin. The variable spacing of these deck beams suggests that this scow schooner was constructed the usual way -- pieced together inexpensively and sometimes even erratically with whatever lumber was available at the time, without any set building plans.

Construction of scow schooners required few carpentry skills, as the vessel was essentially a framed rectangular box built with very few curved boards. One drawback of this simple type of vessel construction was that the wide, flat bow made the ship extremely vulnerable to damage from any collision with logs, trees or other large debris floating in the water.

Attempts at definite identification of this shipwreck commenced immediately. This was clearly a small scow schooner which had carried a cargo of stone, and no human remains were found on or near the vessel. Quickly the likeliest candidate became a ship named the *Ocean Wave*, which

Sunk.

We learn from Mr. CARRINGTON of Bailey's Harbor, that the scow *Ocean Wave*, loaded with stone sunk in Lake Michigan off White Fish Bay and ten miles from shore. The crew arrived safe at the Bay.

was lost on September 23, 1869, with 53 cords of building stone intended for harbor improvements. The vessel had left Mud Bay (today it has a much more romantic name: Moonlight Bay -- just north of Baileys Harbor, Wisconsin) and was bound for White Lake just north of Muskegon, Michigan, on the other side of Lake Michigan. As if the bad weather weren't enough, the *Ocean Wave* struck an object, probably a floating log or tree (called a "deadhead") or some type of wreckage, which holed the hull. Captain Fletcher Hackett from Milwaukee, who owned the vessel, and his crew barely had time to launch their rowboat before the ship sank. Left with only the clothing they wore, they watched the *Ocean Wave* sink, taking with it to the bottom all of their personal property plus a sum of money from the captain reported to be a total of $160 in "greenbacks" (paper currency) left in his cabin. This *Ocean Wave* had been constructed in 1860 at Harsens Island in the St. Clair River, registered 74 tons and measured 73 feet in length with a beam of 20 feet and a draught of seven feet.

The main problem in connecting the *Ocean Wave* to this unidentified shipwreck was that contemporary newspaper accounts stated strongly that the *Ocean Wave* sank about ten miles off shore in 360 feet of water. This newly-located wreck lay in 105 feet of water only about two miles from shore.

The search for another shipwreck candidate continued.

In August, 2004, Wisconsin state underwater archaeologist Keith Meverden explored the shipwreck and saw something which previous divers had dismissed as being simply the broken, splintered end of a wooden board beneath the bowsprit not far from the bow. Close examination revealed this "broken wood" to be a carved figurehead of an open-beaked eagle's head!

Fewer than twenty of the 1,000+ shipwrecks found in the Great Lakes to date carry a carved figurehead. To find such a rarity on a common scow schooner was difficult to believe. A somewhat skilled workman or sailor must have had some time on his hands, as well as pride in his heart, when he decided to add a decorative figurehead to this workhorse vessel.

No contemporary newspaper accounts of the sinking of the *Ocean Wave*

Above: *Deadheads (floating logs and tree trunks) in Lake Michigan have always posed problems for boaters.* **Below:** *The* OCEAN WAVE'S *crew rowed ashore near Cave Point at night in late September, 1869, after their ship sank.* PHOTOS BY CRIS KOHL

indicated that the vessel carried a carved figurehead. In fact, many of the news stories erroneously reported that this *Ocean Wave* was the vessel of that name built in 1853 in Cleveland. Finding the ship's registration or tonnage numbers carved into the forward beam of the main hatch would definitely have identified the shipwreck, but such numbers remained elusive.

In January, 2005, Sturgeon Bay maritime historian/journalist Jon Paul Van Harpen contacted the National Archives and Records Administration in Washington, D.C., and acquired copies of the *Ocean Wave*'s enrollments. When a ship was launched, a formal document called an enrollment was registered with the government, and every time a new owner acquired the vessel, or a fraction of its ownership, a new enrollment was issued. The *Ocean Wave* had a total of six enrollments in her nine-year life. Technical information about the vessel appeared on its enrollment, and in the space provided after the word "head" (meaning "bow" in this case), usually the word "Plain" or "Round" would be written by the ship's owner. That was not the case with this vessel. Van Harpen was pleasantly surprised to find the words "Eagle Figurehead" written on two of the six enrollments, while the remaining four read "Eagle head."

The little shipwreck in Whitefish Bay had been identified using its enrollment documents.

Very few scow schooners as intact and as interesting as this one have been available for shipwreck study. So historically significant and fragile is this financially valueless scow schooner shipwreck that the State of Wisconsin had its team of underwater archaeologists and volunteers in July, 2005, anchor a marker buoy in the lake bottom 40 feet off the shipwreck's starboard bow so that visiting boaters would not damage the *Ocean Wave* by dragging their anchors into it to find it. At the same time, the State, working mostly with volunteers from the Wisconsin Underwater Archaeology Association, spent two weeks surveying the shipwreck site and most of its debris field, and several months later published their work.

Some researchers began questioning the huge discrepancy between the depth of water where the *Ocean Wave* sank and the distance from shore, as reported by Captain Hackett at the time of loss, and the actual depth and distance of the wreck. Reportedly the crew took most of the night to row to shore, so they may have estimated their offshore distance by that fact, as incorrect an estimate as it turned out to be. One researcher found an 1869 newspaper article which indicated that the *Ocean Wave* had been insured for $8,000 only three weeks before it sank. The newspaper account also clearly stated that the vessel was valued at $5,000. Suspicions grew, and it began to look like the ship was purposely scuttled for the insurance money.

Cris Kohl was asked to research if there were any reports in the 1869 Chicago newspapers which suggested impropriety regarding the loss of the *Ocean Wave*. He found none, but the accounts which he did find indicated that the ship had been insured for only $3,000, not $8,000. That made more sense, as no insurance company in those days would have been enticed to insure a vessel for considerably more than it was worth. Indeed, any insurance carried by ships was usually for significantly less than its actual value.

Finding this information was not easy because of the difficulty in reading the damaged, poor quality newspaper microfilms available. Cris slowly became aware that the number "3" in "$3,000" could easily be mistaken for the number "8" on a scratched microfilm of an old newspaper. Perhaps the recent suspicions of insurance fraud came about as a result of faulty

Above: *Joan Forsberg examines the* OCEAN WAVE's *windlass, chain and other interesting details of the bow area.* **Right:** *Randy Wallender, the first diver to explore the* OCEAN WAVE, *secures his boat to the state buoy marker.* **Below:** *Two small anchors lie on the lake bottom at the upright bow.* PHOTOS BY CRIS KOHL

Disarranged portions of the OCEAN WAVE's decking and railing, as well as a large debris field of its stone cargo, lie off the port quarter. Early scuba divers measured the visible length of this shipwreck and found it to be about 65 feet, proportionately matching the OCEAN WAVE's length when one considers that an unmeasured section of the stern, which clearly struck the bottom first, lies broken and buried in the sand. PHOTO BY CRIS KOHL

Scow schooners have sometimes been derided for their basic and inexpensive construction methods, but the workmen who built the OCEAN WAVE did an excellent job of the bowsprit, which has remained upright and outstretched underwater in defiance of gravity for well over 130 years now. Try holding your arm straight out for that long! PHOTO BY CRIS KOHL

Above: *Joan Forsberg gingerly follows the long bowsprit of the* OCEAN WAVE *to its point.* **Below:** *The carved, open-beaked figurehead of an eagle positioned beneath the bowsprit added some unusual artistic flair to what was otherwise considered a wallflower of a wooden workhorse. Ship's figureheads, in Roman times used to frighten and intimidate enemies, were placed mainly on ocean-going vessels as ornamentation. They were rare on Great Lakes ships; of the many wrecks found so far in the freshwater seas, only about 20 carried figureheads. This makes the* OCEAN WAVE *truly unique.* PHOTOS BY CRIS KOHL

south point of Whitefish bay.
The Ocean Wave had a cargo of 28 cords of stone from Mud bay, intended for harbor improvement at White Lake. The depth of water where she lies is estimated at 360 feet, which as a matter of course, will render her a total loss. She was built at Harrison's Island, Michigan, in 1860, measured 73 73-100 tons, new style, rated B 2, and was valued at about $5,000. She was insured for $3,000, in the Republic, of Chicago.

It is easy to see how a researcher could misread the "$3,000" for "$8,000" in the Ocean Wave *story in this old, scratched microfilm.*
Cris Kohl Collection

microfilms.

Any true maritime researcher has spent many hours tediously poring over old newspapers on microfilms in quest of information about ships and shipwrecks. While the value of any newspaper article hinges greatly upon the quality and veracity of its journalist, these common, everyday accounts are often the only source we have of shipwreck news. Unfortunately, the modern tendency to replace original newspapers with microfilmed versions may have cost us much information about maritime history.

After World War II, a new era of modernism developed, and with it came the technique of, and the enthusiasm for, saving vast quantities of information by photographing newspapers onto small rolls of film called microfilm which could be conveniently read by any researcher using an electric microfilm reader, which is actually a mechanical device which both illuminates and enlarges the original microfilm.

Most library and museum personnel were ecstatic. The new micro-filming process would free them from having to sacrifice the space in entire rooms previously devoted to newspaper storage. As soon as their newspaper collections were photographed onto microfilm, the original piles of newspapers were often discarded or destroyed.

Unfortunately, in the 1940's and 1950's, the proponents of saving news-papers on microfilm saw only the advantages (space-saving and easier access) and could not foresee future problems, such as horribly scratched, brittle and torn microfilms (turned that way by overuse, misuse and abuse), which would be costly to replace (about $180 US for each roll today), with microfilm readers in vast numbers needing repairs (two-thirds of the two dozen microfilm machines in the main Chicago Public Library, for example, are closed for repairs on any given day). For some strange reason or lack of vision, people also failed to notice that the microfilming process was done completely on black-and-white film, so that the color artwork printed in many newspapers as early as the 1880's was photographed only in black, white and varying shades of gray on modern microfilm. Many of those original color pages may be lost forever. Often the technicians who originally photographed old newspapers onto microfilm were not adequately proficient in their photography skills, so that some newspapers were photographed far too light and others much too dark to be read. Bound copies of real

The OCEAN WAVE's *low-profile cabin housing lies near the damaged, buried stern of the vessel. Just in front of it is the stern cargo hatch.*   PHOTOS BY CRIS KOHL

newspapers were sometimes not removed from their bindings before being microfilmed, so that newsprint columns in the center where the binding was located are often partially missing, or they are out of focus because they could not be made to lie perfectly flat.

Some individuals clearly recognized this problem. The late Dr. Richard Wright, a History professor at Bowling Green State University in Ohio and founder of the Institute for Great Lakes Research in 1972, began aggressively amassing truckloads of Great Lakes newspapers which were being discarded once libraries and museums had them microfilmed or could finally afford to obtain microfilmed copies of them. He and several student helpers painstakingly searched for and cut out all of the Great Lakes maritime information in these original newspapers. Dr. Wright often took work home with him, spending three or four hours an evening snipping through piles of very old newspapers. Back at the university, he and the students would carefully glue these articles onto sheets of paper with the name of the newspaper and the date typewritten across the top of the sheet. These sheets were then placed into binders which Dr. Wright called "scrapbooks." At the time of his death in 1986, he had assembled hundreds of thousands of Great Lakes maritime articles in over 300 scrapbooks, arranged chronologically, and today they remain the only clearly readable collection of Great Lakes maritime history using primary newspaper materials dating from the year 1818 to the modern age. Several individuals, on a more general level, have been collecting as many original bound newspapers as possible in order to save them for history, since microfilming has proven to be flawed.

With today's computer revolution comes the clamor to make all newspapers, even very old ones, available on-line. Those doing most of this clamoring argue that once on-line, microfilm versions of these old newspapers can be discarded. We must learn from the lessons of the past, and be aware that present-day technology has not yet passed the test of time and may not always be available to us. There are disadvantages to today's technology which may, at this point, be hidden from us. One visible problem lies in putting existing microfilmed newspapers on-line -- they are already faulty, and by placing these corrupted microfilmed versions on-line, we become one more generation removed from the original newspaper. The fate of the original printed word appears to be on very shaky ground in our blind rush to leap into the digital age.

The hushed little wreck of the scow schooner, *Ocean Wave*, has sat silently frozen in time on the bottom of Lake Michigan while the surface world has kept whirling, faster and louder, through more than 130 years of intense and massive progress, leapfrogging from small, wooden scow schooners to thousand-foot steel freighters on the Great Lakes, and snowballing from newsprint to microfilm to digital information. As we escape from the mayhem of the modern world by scuba diving into the soundless, subaquatic solar system of the peaceful past, we pause to appraise what a shipwreck, with its researchable history, truly means to us.

THE *CARRINGTON*
(OCTOBER 30, 1870)

D arkness and fog. This is a combination dreaded by every captain who sailed the treacherous waters around Death's Door. Captain Michael Connell, owner and master of the schooner *Carrington*, had good reason for concern as he approached this area in the wee hours of Sunday, the 30th of October, 1870, because the thick haze was obscuring the few lights that marked the rocky shoals. In the murky darkness, he mistook Eagle Harbor Light for Green Island Light and, believing he was giving the island a wide berth, steered northeast and struck the reef which juts out about a mile from the southwest point of Hat Island. The schooner *Carrington* had reached her final port.

The *Carrington* was built in Ohio in 1853 for Frederick Carrington and measured 120 feet 9 inches in length, 24 feet 9 inches wide and 275 gross tons. The two-masted, wooden schooner changed hands many times until finally, in 1868, Capt. Michael Connell of Chicago purchased her and shortly afterward formed a partnership with his brother. Until her fateful final voyage, the *Carrington* had a relatively uneventful career.

After the schooner was recaulked in her home port of Chicago in August, 1870, she was ready to go back to work. On Saturday, October 29, she picked up a cargo of 190 tons of pig iron and a deckload of 600,000 shingles and left Green Bay, heading for Chicago at about 7:00 PM. Seven and a half hours later, in the haze off the shore of Egg Harbor, the captain's mistake sent the ship aground on the rocks of Hat Island.

By daylight, the vessel had taken on six to seven feet of water, and the deck was under water to the main mast. Capt. Connell secured the ship as best he could and, at 9:00 AM, set off with the crew in a small boat for

No photo of the two-masted schooner, Carrington, *has yet come to light, but this ship, the* Cataract, *very closely resembled her.* Cris Kohl Collection

Menominee about fourteen miles away, where the nearest telegraph station was located. He sent a telegram to the insurance company and to get assistance rendered for the ship. A gale blew in that same night, preventing any attempt to return to the schooner. The next morning, Capt. Connell and crew, in a small sailboat, were able to make it to their vessel. What they found was a sad sight indeed. In the storm, the ship had slid off the shoal, was lying on her beam ends and had broken in two.

Both the ship and the cargo were insured, and the salvagers were busy right away trying to gather up the shingles along the beach, recovering about half of them by November 3rd. The pig iron took longer. Since the *Carrington* was submerged in between thirty-five and fifty feet of water, the salvage work on the wreck was done by a team of hardhat divers in the winter of 1871 and the iron was placed on the ice and hauled to Egg Harbor. By March 30, 1871, 125 tons of pig iron had been salvaged, and even forty years later, there was interest in recovering the remainder of the cargo.

Some of that pig iron can still be seen today, scattered around the shipwreck site. In the 1960's, a diver named Francis Felhofer placed a plaque with information about the *Carrington's* history on the shipwreck so that future scuba divers visiting this site will be able to know something about its background.

THE *MERIDIAN*
(OCTOBER 23, 1873)

In her twenty-five years on the Lakes, the *Meridian* had a most colorful history. Sadly, her demise passed without much notice or concern; she sank to her watery grave with barely a whimper.

This two-masted, wooden schooner, official number 16408, slid down the launch ramp in 1848 at Black River, Ohio, having been built by William Jones. Her length measured 120.35 feet, her beam, 23 feet, and her draft, 8.95 feet. Early in her life, using the old measurement method, her gross tonnage was 244 until after 1867, when tonnage was measured under a new system and it changed to 184 gross tons.

On August 1, 1849, barely a year after her launching, the *Meridian* was the setting for events dramatic enough for a scene from *Mutiny on the Bounty*. The ship was heading from Cleveland to Chicago, its home port, and was off Port Washington, Wisconsin, when the Second Mate, James Bain, attacked Capt. Seamour. The First Mate, Harvey Rummage, came to the captain's aid, but Bain grabbed him and threw him overboard. Other members of the crew brought Rummage back on board, but Bain apparently was still intent on a fight and grappled the First Mate. In the ensuing melee, Rummage swung a mighty fist at Bain, killing him instantly. Rummage requested that the ship pull into the port of Milwaukee so that Bain's dead body could be attended to and so that he could surrender to the authorities. What happened to First Mate Rummage is lost to history, but we certainly hope that the captain spoke up in his defense and that this brave mate was exonerated.

In 1852, spring arrived late. Near Buffalo in May, five propellers, two paddlewheelers and many other vessels were frozen in. Despite the

The twin-masted schooner, MERIDIAN, *built in 1848, may have never been photographed, but this lookalike ship, the schooner* FEARLESS, *gives a good idea of what the vessel looked like.*   CRIS KOHL COLLECTION

unseasonably cold weather, the *Meridian* sailed through the lower Detroit River on May 20, 1852. Disaster struck the schooner when she collided with a shipwreck and sank in the cold water near Malden, Ontario. She was recovered and returned to service.

Another grim story in the *Meridian's* history concerned a body that washed onto Chicago's shore on the morning of Saturday, May 2, 1868. The body was that of a sailor named Harris who was lost from the ship on the 13th of April. The circumstances surrounding the drowning of this poor man were not reported, but sailors falling off their ships, or being swept off by waves, were, unfortunately, common occurrences.

In spite of her dramatic history, the final loss of the schooner *Meridian* seems not to have attracted the attention of the media at the time. Was it just another of the many, many schooners that stranded on a reef and was considered a total loss? Were they viewed as past their primes, both in chronological age and in technology, that they were not worth the salvage effort? The heyday of sailing ships was about to begin its descent, replaced slowly but surely by steam-powered, propeller-driven vessels as the stars of Great Lakes shipping. *Inland Lloyds* reported the *Meridian's* value in

Above: *The Sister Islands near the* MERIDIAN *are among the many ship-snaggers in Green Bay waters. Named after the two daughters of an early Goodrich Line captain, and lying less than one mile off shore, these two narrow, low-lying islets, about one-quarter mile each in length and only about 170 feet in width, run in an east-to-west direction with low brush struggling to grow on their rocky surfaces (1860's reports described these islands as being heavily wooded). The unlucky, wrecked schooner,* MERIDIAN, *lies between the boat and the island on the right in this photo. Green Bay waters may appear blue on the surface, but underwater, they live up to their name (see photo below).* PHOTO BY CRIS KOHL

Below: *The most intact, identifiable and interesting part of the wreck of the* MERIDIAN *in 40 feet of water is the bow, here being explored by Joan Forsberg.* PHOTO BY CRIS KOHL

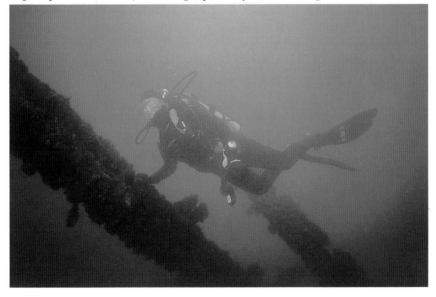

As with many of the shipwrecks which lie in Green Bay, the wreck of the Meridian *on most days will challenge the visiting underwater explorer with less visibility and less light than is generally found on shipwecks on the Lake Michigan side of Death's Door.*

PHOTO BY CRIS KOHL

1873 to be only $4,000, and her insurance rating was only C1, which meant that she was not in the best condition.

On October 23, 1873, the *Meridian*, fighting a heavy gale, stranded on Sister Reef in Green Bay off the southern end of Little Sister Island, not far from the town of Sister Bay, Wisconsin. The propeller *Oconto* reported seeing her broken up from the ravages of the storm. The *Meridian's* final owner, J. Downey, declared her abandoned.

At the very least, modern-day adventurers in the form of scuba divers can appreciate the remains of this once-lively ship. This shipwreck lies in about 45 feet of water, with wreckage rising at the bow to a height of 17 feet above the bay bottom. The rest of the shipwreck is broken and scattered on a sand and clay bottom.

The *Meridian* lies quietly in her final resting place, all the drama of her life ended.

THE BIG BLOW OF **1880**
(OCTOBER **16-17, 1880**)

One of the storms that have great cause to be remembered in lake shipping circles swept over Lake Michigan October 16, 1880.... Violent southwesterly gales on Lake Michigan raged all day of the 16th and part of the 17th. The temperature dropped from 65 degrees to the freezing point, and snow fell as far south as Chicago. The loss of life was very great, nearly 100 souls going down on the Goodrich liner *Alpena*, Grand Haven to Chicago.... In all about 90 vessels were wrecks or badly damaged, and 118 lives were lost as a result of this storm.

This is how John B. Mansfield, in his epic two-volume, 1899 set of books called *The History of the Great Lakes*, described this severe storm which struck Lake Michigan. The Big Blow of 1880 is also known as the Alpena Storm because of the tragic loss of life when the steamer, *Alpena*, disappeared with all hands in lower Lake Michigan during this furious upheaval. It is probably the worst storm in recorded history to hit the Death's Door region, exhibiting greater fury, stronger gales and more destruction in terms of ships lost than any other sustained gale, including the Great Storm of 1913, which wrought most of its fury on Lake Superior and Lake Huron.

The wooden propeller, *Northern Queen,* steamed through the waters near Death's Door during the storm, and that story appeared in the *Chicago Inter Ocean* on October 19, 1880:

> ...Captain Campbell was obliged to make the most of any opportunities for shelter, and, as every anchorage was occupied by vessels, he ran the steamer down the shore to Washington

Island, reaching there at 5 o'clock in the evening. The captain declares that he never encountered such a sea on the lakes during his career of twenty-eight years as a master. It was highest at 4 on Saturday afternoon, and off Death's Door the water was breaking in five fathoms, he believed. While at the island, a large steambarge loaded with ore anchored there, her rails tattered and her foreboom broken.... At every point Captain Campbell found proofs of the extraordinary violence of the gale. At Detroit Island three schooners were stranded and three were at anchor with signals of distress flying, every one...disabled.... The sea was still too high to attempt the relief of any of the craft....

The *Northern Queen* survived this storm unscathed, only to experience problems here one year later (see Chapter 12, pages 131-134).

On October 21, 1880, the *Chicago Inter Ocean* reported, under the heading "News from the Wrecks at Baileys Harbor and North Bay," on some of the many ships still facing problems due to the storm:

...The first vessel on was the *Josephine Lawrence*.... The vessel and cargo will prove a total loss.

The next was the *L. J. Conway*,... she had three anchors and all her chain out, but steadily dragged.... went ashore on the sand beach about 3 o'clock p.m. Having lost her yawl the crew had to stay aboard all night, but were taken off in the morning all safe....

Next was the little schooner *Lettie May*, of Green Bay.... her chain parted. They... let go another anchor, but she went right ashore and washed up high enough for the crew to wade ashore.

...The schooner, *Pauline*, of Manistee,... came in about 6 p.m. on the 16th and let go her anchors, but carried away her chain and windlass and went ashore on sand beach about 7 p.m. The crew had to take to the rigging, and stayed there all night, and were taken off in the morning by the pound boat....

...Also in Mud Bay is the schooner *Contest*,... loaded with ties and poles, bound for Chicago. She went ashore about noon on the 16th and lays up on the rocks on the north side of the bay. The vessel and cargo are all right, and will be saved....

The schooner *James Platt*... parted her small chain and dragged ashore at this place [Baileys Harbor]... All hands safe. Shipped a heavy sea coming in that carried yawl away and steering gear and opened the decks. Canvas badly torn....

The schooners *Cascade* and *Alice B. Norris* are here with canvas stripped but all right. Tow barge *Brunette* is here. Shipped a sea coming in that carried away the house and foresail, and broke the captain's leg....

Schooner *Lem Ellsworth*, also on the beach, light and not injured. Schooner *Florette*, lumber-laden, sunk. Schooner *T. W.*

Left: *Although not from the 1880 Storm shipwreck of the* Perry Hannah *which this marker in a Jacksonport waterfront park commemorates, this small anchor and capstan were found nearby by scuba divers.*

Below: *This anchor at Gordon Lodge at Baileys Harbor supposedly came from the 1880 storm wreck of the schooner,* Two Friends. *If it did, the rest of the shipwreck did not stay behind, but was salvaged, returned to service, and renamed the* Pewaukee. *This anchor could also be from one of the other shipwrecks at Baileys Harbor, such as the* Ebenezer. **Photos by Cris Kohl**

119

Avery, foresail gone. Schooner *Naiad*, big anchor and rudder gone. Schooner *Montauk*, bowsprit and jibboom gone and quarter gone.... *D. A. Van Valkenburg*, masts all gone.... The *Two Friends* (Canada vessel), grain-loaded, is also on the beach full of water....

The *Two Friends'* crew nearly died during this storm. Their stranded ship lay on its side, pounded by the waves several hundred feet from shore, the crew trapped in the angled rigging, the few men on shore seemingly helpless. But one of them, a Sister Bay fisherman named James Larson, sprang into action. His attempts to throw a small line failed, so he persuaded a local man to let him use his rowboat (something Larson accomplished only by leaving enough money with the man to cover the boat's possible loss). In seven successive trips alone in a 14-foot boat through the pounding surf at night, Larson brought each of the seven crew back safely to shore. For his 90 minutes of brave, furious work in rescuing the crew of the *Two Friends*, Larson was awarded a gold medal from the Life-Saving Service.

The large cargo of salt in the *Two Friends* unfortunately converted the waters of North Bay into brine so strong that it was rendered unfit for drinking purposes. One local fisherman complained that he had to go several miles to find drinking water for his household.

The *Two Friends*, of all these ships, seems to have the most steadfast, although incorrect, reputation for being a shipwreck near Death's Door. This vessel was salvaged and returned to service under the name *Pewaukee*. It was converted first to a steamship and later to a barge, finally being abandoned at Sturgeon Bay in 1913. It lies in the ships' boneyard there.

The permanent victims of the Big Blow of 1880 in the Death's Door region were all schooners: the *Josephine Lawrence*, the *Ebenezer*, and the *Perry Hannah*. The 88-ton *Josephine Lawrence* of Port Washington, Wisconsin, loaded with rubble stone from Washington Island to Chicago, dragged her anchor, parted her chain and went ashore on the sand beach at Baileys Harbor. All hands took to the rigging, including the captain, his wife and child, and lashed themselves securely until a pound boat removed them to safety. The 120-ton, twin-masted, 17-year-old *Ebenezer* (91'6" x 22'3" x 8'7") with a stone cargo, was dragged ashore on the rocks at Mud Bay. The storm drove the 220-ton *Perry Hannah* (125' x 26' x 10'6") up against the south side of Reynolds' pier, destroying it, at Jacksonport.

After the storm, the lighthouse keeper on Pilot Island reported that Lake Michigan's water around the light was white for a week. He theorized that the violent, prolonged storm had broken and ground up many of the limestone rocks lying just beneath the surface around the island, and that the white, lime powder remained suspended in the agitated lake waters for several days before finally settling to the bottom.

The *D. A. Van Valkenburg*
(September 16, 1881)

Front page ink on a New York City daily newspaper is not usually the kind of wide-ranging attention given to a Great Lakes shipwreck, but when that shipwreck sustained the worst loss of life of any on the Lake Michigan side of the Death's Door area, attention is understandable.

Page one of the *New York Tribune* on Sunday, September 18, 1881, announced succinctly:

> ### A SCHOONER AND HER CREW LOST
> Chicago, Sept. 17.---News was received here to-day that the schooner *D. R.* [sic] *Van Valkenburg*, corn laden, for Buffalo, went down with all hands, off Whitefish Bay yesterday. No particulars given. The crew probably consists of half a dozen persons.

Surprisingly, John Mansfield completely overlooked this vessel and its tragic loss in his massive *History of the Great Lakes* in 1899. Considering the scope and detail of his two-volume work, it can only be viewed as a serious oversight that the worst shipwreck disaster which he describes for the year 1881 is the sinking of the *Carlingford* and the *Brunswick* by collision in Lake Erie when four lives were lost. The *D. A. Van Valkenburg* sank that same year near Death's Door in Lake Michigan with the loss of eight lives.

Launched at Tonawanda, New York, in 1866, the massive, 538.78-ton, three-masted schooner, *D. A. Van Valkenburg*, departed Chicago on Wednesday, September 14, 1881, at about 4 P.M., with an enormous cargo of 30,000 bushels of corn bound for Buffalo. An average-sized Great Lakes schooner would have operated with a total of five or six sailors on board, but this large vessel was beyond ordinary. It required a crew of nine.

The magnificent, 535-ton vessel, Stuart H. Dunn *(173'6" x 26'8" x 12'7"), seen here being towed out of a harbor while light, that is, riding high without a cargo, is representative of what the large, 539-ton* D. A. Van Valkenburg *would have looked like in the 1880's. The* Dunn *was scuttled in deep water in Lake Ontario in late 1925.* Cris Kohl Collection

The *Van Valkenburg* was driven off course by strong easterly winds and struck rocks on the north side of Whitefish Point at seven P.M. on Thursday, September 15, 1881.While the ship stayed stuck fast and helpless in that position, the wind increased and shifted to the northeast, a direction generally considered dangerous for sailing on the inland seas. The crew spent a restless night stranded while facing strong winds and agitated seas. Come daylight on Friday, aware that the serious pounding had begun to break up their ship, the nine crewmembers filled and launched the ship's yawlboat, ready to take it out into the lake (away from the inhospitable-looking shore), only to have the wind and waves capsize it almost immediately. Only six men managed to get back into the yawlboat, the other three having been swept away by the strength of the wild waves. A few more relentless billows emptied the yawlboat permanently.

The bodies of the *Van Valkenburg* crew washed up along the heavily forested, rocky, crag-lined shore at Cave Point. With large, forceful waves fiercely pounding the embankment and streaming with a relentlessly danger-ous rhythm in and out of the swirling recesses of the dents and coves crenelating the 30-foot-tall cliffs, this was the most inhospitable place on the lake. Even if a crewmember did not drown in the raging seas, death by dashing on the jagged rocks was likely.

At Jacksonport, three miles north along the shoreline from where the shipping accident occurred, a bewildered stranger, appearing confused, staggered into town. Royal Erskine, a resident, approached the man and asked him what was the matter. The man had difficulty speaking, but he conveyed some vague information about a nearby shipwreck. A search party quickly formed and started down the beach, where they found half a dozen bodies, a couple of them high and dry on the rocks, and the rest tossing about in the surf and coves.

The stranger who had wandered into Jacksonport was crewmember Thomas Breen, by luck the sole survivor from the nine-man crew of the wrecked *D. A. Van Valkenburg*. Although physically spent and seemingly mentally damaged, Breen recalled that, as he became caught up in the repeated cycle of the heavy seas dashing him against the rocks and the undertow carrying him out again, he managed to seize hold of a boulder as the water receded. He soon landed on the shoreline, more dead than alive, fading in and out of consciousness. Eventually, and without a clue about his location, Breen wandered inland through the thick underbrush and eventually reached the road which he took north into Jacksonport.

A TERRIBLE COAST.

That Where the Fine Ship Van Valkenberg Went Down with Her Crew.

A Connected, Graphic Account of the Disaster from Captain MacMillan, Now at the Scene.

A Precipice of Solid Rock, with the Poor Seamen Struggling Below.

The Great Staunch Vessel Broken in Fragments and Strewn Along the Coast.

A Full Statement from Breen, the Only Survivor of the Entire Company.

General Marine News—A Fierce Squall Yesterday—A Bridge Blown Down.

THE VAN VALKENBERG.
THE ADA MEDORA'S REPORT.
The schooner Ada Medora, Captain Fred Gunderson, which left Chicago with the ill-fated schooner D. A. Van Valkenberg, is back in port

The newspapers of that era, highlighting story details with multiple subheadings, offered their readers dramatic (and often too graphic) accounts of shipwreck losses. The grim fate of the **D. A. VAN VALKENBURG'S** *crew reached many members of the public by means of this account in the* CHICAGO INTER OCEAN *on September 25, 1881.*

CRIS KOHL COLLECTION

The town's search party spent all day Friday recovering as many bodies as they could find, a particularly demanding job when they looked down and saw a body being pounded by harsh waves in a small cove with difficult access. The bodies were carried on stretchers through the underbrush to wagons waiting on the road to convey them to Jacksonport. Several men in town spent Friday night making coffins. On Saturday, the six bodies, which had already turned black, were buried at Jacksonport. The town's generous residents provided everything: coffins, pallbearers, ceremony and plots.

On a summer day, the Cave Point shoreline and Lake Michigan almost appear friendly. But the waves are not whitecaps -- they are breaking on the shallow shelf of hard rock extending just beneath the water's surface around the entire point. When storms develop, even during summertime, this area becomes potentially life-threatening to mariners -- as the eight victims of the D. A. Van Valkenburg *discovered.* PHOTO BY CRIS KOHL

When some people in Sturgeon Bay heard that steward Richard Harlow was a Freemason, they reburied him in a fine, rosewood coffin with Masonic honors in Sturgeon Bay. The three sailors who were members of the Seaman's Union (Robert Keith, Peter Hennesey and George Curtis) were also reburied in Chicago at the expense of the union.

Survivor Breen remembered his crewmates only by their first names. He identified the bodies and was able to tell which positions they held on board the ship. Papers found in the pockets of the deceased further helped identify them. Breen was, however, unsure of the captain's surname, but he thought it was Keith (the bodies of the captain and the first mate were still missing). In fact, at this point, Breen was not even certain of the ship's name. He did think, however, that there had been something wrong with the ship's compass, and that was why the vessel ended up off course.

The search party on land saw nothing of the shipwreck, but the corn cargo was washing ashore, suggesting that the ship broke up quickly.

The Chicago owners of the *Van Valkenburg*, Thomas Hood and Capt. William MacMillan, unaware of their vessel's fate, received this telegram:

> Do you want any assistance at the schooner *Van Valkenberg*[sic]? I have wrecking apparatus and the tug *Dennis Brothers*.
> Joseph Dennis, Sturgeon Bay, Wis., Sept. 16.

Joan Forsberg carefully watches her step as she approaches huge, relentless waves pounding in one of the small coves at Cave Point where bodies from the schooner **D. A. Van Valkenburg** *were churned on the rocky shore after the ship sank. Only one man escaped these nightmarish waters and hostile shoreline, just barely able to cling to a rock and pull himself up to safety.* PHOTO BY CRIS KOHL

Of course, the ship's owners did not understand the telegram's meaning. A second telegram finally arrived which explained the lamentable situation:

> Notify the owner of the bark *D. A. Van Valkenberg* [sic] that she went ashore near Whitefish Bay Point at 7 o'clock last evening--- Thursday. (The wires have been down.) All hands were drowned except a sailor named Breen. She was loaded with corn, and has probably gone to pieces by this time.
>
> Charles Reynolds.

Capt. MacMillan quickly visited the scene of the disaster, interviewed the sole survivor, and made notes about the ship's remains. The following accounts appeared in both the *Chicago Inter Ocean* and the *Door County Advocate* in late September, 1881:

> The deck beams and decks and houses and taffrail and some of the timber-boards, rudder, pieces of the cabin, etc., are strewn along the shore on the rocks and stony beach. The masts, yards, and other spars are floating over the balance of the wreck. I saw the ends of the anchor stocks sticking out of the water yesterday, but to-day they are not to be seen, but the spars have turned them over, as it is blowing a strong breeze to-day. The stern-post and a piece of the keel attached has broken off, and is floating around among the spars to-day. If the water becomes smooth, the anchors and chains and a great many blocks might be saved, as the mainmast, mizzenmast and some of the gaffs and booms, the bowsprit and jibboom are just as they were when in their proper places, but of course floating around among the rest of the spars, and only held to the wreck by the bobstays.
>
> The corn is being scooped out of the lake with dip nets from the top of the rocks, and some of them [the local residents] have long ladders made to go down to the edge of the water with which to get the corn. Of course the corn has all been washed out of the wreck....

Reportedly every available vacant building and shed was filled with the corn which was washed ashore from the *Van Valkenburg* and recovered by the local residents, as much as 30 wagons of corn in one day.

The eight shipwreck victims were Capt. Andrew L. Keith, of Chicago; his 25-year-old son, Robert Keith, who worked as second mate; A. S. Kalloch, the first mate; Richard Harlow, steward/cook; Peter Hennesey; George Curtis; Thomas Keegan; and a young German sailor.

Concern over the *Van Valkenburg's* survivor continued. The *Cleveland Herald* wrote that, "Thomas Breen, the sole survivor..., is so badly injured that his mind is confused and he cannot give a clear account of the disaster...." Breen, however, appearing much more clearheaded than he did on the day of the disaster, gave surprising details of the ship's final operations and ultimate loss to Capt. MacMillan:

...The course that I steered when it was my trick at the wheel was north by east.... I did not have another wheel [a turn at steering]. The vessel struck the rocks before my turn came, but I heard the men that were steering say that she would break off sometimes to northwest for a little while and then come right back to her course again.... I went into the forecastle and lay down on the locker and had a smoke, and was waiting for eight bells to go to the wheel. I heard the second mate telling the man at the wheel to give her a half a point better full, and immediately afterward I felt the vessel strike, and I thought we were giving her center-board.... They then sounded the pump and found twenty-two inches of water in her. We took in all sails but the mizzen. The vessel was then pounding with her bilges against what seemed to be a ledge of rocks, and was striking heavily forward and aft. Before this the wheel was partly unshipped. Afterward the captain said take the wheel off, and we took it off and laid it down on one side. While the men were aft the captain said: "I see the Manitous." He then said: "Go below, boys; we can't do anything more now." ...About 2 A.M. the mate called all hands to get the boat alongside, and got the bags with our clothing ready and the boat provisioned and everything ready to leave the wreck. We got some coffee and something to eat. All hands then made into the boat, ready to leave for the lake, as we saw nothing but a precipice of rocks ashore and no place to land in sight. The second mate said, in a little while: "Father, we had better leave. The mainmast is going to tumble over on us." The captain then called out to the man in the boat to "stand by and cut the bowlines as soon as that big sea goes past." And when it passed he cut the line, and we pulled out in the lake about two lengths of the vessel from the vessel. We got over a number of seas when a big roller came along on the reef that extended away outside of the vessel and raised the bow of the boat high out of the water and the stern went under at the same time. The sea rolled over both gunwales, and she went down and came up bottom up. When I came up I had hold of an oar. I saw that it was of no use to me, and I swam to the boat and got hold of the keel. I then looked around to see who were with me, and I saw Hennesey, Curtis, the mate, and the captain. The next sea that came along washed us all off but the captain, who had hold of the ring in the stern of the boat. The next time I caught the boat there was Hennesey, Curtis, and the captain. I heard the mate say, "Oh, God!" that was the last I saw or heard of him. A number of seas came along, and we had hard work to hold on. I think the captain was struck by the stern of the boat on the breast. A little while after the bow of the boat struck the rocks I said to Hennesey and Curtis, "She has struck bottom." They said, "Has she?" Hennesey said to Curtis, "How do you feel?" Curtis said, "I am getting very weak. I wish I had these coats off." (He had an undercoat and an oil-cloth on.) I said to him, "Then keep well forward on the boat." (The boat's bow was out, head to the sea all the time.) A big sea came along and washed me off, and I saw them no more alive. Just before this happened I saw George with a bag of clothes under his arm, and an oar under his other arm. I then saw a spot on the shore among the rocks, and I made up my mind that if I did not reach it I would never get ashore alive. I succeeded in reaching a rock, and held myself on it about a minute to rest. The sea kept washing me in every sea that came, and I never let go of the rocks until I got out of the water....

About ten days after the disaster, a local resident took a small boat to the wreck site and found the hull split in two from stem to stern, and concluded that the wreck "will undoubtedly be completely used up by wearing and grinding on the jagged rocks which line the beach for some distance."

During the first week of October, 1881, Capt. MacMillan's efforts to recover the anchor, chains and other items from the wreck were foiled by bad weather. However, the ship's bell, which weighed between 40 and 50 pounds, washed ashore and was recovered intact. By mid-October, with calmer weather, the anchors and chain were recovered from the site.

First Mate Kalloch's body was found in late September and sent to Chicago for burial, leaving only the captain missing. Capt. William Keith of Chicago had gone to Whitefish Bay and spent many days combing the shoreline in search of his brother, Capt. Andrew Keith's, body, but returned home frustrated. Several weeks later, on Saturday, November 12, 1881, Jacksonport resident William Brabazon, found the captain's body on the beach one and one-half miles north of the place where the ship was wrecked. The last of the eight bodies had been recovered; it was sent home for burial.

The *D. A. Van Valkenburg* had new decks, some beams and other repairs made only three years earlier, and was overhauled just a few months before her demise. Rated B1 by the insurance companies, the ship was valued at $16,000 and insured for $12,000. A year earlier, the *Van Valkenburg* was coincidentally at Whitefish Bay when it was caught in the Big Blow of 1880, losing her masts in the storm. The initial cost of repairing the dismasted vessel was given as $800 (in the official "Wreck Report"), later increased to $4,000 (*Chicago Inter Ocean*, October 26, 1880), and still later, placed at $8,000 (*Door County Advocate*, November 18, 1880). It is not known how high that particular repair bill went.

However, the ship had opened that season of 1881 on a Friday, a fact reported by a shocked Chicago newspaper which chided Capt. Keith and the owners for "tempting the fates." The old superstition about starting the first trip of the season on a Friday forever dooming that ship to ill luck was true in the case of the *Van Valkenburg*.

Years later, in 1909, a writer suggested that this tragic loss of lives was responsible for opening government eyes to the necessity of building a lighthouse at the lake entrance to the Sturgeon Bay Ship Canal eight miles south of the wreck site. This lighthouse, however, was already nearing completion when the *Van Valkenburg* sank (it opened officially in May, 1882).

The massive *D. A. Van Valkenburg* was reputedly a solid vessel, but the gales and rocks of Death's Door proved far more powerful. Two months after she sank, surprisingly little remained of her at the site: "...A portion of her bottom can be seen on the bottom of the lake in clear weather. This lies about nine feet below the surface, where it is held down by the iron and will probably remain for years."

THE *JENNIBELL*
(SEPTEMBER 17, 1881)

E arly on Saturday morning, September 17, 1881, a sudden, fierce squall out of the south capsized the two-masted schooner, *Jennibell*, in Death's Door Passage near Plum Island. The crew desperately clung to the sides of the ship, praying for rescue. Fortunately for them, Capt. Burnham of the tug, *Gregory*, which was at anchor nearby, witnessed the catastrophe and sped to the distressed ship. The *Gregory* picked up the crew and took the *Jennibell* in tow, heading for Sturgeon Bay instead of the nearer harbor of Ellison Bay so that the ship could be raised and pumped out, as requested by the schooner's master, Capt. Jacobson.

The *Gregory* headed around the western side of Chambers Island because the water was too shallow on the eastern side to clear the capsized *Jennibell's* masts. Coming abreast of the island, the rescuers found themselves fighting a gale so severe that they had to release the stricken schooner which, with her waterlogged cargo of green wood, went to the bottom.

A few days later, the *Gregory* returned to the wreck of the *Jennibell* to try to pull her off the bottom of Green Bay, but after considerable effort and time, the line broke, leaving the sunken vessel where she lay. At the time, it was thought that since the schooner's anchors were overboard, it was impossible for the tug to raise her.

The 94-foot-long, 132-ton schooner, *Jennibell*, had left Egg Harbor the day before with a cargo of green cordwood and a deckload of hemlock bark. Apparently Capt. Jacobson disregarded the old sailor's superstition that it is bad luck to leave port on a Friday. This voyage certainly proved to be unlucky for J. J. Barringer, the owner of the uninsured deck cargo valued at $500 (the below deck cordwood's value was not given), and for J. and C.

Left: *This lookalike schooner, the* JOSEPH DUVALL, *had very similar dimensions to the* JENNIBELL. *The* DUVALL *sank in the St. Clair River in 1905 after a collision with the steel whaleback, the* JAMES B. COLGATE.

CRIS KOHL COLLECTION

Below: *In the 1960's, scuba divers attempted to raise the* JENNIBELL, *but unfortunately, the ship broke in two when it was lifted from the bottom. Only a mast and the bowsprit were recovered.*

PHOTOS BY FRANCIS FELHOFER, COURTESY OF JON PAUL VAN HARPEN

Christianson, owners of the ill-fated *Jennibell*, valued at $2,500 at the time of loss. The *Jennibell* had been built in Sheboygan, Wisconsin, in 1863.

The unfortunate history of the *Jennibell* did not end with her sinking. George O. Spear, the famous shipbuilder who owned the *Gregory*, sued the schooner's owners for services rendered amounting to $600. Although the Christiansons countersued for $3,000, the value of their lost vessel and its deck cargo, the court in 1885 found in favor of the tug's owner, who was awarded a portion of his claim.

The *Jennibell* rested undisturbed for 80 years until 1961 when she was located by Egg Harbor diver Frank Hoffman and his team. Hoping to succeed where the *Gregory* had failed 80 years earlier, they placed cables under the schooner's hull and tried to raise her. But this 1963 recovery attempt would fare no better than the tug's; in fact, it fared much worse. The *Jennibell* broke in two and dropped back to the bottom in 105 feet of water. Today, this site is visited by scuba divers who enjoy viewing 1860's nautical items such as the anchor chain wrapped around the windlass, a centerboard winch, and even her 1881 cargo of cordwood below deck.

THE *LAKE ERIE*
(NOVEMBER 24, 1881)

I shall never navigate the lakes again," pronounced Capt. J. M. Johnson of the propeller *Lake Erie*. Usually "the jolliest and newsiest of Canadian captains... his thin countenance, worn look, and the absence of his hale and hearty manner told, more than words, the effect the miraculous escape from an awful death had upon him." So reported the *Chicago Inter Ocean* of December 1, 1881, after interviewing the captain about the disastrous events that had just occurred.

Our story of the tragic *Lake Erie* actually begins on September 10, 1881. Carrying corn, sundries and a few passengers from Chicago to Collingwood, Ontario, the propeller, *Columbia*, sank in a storm off Frankfort, Michigan, with the loss of 16 of the 23 people aboard. Shaken by the loss, its Toronto owner, the New England Transportation Company, insisted that, drawing near to the end of the shipping season when the lakes were the most dangerous, its ships would travel together.

Thus, on Tuesday, November 22, the propeller, *Lake Erie,* and its sister ship, the *Northern Queen*, both carrying corn cargoes, left Chicago together so that in case of an accident to one of them, the other could render assistance. It was a good and safe plan, except for the northwest gale-force wind, mist and snow that overtook the vessels in the pre-dawn of November 24th while they were nearing Point aux Barques. The weather had already been so cold that ice four inches thick was reported in the Sturgeon Bay Ship Canal. But the *Lake Erie* and the *Northern Queen* pressed on. Unable to see each other or communicate their locations, the sisters in the storm were doomed. Capt. J. M. Johnson of Collingwood, Ontario, master of the *Lake Erie,* described what transpired:

> ...It was a horrible night. It snowed and rained together, and the air was permeated with mists and smoke so that the ship lights were hardly distinguishable. The *Lake Erie* was ahead, and I on deck. I blew the whistle to indicate a change in our course toward Beaver Islands. No response came---the sound had no chance in that gale. I gave the order to port the wheel. Observing that the *Queen* did not respond I ordered the mate to starboard the wheel. The second change of course was fatal. The *Queen* bore down upon us. She gave two warning whistles and there was a sudden crash, shaking the ship from stem to stern.... In an instant all hands were on deck. I sounded the water forward and found four inches, but aft it had crept above the fire hold of the floor.... Five minutes later the fires were out.... An examination showed that the steampipe was broken, the machinery useless, and we were at the mercy of the waves....

The *Northern Queen* had rammed the *Lake Erie* twelve feet forward of the aft gangway. Within minutes, its propulsion extinguished, the *Lake Erie* bobbed helplessly in the wind and waves. At first, the *Northern Queen* attempted to throw a line to the *Lake Erie* in hopes of being able to tow her into shallow water, but the ferocious weather would not permit that. The *Queen* pulled alongside in the tremendous seas and rescued the entire crew, including one sailor, William Forbes of Hamilton, Ontario, who had been horribly scalded by the steam. Twelve miles off shore, after a two-hour struggle, as the 136-foot-long, wooden *Lake Erie* sank at dawn on Thanksgiving Day, Capt. Johnson described the dreadful scene:

> She rose on her keel, the main mast crashing down, and sunk out of sight stern first. I shall never forget that instant, nor the pang of horror that thrilled me when I saw her disappear.... We sounded where she went down but found no bottom.

Determining that the *Northern Queen* was not badly damaged, but that the injured sailor was in desperate need of medical care, Capt. A. C. Cameron, also from Collingwood, Ontario, steered his vessel towards the nearest harbor. Two miles south of Manistique, the injured sailor unfortunately died before help could be reached. By this time leaking badly, the *Northern Queen* was steered into Manistique Bay. Capt. Johnson and his *Lake Erie* crew felt the terror of a second ship sinking under their feet:

> Between the strong current setting out and the gale and sea running in, the *Queen* whirled twice around, the stern striking the end of the pier. Great swells crashed over her and as she was

The 427-ton, wooden steamer, Lake Erie *(136' x 23'4" x 7'3"), sank at 5 AM on November 24, 1881, in a collision after passing Death's Door. The ship had been constructed by Melancthon Simpson at St. Catharines, Ontario, in 1873.* Cris Kohl Collection

> pounding to pieces, the captain scuttled her to save at least a remnant. The sea broke in her windows and carried away her cabins...Now came the struggle for life...We launched the yawl and in an instant were driven out into the surf. By a great effort a line was thrown us and we were drawn in, drenched to the skin.

For the next three days, the 36 members of the two shipwrecked crews stayed in Manistique where they were sheltered by the locals and they buried their shipmate. The adventures of the men of the sister ships were not at an end, however, as they set out in sleighs to travel the 60 miles to civilization. Capt. Johnson continued his thrilling tale:

> We traveled 23 miles when the snow disappeared. Night had arrived and we were in the midst of a great forest. Procuring a guide we started out on the remaining distance on foot. Wolves and wild animals beset us on all sides, but our force was large, and they dared not attack us. Over the rough roads and through the gloom we fought until Day's River was reached, and we were at a railway station at last.

It had been a horrible season for the New England Transportation Company. They had lost three ships in three months, three-fourths of their fleet, and 18 souls had gone to their graves. With only one ship left, the

Canada, the shipping line itself was in peril.

The *Lake Erie* was insured for $18,720, with her main cargo of 16,000 bushels of corn covered for $10,850. The sundry cargo, comprising 50 barrels of corn-meal, 20 barrels of mess pork, 50 bales of broom-corn and 11 sacks of oil-meal, were insured for a total of $3,325.

The *Northern Queen*, launched at Marine City, Michigan, in 1872, as the 340-ton, wooden bulk freighter, *Robert Holland* (149'6" x 28'2" x 11'8"), was renamed in 1878 upon conversion at Manitowoc to a combination passenger and package freighter. The *Queen* was valued at $13,600 at the time of loss, and insured for about two-thirds of her value.

Ironically, the *Northern Queen* was raised from the depths of Manistique harbor in 1882 and was successfully returned to service as a bulk freighter under a new name -- the *Robert Holland,* the ship's former name before she became the *Northern Queen*! For over 30 years, this vessel served the Great Lakes with only minor mishaps until May 11, 1915, when she burned to a complete loss at Sturgeon Bay, where she lies today with other boneyard ships. An 1897 newspaper article headlined "Relic of an Old Wreck. Parts of the *Northern Queen* Dredged up at Manistique" was incorrect, with the dredgers and the writer unaware that the *Northern Queen* had been raised and returned to service under a new name. The true identity of this "Old Wreck...at Manistique" remains unknown.

In early December, 1881, a tugboat captain reported that the life preservers and the piano from the *Lake Erie* were washed ashore at the Beaver Islands.

The story of the *Lake Erie* and the *Northern Queen* is full of tragic irony. The calamitous accident to the *Lake Erie* deckhand caused the leaking *Northern Queen* to seek assistance ashore, rather than continue its journey out into the open lake, where it would have found no help when it needed it. The November 30, 1881, *Chicago Inter Ocean* summed up the disaster:

> The most remarkable thing about this matter is the extra precaution taken to ensure the safety of the propellers... both boats... kept in sight of each other until a blinding snowstorm intervened and in a fatal moment the faster running craft crashed into the slower one with terrible effect to both.
>
> The case forms a precedent among others in the whole history of the lake marine. Three propellers of the line lost within as many months, one carrying her crew to the bottom, another running into and sinking the third, and the last bearing the crews to a point of safety and then disappearing out of sight.

13

THE *F. J. KING*
(SEPTEMBER 15, 1886)

T he *F. J. King* was constructed for the timber trade, and strength being the main consideration, less beauty of symmetry was perhaps expected, but we believe in both respects she more than realizes the expectations of her owners. Her dimensions are, length, 144 feet, beam, 26 feet 2 inches, depth of hold 12 feet, and measures about 285 tons. The timber used in this vessel is of a quality superior to that generally used....and in every part the greatest attention was given to render the hull as staunch as possible. The cabin is large...the skipper's quarters neat, cosy and cheerful, nicely carpeted, and the other rooms are furnished in good taste, everything bearing testimony to the skill of a master builder.

Clearly, the reporter for the *Toledo Blade* of June 18, 1867, who was present at the launching of the *F. J. King* the day before, was very impressed with the latest addition to the cadre of Great Lakes schooners. Stoutly constructed by George R. Rogers of Toledo for the proud owners, the Wilcox Brothers, the *King* was about to begin a very successful, profitable career. Her first master was Capt. Charles Cramer, described by the *Blade* as "a capital fellow." After the launch, the schooner was towed to the Wilcox dock and a sort of "open house" was held. M. I. Wilcox, Esq., invited Mayor King (for whom the ship was named) and members of the Board of Trade to join him on board, and everyone enjoyed "wetting" the new vessel.

Thus launched in grand style, the *F. J. King* began a solid career hauling lumber and eventually carried a variety of cargoes.

Attempting one last run of the season in December, 1869, the *King* was sent to a port on Lake Ontario for the first time, which meant traversing the Welland Canal. However, when she reached Port Colborne, Ontario, downbound, it was discovered that she was a bit too long for the locks, and the corners of her stern had to be cut off. The Toledo owners planned to give her a rounded stern during the winter so that she would be what was termed a "canal vessel." A length of 140 feet was about the maximum for a ship to pass through the Second Welland Canal, which had been completed in 1845. The Third Welland Canal, with clearance for 250-foot-long vessels, would not be constructed and opened until 1887. However, that year would be too late for the *F. J. King*.

It was not unusual for a Great Lakes ship to pass through several owners and masters in its lifetime, but the *King* had few changes of ownership. Capt. J. S. Dunham purchased her in 1871 and owned the vessel until her demise. By 1886, Dunham and Capt. William Griffin were partners in the vessel, with Griffin, the master, holding a one-third interest. In the winter of 1886, the nineteen-year-old ship was given a complete rebuild which brought her value up to $10,000, and she was given an A2 rating by the underwriters, quite high for an aging schooner.

There is some discrepancy among contemporary newspapers relating to the exact time and date of the disaster which befell the *F. J. King*, but the *Door County Advocate* claimed to have learned the details directly from Capt. Griffin. According to the captain, they left Escanaba with a load of iron ore on Tuesday, September 14, 1886, at 1:00 in the afternoon, bound for Chicago. At first pleasant, the weather changed for the worse as soon as the vessel made it into Lake Michigan, and a southeast wind pounded hard on the ship. By the next morning, abreast of the Sturgeon Bay Canal, the schooner's wooden seams opened and Capt. Griffin gave orders to come about and run the vessel before the wind. He hoped that he could beach her on sandy ground in the shelter of North Bay, but the seas were so heavy that the ship was rolling terribly and becoming unmanageable.

Four miles east of Cana Island, the wind died down, but the waves were still so high that the *King* broached to and was carried two miles further out when she began to sink. The pumps were not able to keep up, despite heroic efforts by the crew, and the captain knew that the schooner was doomed. Luckily, another ship was passing by, a schooner named the *La Petite*, and Capt. Griffin signalled her for help. The *La Petite* changed course and headed for the stricken *King*.

After Capt. Griffin gave the order to abandon ship, his eight-man crew gathered a few of their belongings before taking to the yawl boat. The captain was the last to leave his sinking schooner. Twenty-eight minutes later, on Wednesday, September 15, 1886, at 1:00 in the afternoon (exactly 24 hours

The three-masted, 265-ton, 135-foot-long schooner, HATTIE HUTT, *was very similar in size and appearance to the 280-ton, 140-foot-long* F. J. KING .   CRIS KOHL COLLECTION

after they had left Escanaba), the crew watched their ship sink bow first, and they heard an explosion as the trapped air blew outward, causing some of the captain's papers from his cabin to fly fifty feet into the air. Then the *F. J. King* was gone.

The *La Petite* brought the captain and crew safely to the wharf in North Bay that same afternoon.

The men went by stage to Sturgeon Bay, where the crew, except for the captain, boarded the schooner-barge, *Westchester*, in tow of the tug *T. H. Smith*, and headed for Chicago. Capt. Griffin, however, went to Menominee and, with a heavy heart, took a train to Chicago. He had lost a ship which had served its owners well, had suffered no major calamities until now, and had always been a moneymaker. He knew that, because of the extreme depth where the *King* had foundered, and because the cargo was heavy, bulky iron ore, there would be no salvage attempt. This would be an especially hard loss for his partner, Capt. James Dunham, who had suffered three other wrecks in a little over three years. In 1883, in a savage spring storm off Chicago, Dunham's schooner, the *Wells Burt*, tragically sank with the loss of all eleven crew. One can be certain that Dunham and Griffin were relieved beyond words that the entire crew of the *F. J. King* was saved, but the *King* was the only vessel in the Dunham fleet that was uninsured, although Griffin had insured his one-third interest. Dunham, despite his loss, remained optimistic, and continued in the shipping business for years.

WANTED

GPS OR LORAN

F. J. KING

$1,000.00
REWARD

THIS IS NOT A JOKE!   YOU WILL RECEIVE $1,000.00 CASH
AFTER VERIFICATION OF FIND BY
THE CLUB SHIPWRECK COMMITTEE.
FOR MORE INFORMATION CHECK OUT
WEB SITE: www.neptunesnimrods.org

*The reward offered for the location of
the* F. J. KING. COURTESY OF THE NEPTUNE'S
NIMRODS SCUBA CLUB

The keeper of the Cana Island light, William Sanderson, reported to the Milwaukee collector of customs that the *F. J. King* mastheads were sticking out of the water and presented a hazard to navigation. The revenue cutter, *Andy Johnson*, would have been dispatched to remove the obstruction, but a further message in early October from Capt. Sanderson reported that the masts were no longer visible. All that remained floating on the surface of the water was a portion of the square sail, as if the *King* were vainly trying to mark the spot of its watery grave.

Today, the exact location of the *F. J. King* is unknown. No eyes have seen her since the crew witnessed her sinking. The *King* is one of the most hunted shipwrecks in the Great Lakes, largely because it is believed that she will be found in extremely good condition. She was staunchly built, was not especially old, was well-maintained and suffered no catastrophic damage on the surface (such as from a collision, from crashing onto the rocks, or from being crushed by ice). Sinking in deep water, the ship has probably not been pounded to pieces, as have many shipwrecks in the shallows. Finding this shipwreck has become so important that a Sturgeon Bay area scuba dive club, the Neptune's Nimrods, has offered a reward of $1,000 for anyone who produces coordinates which can be verified as being the location of the *King*. The Neptune's Nimrods is the oldest scuba diving club in Wisconsin and its members are excellent stewards of the shipwrecks in their local waters.

The *F. J. King* will be a true historical treasure when she is found, and humans can set eyes upon her for the first time in over 120 years.

14

THE *FLEETWING*
(SEPTEMBER 26, 1888)

C aptain Andrew McGraw was faced with a choice that evening of the 26th of September, 1888: to take the safe route from Green Bay to Lake Michigan through the Sturgeon Bay Ship Canal, or to try to guide his schooner, the *Fleetwing,* through one of the most perilous stretches of water in the Great Lakes -- Death's Door Passage. It was dark and the wind was blowing at gale force. He chose Death's Door.

At the time of the launching of the two-masted, wooden schooner, *Fleetwing,* at Manitowoc, Wisconsin, on August 10, 1867, a reporter for the *Manitowoc Pilot* declared the ship to be sturdily built and "very handsome in the water." She was 136 feet long, had a beam of 28.5 feet and sported an eagle figurehead.

Other Door County shipwrecks, proudly and perhaps surprisingly, bore figureheads: the scow schooner, *Ocean Wave,* carried an eagle figurehead (see pages 99-110), the *A. P. Nichols,* wrecked at Pilot Island, had one (pages 79-92), and perhaps the historic *Columbia* (pages 77-78), lost at Death's Door in 1859, also carried an example of such carved, wooden artwork.

Henry B. Burger built the *Fleetwing* for S. Goodenow and Peter Johnson of Manitowoc for use in the grain trade. After the Civil War, Great Lakes shipping was booming, and Goodenow and Johnson were eager to own one of these fast and well-built schooners to transport grain from Chicago to Buffalo. Unfortunately for the *Fleetwing's* owners, grain prices and the shipping boom had begun to soften by the time the ship set sail for the first time. They brought in Capt. James Pederson as master and part owner in 1874.

The noble schooner, Fleetwing, soundly constructed at Manitowoc, Wisconsin, shortly after the Civil War, was bound for Death's Door Passage 21 years later when her captain temporarily lost his bearings -- and, permanently, his ship.   Cris Kohl Collection

By 1880, the Chicago lumber merchants, John Spry, John C. Spry and H. H. Gardner bought out Goodenow and Johnson (Pederson remained master-owner) and yanked the *Fleetwing* out of the grain trade. Instead, she hauled lumber, a more lucrative cargo, from ports in Michigan to Chicago. Their partnered stewardship, however, did not last long.

One wonders if the many tribulations of owning a schooner in Chicago's busy harbor caused Pederson and his partners to decide that the *Fleetwing* was more trouble than she was worth. With Capt. Pederson at the helm, the *Fleetwing* had suffered collisions two days in a row: on Thursday, September 2, 1880, the propeller *John Pridgeon* was running too fast in Chicago Harbor and ran into the schooner. On Friday, September 3, the propeller, *Badger State* hit her. Although both incidents produced only minor damage ($50 and $100 respectively) to the *Fleetwing*, Capt. Pederson certainly sounded cranky in his statements on the *Wreck Reports* when he said the "pure carelessness on the part of the master" of the *Pridgeon* and the "bad steering" of the *Badger State* caused the collisions.

John Spry and Capt. Andrew McGraw in March, 1881, alone became the final owners of the *Fleetwing*.

Heavily loaded with lumber, the *Fleetwing* left Menominee at dusk on Wednesday, September 26, 1888, bound for Chicago. Under pressure to

140

make a lucrative trip, Capt. McGraw headed his vessel, under full sail in very strong winds, towards Death's Door Passage, which, even in the best of weather, required first-rate seamanship.

It was becoming more difficult for owners to make a reasonable profit in shipping. Some vessel owners even forbade their captains to use the Sturgeon Bay Ship Canal, formally completed in 1881, because of the canal toll and the high cost of a tug's towing services. Even though heading for Death's Door meant putting his ship and crew in harm's way on such a foul night, Capt. McGraw, part owner

WRECKED BY THE WINDS.

Death and Destruction Mark the Course of the Northwestern Gale.

While Rescuing a Crew a Surf Boat Capsizes and Five Lives Are Lost.

Loss of the St. Clair, Brandon, and Other Marine Casualties—General News of the Lakes.

THE GALE.

The wind veered about due north here yesterday and continued strong all day. The schooners Levi Grant, Jessie and George J. Boyce,

The gale which ultimately destroyed the stranded FLEETWING *proved disastrous for other ships, too.* CRIS KOHL COLLECTION

and total master of the *Fleetwing*, chose not to use the canal and incur the fees of about $30. Perhaps he was remembering a fateful trip through the Canal virtually a year earlier. The *Fleetwing* was attempting to transit the Canal under full sail shen she ran aground at the north end early on the morning of September 28, 1887. She was displaying a signal of distress, but had all her sails set. Capt. Jacobs of the tug *Piper*, towing the lumber-laden schooner *Surprise*, did not realize the *Fleetwing's* situation until it was too late. The *Surprise* struck the *Fleetwing*, causing the former to lose her dolphin-catcher and sustain damage to her standing rigging. The *Piper* towed the *Surprise* back to Sturgeon Bay for repairs, and the *Fleetwing* was held responsible for the collision.

In the darkness of this night a year later, Capt. McGraw made a very serious error: he mistook Death's Door Bluff for Table Bluff, and sailed straight into the dead end of Garrett Bay. At 11:00 PM, the ship struck the rocky shallows with tremendous force, shearing off the mizzenmast. Hard aground, she settled by the stern in about nine feet of water, which began to fill the holds.

Luckily, because of the shallow depth and close proximity to shore, the entire crew, which usually numbered eight, was able to make it safely to land. They even had time to gather up their belongings. The wet, cold, and glad-to-be-alive crew, including a woman cook, was taken in by the Nelson family who lived nearby and owned the local dock, which had also been damaged by the storm. The newspapers at the time described this storm as

Left: *On the shoreline of Garrett Bay, a colorful Joan Forsberg begins to suit up in anticipation of exploring the wreck of the* Fleetwing, *lying in calm, clear, shallow water just a few feet away.*
PHOTO BY CRIS KOHL

Below: *The wreckage of the schooner,* Fleetwing, *lies broken up and scattered over a 500-foot area in 8 to 30 feet of water.*
PHOTO BY CRIS KOHL

Enough large and identifiable sections of the FLEETWING *exist to offer visiting snorkelers and scuba divers unique opportunities to study 19th century wooden vessel construction. This large segment lies in only eight feet of water. The State Historical Society of Wisconsin, besides buoying this and other nearby shipwreck sites annually, has erected a historic "Underwater Trails" information sign on shore near the wreck.* PHOTO BY CRIS KOHL

the worst of the year so far. Andrew Nelson conveyed the crew to Ellison Bay the next day so they could return to their homes.

Since the crew was safe, attention turned to saving the ship and cargo. The tugboat, *Jesse Spalding*, was summoned, but due to the storm, couldn't leave Sturgeon Bay until Sunday, September 30th, three days hence. The *Spalding* arrived with steam pumps, lighter, hawsers and complete confidence that the schooner, because of its staunch construction, could be pumped out, refloated, and returned to service.

But the *Spalding* had barely installed the pumps on the *Fleetwing* when another gale blew in and forced the tug to seek shelter at Eagle Harbor. When the storm subsided, the tug returned to find that the *Fleetwing* had been pounded to pieces on the rocks. The tug was able to recover the pumps, but nothing could now save the once-sturdy schooner.

When the owners of the *Fleetwing's* cargo, Wells, Ludington and Van Schaick, received notification of the wreck of the *Fleetwing*, they immediately dispatched the tug, *Burton*, and two lighters to retrieve the lumber. With assistance from the steambarge, *City of Nicollet,* the cargo was quickly recovered and returned to Menominee. However, the *Fleetwing's* owners, Spry and McGraw, were not as fortunate. They had been offered $8,000 for the *Fleetwing* the previous winter, but instead of taking the offer, the owners put $6,000 worth of repairs into their ship. At the time of her sinking, she was insured for only $3,000. By October, the captain of the schooner, *Conquest*, had salvaged any rigging and usable equipment, and the remainder of the *Fleetwing* was abandoned.

In 1986-1987, Wisconsin State Underwater Archaeologist David Cooper directed an underwater archaeological survey of the *Fleetwing* site and found the remains of the ship to be extremely useful in providing information about schooner construction. In his detailed and thoroughly researched report, Cooper noted that there were three mast steps found at the site, indicating that the third mast must have been added in a re-fitting. A widely-circulated photograph of what is believed to be the *Fleetwing* taken in 1887 (see page 140) clearly shows her with three masts -- and that she was a truly beautiful lake boat.

The loss of the *Fleetwing* and so many other fine ships in the treacherous Death's Door Passage caused more captains to choose the Sturgeon Bay Ship Canal as the safer course. The October 6, 1888 edition of the *Door County Advocate* futilely called upon the government to build a lighthouse at Door Bluff because "there is no beacon within many miles of this dangerous coast, and as a great deal of shipping passes through this waterway, every facility and protection should be afforded." But it was already too late to save the *Fleetwing*.

THE *ERASTUS CORNING*
(MAY 21, 1889)

In the first few years after her launching in Tonawanda, New York, on April 24, 1867, the *Erastus Corning* attracted attention in every port into which she sailed. The *Milwaukee Sentinel* in 1868 described her as the largest sailing vessel on the Great Lakes. Built by F. N. Jones and John Humble, her hull was 204.3 feet long, 35.3 feet wide, had a draft of 14.5 feet and a huge gross tonnage of 832. She was said to be capable of carrying more than 50,000 bushels of grain. Not only did her size make her unique, but the three-masted vessel was rigged as a barkentine: square-rigged foremast and schooner-rigged main and mizzenmasts. And she was fast! She sailed from Chicago to Detroit in only 60 hours in September, 1868, when typically a schooner would take four or five days for such a trip. She must have been quite a sight to see, in full sail out on the lake.

Mr. Horton of Buffalo, New York, was her proud owner in her early years. In 1871, she was rated A1 by the underwriters and was worth $50,000, a handsome sum in those days. By 1875, under new owner A. C. Taylor, her value had declined to $34,000 and her rating had slipped a bit to A2. Taylor had the rig changed from barkentine to schooner at Buffalo on May 10, 1877. The time of her proud size supremacy was approaching an end.

The largest schooner ever to sail on the Great Lakes was launched at Toledo, Ohio, on April 21, 1881: the leviathan, *David Dows*. The *Dows* sported five masts, was 265 feet long and could carry 140,000 bushels of grain. The *David Dows* eclipsed every other sailing ship on the lakes, including the *Erastus Corning*. Huge cargoes were becoming more frequent. The June 5, 1883, edition of the *Cleveland Herald* reported:

The barkentine-rigged Erastus Corning *early in her career.* Cris Kohl Collection

The recent cargo of the schooner *David Dows* amounted to 73,283 bushels [of] wheat, and was the largest cargo ever brought down the Sault Ste. Marie River.

And even more remarkably:

The [steamer] *Onoko* took out of Chicago Saturday 47,000 bushels of corn and 84,000 bushels of oats, a total of 132,000 bushels. This is the largest cargo of grain ever carried by a single vessel on fresh water.

Ironically, the newspaper stated:

Captain Clark, of the schooner *Erastus Corning*, declined to load his vessel yesterday, on account of its being Sunday.

By 1889, this once-glorious ship had been demoted to a schooner-barge. Loaded with iron ore, she left Escanaba on Tuesday, May 21, in tow of the steamer *Roumania*. (The *Roumania*, launched in 1887, had the first triple expansion engine ever installed in the Great Lakes, but ironically, she herself would be converted to a tow barge in 1918.) That night, the *Corning* hit Gull Island Shoal, causing the tow line to part. To try to prevent her from sinking, the captain ordered the ship, leaking badly, to be run aground on Poverty Island. But the *Erastus Corning* was no match for this dangerous, rocky shore. The propeller *Manchester* rescued the crew and brought them back to Escanaba on Wednesday, but the ship could not be saved. Sent to release her from her precarious position, the tug *Winslow* reported that the schooner was in such bad shape that it was impossible to free her. The grade was so abrupt there that the *Corning* was practically standing on her stern end with her bow in twelve feet of water.

A month later, the salvage contract was awarded to the Poverty Island lighthouse keeper, who planned to recover the iron ore cargo, but the ship was a total loss.

Fully aware that schooner days were reaching sunset, the *Door County Advocate* of June 1, 1889, sadly noted:

The *Corning* was at one time the pride of the lakes, she being a full-rigged ship when the glory of the inland marine consisted almost wholly of sailing vessels.

16

THE *WINDSOR* AND THE *E. P. ROYCE*
(SEPT. 30, 1893 AND NOV. 26, 1893)

The *Windsor* should have been named the *Phoenix* because, like the mythical bird, she was consumed by fire but arose from the ashes, an old spirit reborn in a new body.

In 1866, the harbor of Detroit, Michigan, was the busy transfer point for the booming commerce between Canada and the United States. Passenger and commercial traffic had increased so dramatically in the mid-1800's between Windsor, Ontario, and Detroit, on opposite sides of the mile-wide Detroit River, that the ferry business between these two cities was a very important connecting link. Constructed as a sidewheel ferry boat by Jenkins of Detroit in 1856, the *Windsor* ferried passengers and freight between the Great Western Railway ferry docks in Windsor and the Detroit and Milwaukee Railroad on the Detroit side of the river.

Just before ten o'clock on the evening of April 26, 1866, the *Windsor* was unloading its cargo at Detroit's Brush Street depot dock. Freight handlers were in the process of loading 25 barrels of naphtha onto a freight car which was standing next to a passenger train full of people, ready to depart at 10:00. A man with an open lantern began to examine a leaking barrel, suddenly causing the naphtha to explode violently in all directions. The other barrels, some already in the freight car and some still on the pier, began, one by one, to detonate, spewing the volatile, flaming naphtha onto the passenger train and the nearby buildings. Men jumped into the river to escape the holocaust and 35 people vaulted into the hold of the ferry, hoping for safety. But within minutes, the *Windsor* was ablaze, trapping the people aboard. The mooring line burned and the flaming ferry started to drift

147

uncontrollably down the river.

Capt. Innes of the ferry, *Detroit*, witnessed the entire horrific scene. He sent his crew into lifeboats to rescue desperate men and screaming women jumping over the *Windsor's* rail into the water. The captain attempted to tow the fiery *Windsor* away from shore, but the tow line parted, and he knew the buildings and docks along the entire river front were in peril. Acting quickly, Capt. Innes decided on a dangerous, desperate course of action. Even though he was short-handed, and he had 20 passengers aboard his ship, he decided to ram the *Windsor* and force her down

This vessel, the ERIE STEWART, *very closely resembled the schooner,* WINDSOR. CRIS KOHL COLLECTION

the river. He ordered the *Detroit's* decks to be wet down and then steamed full speed ahead, crashing into the raging inferno in a hail of sparks and blazing timbers. His passengers and remaining crew fought the flames on board the *Detroit*, which stuck fast to the *Windsor* and successfully pushed her out into the middle of the river, heading for Sandwich Point. They beached her there where she burned to the water's edge.

The conflagration on board the *Windsor* and in buildings in Detroit harbor took a terrible toll in human life and property destruction. There were 18 confirmed deaths (17 of which were on board the *Windsor*), and nearly $1,000,000 in property damage, a huge sum in 1866 dollars. The *Windsor* was a total loss.

The heroic Capt. Innes politely refused the $1,000 in gold that a group of grateful Detroit citizens tried to press upon him. Years later, he recalled, "I...laughed 'em out of the notion. Why, anybody who was half a man would have done his best that night of the fire of '66."

Five years later, the *Windsor* emerged from her ashes. A trio of Detroit businessmen decided her hull was sturdy enough to be rebuilt and returned to service. And so she operated as a barge until 1876 when, after an ownership change, the ship was re-rigged with two masts to begin another new life as a schooner! The 115-foot-long, 30-foot-wide ship served in the booming lumber trade into and out of Chicago for more than 20 uneventful years. Until September 30, 1893, near Death's Door.

Hauling a cargo of cedar posts and telegraph poles from Snow Island (one of the 30,000 islands in Georgian Bay near Parry Sound, Ontario) to Chicago, the *Windsor* ran into heavy seas near Ahnapee (Algoma), Wisconsin. Capt. Williams ordered the ship to come about and headed for

This drawing of the MARY EVERETT *(126' x 26' x 8'1", built in 1865 at Wallaceburg, Canada West -- later Ontario) is a close look-alike of the three-masted schooner,* E. P. ROYCE *(124' x 29'1" x 8'8", constructed in 1873 at Sac Bay, Michigan), which was destroyed in late 1893 while attempting to salvage the cargo of the wrecked schooner,* WINDSOR.
CRIS KOHL COLLECTION

the safety of North Bay, but the schooner was leaking, and although the pumps were steadily manned, the vessel became unmanageable by the time they reached Cana Island. At 2:00 AM, on the 30th of September, the *Windsor* struck hard aground on the reef at the southeast end of the island.

Tragedy struck immediately when a huge wave crashed over the deck, sweeping a sailor and part of the deck cargo into the water. Capt. Williams, certain that his ship was doomed and that the yawl boat would not be able to withstand the heavy surf, in desperation, put a message on a piece of board and threw it into the raging water. It read, "Send for the Sturgeon Bay life-saving crew to come at once; we will not stand much longer; the schooner is going to pieces."

Having witnessed the stranding, Cana Island lighthouse keeper Jesse T. Brown followed the board along the beach in the gale and, after about two miles, was able to retrieve it and realize the *Windsor's* true predicament. He immediately sent a messenger to Baileys Harbor. By the afternoon, Capt. Boutin of the Sturgeon Bay Life-Saving Service had been wired for assistance.

Not daring to launch a lifeboat in such a gale, Capt. Boutin loaded the equipment onto horse-pulled wagons for the 30-mile overland trek. Thick woods, mud roads, breakdowns, darkness and pouring rain caused delays and extreme difficulty for the life-savers. They finally arrived at the shipwreck scene at 12:30 AM on October 1, seven hours after leaving Sturgeon Bay.

The life-savers made several attempts with the Lyle gun to shoot a line out to the stricken schooner, but because of the darkness, the storm and the 1,200-foot distance, they failed to reach the *Windsor*. Their only hope was the lifeboat, but unfortunately, it had been damaged during the arduous trip. Hasty repairs were made and the boat was launched into the pounding surf. The brave life-savers reached the schooner which was going to pieces and, in the nick of time, saved the five remaining *Windsor* crew.

The tragic history of the *Windsor* had one final chapter. Martin McNulty, a Chicago liquor dealer who owned the 20-year-old, 124-foot-long schooner, *E. P. Royce,* named for Escanaba businessman, Eli P. Royce, decided the *Windsor's* cargo was worth salvaging.

Four years earlier, the *Royce* had had a close call, as described by the *Chicago Inter Ocean* of May 16, 1889:

> The schooner *E. P. Royce*, Michael [sic] McNulty's boat, arrived here yesterday afternoon with her decks flush with the water. She sprang a leak in midlake on her way down. The crew was a sorry looking set of men as the boat made fast to the North pier. They had been kept at the pumps day and night, and were ready to jump ashore as soon as she landed and go to sleep. Had the vessel been flying light nothing could have saved her from foundering. Her load of dry lumber alone kept her afloat.

Even though the *Royce* had a history of near-tragic misadventures, McNulty sent his ship to the rocky, treacherous Cana Island coast.

The *Royce* arrived at the location of the *Windsor* wreck in late November, 1893, ready to recover the lumber before winter weather made it impossible. The salvage progressed well, with the *Royce's* holds full and her deck loaded high with the cedar and telegraph poles. One day more of good weather was all Capt. Worfel needed to finish the job, but the gales of November would have the final say for the schooner *E. P. Royce*. A fierce storm on November 26th drove her onto the beach at Little Harbor just south of Cana Island. The crew were able to launch the yawl boat and just barely make it safely to shore at Mud Bay (now Moonlight Bay) where they were boarded at a lumber camp until they were able to arrange their return to their Chicago homes. Over the next few months, every east or southeasterly wind caused the *Royce* and its salvaged cargo of lumber to break up a little bit more. The ice-bank-lined shore prevented the lumber from washing up on the beach where it could be recovered, and ultimately most of it was carried out into the lake. The schooner *D. L. Filer* recovered masts, sails, yards, blocks, ropes and other "paraphernalia" from the wreck of the *Royce* the following summer.

The disastrous tale of the two schooners, the *Windsor* and the *E. P. Royce*, had a sad postscript. On May 26, 1894, half a year after the ships were lost, the body of an unknown man washed ashore in Mud Bay. The remains, which had evidently been in the water for a long time, were partly covered by a pair of tattered pants. The coroner's inquest determined that this was the sailor who had been swept overboard when the *Windsor* stranded. The unfortunate victim was buried in the town cemetery at Mud Bay.

The *E. R. Williams*
(September 22, 1895)

Numerous vessels failed to make it through the passages which connect Green Bay and Lake Michigan. The reasons for this failure varied, but the most common one was foul weather. When the winds increase in speed and the waves grow larger, sailors know that their ships are at risk. One vessel which fell victim to the force of these gales and waves was the three-masted schooner, *E. R. Williams*.

On Sunday, September 22, 1895, the relatively new steamer, the *Santa Maria*, towed three considerably older ships, the former schooner named the *Thomas Gawn*, the barge *Teutonia* and the schooner *E. R. Williams*, out of Escanaba harbor. All four ships were heavily loaded with iron ore and were heading for Lake Erie.

The sea ran heavily from the south on Green Bay, and all four vessels, laden deep in the water while moving towards Poverty Passage into Lake Michigan, experienced difficulty making headway. Soon a full-fledged storm swept across the area, so severe that in nearby Manistique, acres of trees were torn up by their roots, windows were smashed and fences were blown down.

At least one newspaper reported that all four of these ships, deciding to ride out the storm, dropped their anchors, and that it was while at anchor that the *Williams* sank. But numerous other accounts disagreed with this.

The *Chicago Inter Ocean*, for example, wrote, in an article datelined Escanaba, Mich., Monday, September 23, 1895, that

> ...up to 9 o'clock last night, the schooner's lights could be
> seen by the crew of the *Santa Maria*. Shortly after that time, the

The **E. R. Williams,** *closely resembled the* **Pensaukee,** *pictured here under full sail. Surprisingly, no photographs of the* **Williams** *seem to exist.* Cris Kohl Collection

tow line parted, and the *Williams* disappeared from sight. The *Santa Maria* cruised around for some time, trying to find the *Williams*, but it was not until daylight that her topmast was discovered sticking out of the water under St. Martin's Island. No trace of the crew could be seen. The *Santa Maria* returned here this afternoon, and Captain E. E. Rathburn reported the wreck....

Capt. Rathburn reportedly claimed that "it was impossible for any of the crew [of the *E. R. Williams*] to reach shore in the big sea." One newspaper wrote that "all on board are supposed to be lost, as it would be impossible for them to reach shore in such a furious sea." Exactly when things appear to be at their worst, something unexpected and wonderful occurs.

The entire crew of the *E. R. Williams* -- Capt. Hunton of Cleveland, Maggie Bennett, the stewardess (cook), also from Cleveland, six sailors who remained unnamed, and even the ship's dog -- were found alive and well by the steamer, *Osceola*, under the command of Capt. Fred Jarvis, on Big Summer Island.

The *Detroit Free Press*, in successive articles published on September 25th and 26th, 1895, related the crew's experiences:

> ...Capt. Hutton [sic] states that the *Williams* sprung a leak
> Monday night [Authors' note: This should read "Sunday night"]

152

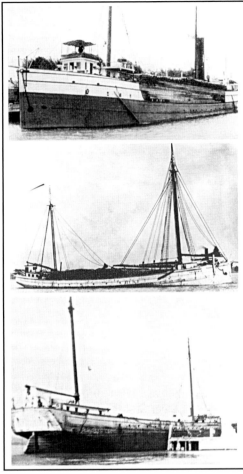

MARINE

SUNK IN GREEN BAY

THE SCHOONER E. R. WILLIAMS
WENT DOWN IN A GALE.

IT IS THOUGHT THAT ALL ON BOARD
THE VESSEL PERISHED.

The two-year-old wooden steamer, Santa Maria (**top left**), *was towing three old vessels, the 15-year-old* Teutonia (**middle left**), *the 23-year-old* Thomas Gawn (**bottom left**), *and the 22-year-old* E. R. Williams *when the latter sank on September 22, 1895. The* Detroit Free Press (**above**) *of September 24, 1895 feared disaster for the missing crew.* Cris Kohl Collection

and three feet of water came into the hold in five minutes. She then broke in two and went down in twenty fathoms of water.... himself and crew had scarcely time to get into the yawl before the schooner sank. The crew...headed towards Big Summer Island, which is about thirty miles from Escanaba. They were unable to land until daylight, and for two hours were tossed about in one of the worst storms ever seen on Lake Michigan. As soon as there was light enough to see, a safe landing was made. Neither captain nor crew can understand how it was that the yawl did not capsize in the breakers, especially in view of the fact that they had only one oar and a small piece of another, while the distance from the wreck to the island is about nine miles [Authors' note: The distance is closer to six miles.]....

Old vesselmen who had experienced the recent bad weather also found it difficult to believe that a 20-foot yawlboat containing a crew of eight,

Left: *Both wooden-stock bow anchors of the* **E. R. WILLIAMS** *remain on the site, the portside one still showed in place along the rail, and the starboard one lying on the deck.*

PHOTO BY CRIS KOHL

Below: *The flowing lines of the* **E. R. WILLIAMS** *in 105 feet of water are accentuated by the long bowsprit and its accompanying chains, all still upright and in place.*

PHOTO BY CRIS KOHL

Above: *There is much to see, big and small, on the wreck of the schooner,* E. R. WILLIAMS. *The stern portion of the vessel has broken, probably from the ship hitting the bottom of the bay stern first. Visiting scuba divers have placed many small ceramic and porcelain items of interest on a bench near the starboard quarter.* PHOTO BY CRIS KOHL

Below: *The mast stubs on the* E. R. WILLIAMS *still retain their original wooden mast hoops which were used to hold the sails close to the mast.* PHOTO BY CRIS KOHL

plus a dog, could live in such a storm. The *Door County Advocate* of November 16, 1895, gave some interesting details of how this survival transpired:

> ...In this instance, the use of oil to reduce the effect of the big waves was resorted to, and after leaving the schooner in the yawl, cups of oil were thrown out whenever a very large wave was encountered, and this is what saved the yawl from being swamped.

The *E. R. Williams*, owned by F. W. Fay of Elyria, Ohio, was valued at only $3,500 at the time of her loss, and the ship was not insured. Her cargo of 570 tons of iron ore, consigned to M. A. Hanna & Company of Cleveland, was fully insured.

When the staunch, three-masted schooner, *E. R. Williams,* was launched at Toledo, Ohio, on Saturday, May 24, 1873, the formal, lavish ceremony received much newspaper coverage. More than 100 of the invited guests rode the vessel down the launchramp, and they later enjoyed an elegant banquet in the vessel's completely finished interior cabins (ship interiors were normally completed after, not before, the ship was launched). That the *E. R. Williams* was special was known by many, including those formal guests, the newspapers which described the vessel in such glowing terms, and the owner who named the ship after himself.

The *E. R. Williams* immediately began hauling large quantities of grain, living up to all of the praise and publicity it had received at the launching.

In the late 1990's, the location of a shipwreck, supposedly that of the *E. R. Williams,* lying in state of Michigan waters just north of St. Martin Island, surfaced through the combined work of a commercial fisherman and a scuba diver. This schooner wreck sits upright and amazingly intact in 105 feet of water (contemporary newspaper accounts claimed that the *Williams* sank in "20 fathoms," which is 120 feet, of water, close enough for this shipwreck to qualify). The cargo does appear to be iron ore. The stern end of this wreck is broken off (with the ship's iron stove sitting on the lake bottom 40 feet away from the back of the wreck), consistent with the report that the *Williams* broke in two just prior to sinking. The fact that the two anchors on this wreck's bow were not deployed proves that either a) the contemporary newspaper account which claimed that they were at anchor was wrong, or b) this shipwreck is not the *E. R. Williams.* Obvious identity giveaways, such as a nameboard, or the ship's official number (8987) or tonnage number (293.64) carved in the foreward-most beam of the foreward-most hatch, have not been located. There may be no smoking gun yet, but there is certainly plenty of smoke to indicate that this impressive shipwreck is indeed the schooner *E. R. Williams.*

THE *OTTER*
(OCTOBER 10, 1895)

T he six-man crew of the schooner, *Otter*, expected another routine run with a lumber cargo for the ship's Chicago owner, J. Caesar. Even an impending storm was not worrisome for the sailors, seasoned veterans all. They loaded 130 cords of wood at the Mashek Company dock in Whitefish Bay on Wed., October 9, 1895, and hoped for a fast run to Chicago. Little did they know that, on the next day, they would be fighting for their lives as their ship was being dashed to pieces under them.

Launched one month after the horrors of the Battle of Gettysburg in 1863, the two-masted schooner, *Otter,* would serve her first owners, Tremain and Gallagher, far from the battlefields of the Civil War raging further south. The 106-foot-long, 25-foot-wide ship slid down the launch ramp in Newport (now called Marine City), Michigan, to be part of the heyday of sailing vessels on the Great Lakes. Worth $10,000 at the start of her career, her value steadily declined until thirty-two years later, the 260-ton wooden ship was practically worthless, with no rating and no insurance.

Knowing the *Otter* was not in good condition, Capt. William Kaufman decided to weather the storm at anchor in Whitefish Bay rather than risk his boat and crew trying to reach Chicago in the increasing gale. They made it through the night, but at 8:00 in the morning on the 10th, the anchor chains broke, and the *Otter* was helpless and adrift in the ferocious storm and enormous seas. She struck broadside on the rocks 300 feet from shore and the captain and crew knew their vessel was doomed. Launching the yawl boat failed; a wave filled and capsized it. The desperate men climbed into the *Otter's* rigging as they felt the ship going to pieces under their feet. Fishermen on shore tried to launch a boat, but the waves drove them back.

The rescue of the sailors of the stranded OTTER *involved the Life-Saving Crew setting up a breeches buoy and removing the men from the ship one-by-one. Here Capt. Kaufman is hauled to shore.* DOOR COUNTY MARITIME MUSEUM AND LIGHTHOUSE PRESERVATION SOCIETY, INC.

The *Milwaukee Sentinel* on October 11, 1895 wrote:

> ...The only hope lay in the life-saving crew at the canal and a telephone message was sent for their assistance, Capt. Anderson responded quickly and loading his detachable wagon in the surf boat, the crew were brought to this city [Sturgeon Bay]. The boat was loaded on a wagon, with four horses attached, and a like number on the supply wagon.
>
> The twelve miles overland to the wreck was covered in less than an hour and a half. The cannon was brought to bear on the wreck, and with the first shot the line fell over the craft. It was only the work of a few minutes to run out the breeches buoy, and in this way the crew of six men were safely brought to shore. The last man to land stated that the craft would not last two hours more and was going to pieces when he left her, every sea wash making a clean sweep over the doomed vessel. She will prove a total loss....

Every man on board the *Otter* owed his life to Capt. Anderson's decisive action, his heroic Life-Saving Service crew and the wonderful invention called the breeches buoy. A small cannon on the beach shot a long line to the stricken ship, and the crew then fastened it to the mast. The breeches buoy, a pair of canvas pants suspended in a life preserver, was then swung out to the vessel by means of a pulley system. A sailor was then securely tied into the pants and pulled ashore to safety.

The cargo and rigging were salvaged. Within a few months, nothing could be seen of the wreck of the *Otter*, and the beach, the scene of such thrilling drama, was quiet once more.

THE *AUSTRALASIA*
(OCTOBER 17, 1896)

N amed after two continents -- a combination of the smallest and the largest -- this enormous wooden steamer, when she slid down the launchramp, was termed "monster" and "leviathan." Even 34 years after this ship's demise, Norman Beasley's 1930 book, *Freighters of Fortune*, proudly proclaimed that this vessel "was the largest craft on fresh water."

That the 282-foot-long (keel length), 1,829.32-ton *Australasia* was absolutely immense for a wooden steamship is not in dispute, but she was not ever the largest ship on the Great Lakes. When she was launched at West Bay City, Michigan, on September 2, 1884, the title of the "largest craft on fresh water" at that time went to the 2,164-ton, iron *Onoko* (287'3"--keel length--x 38'8" x 20'7"), launched at Cleveland on February 16, 1882.

The *Australasia*, however, was the largest WOODEN craft on the lakes at the time of her launch. There had been a larger one, the *Western Metropolis* launched at Buffalo on April 23, 1856. That 321-foot-long, 1,860-ton wooden steamer was converted to a 273-foot-long, 1,341-ton bark in early 1863. This sailing ship, which was actually larger than the famous five-masted *David Dows* built in 1881, was wrecked near Chicago in September, 1864.

Construction of the *Australasia* commenced at the James Davidson shipyard in West Bay City, Michigan, on November 1, 1883, when several dozen workers carefully laid the important keel, or spine, of the ship. For the next ten months, between 75 and 150 men worked on the vessel at any given time. Although the *Australasia* was built for use in the iron ore and grain trades, her first scheduled cargo was salt to be taken to Chicago.

The *Cleveland Herald*, on August 30 and September 3, 1884, provided these interesting facts about the *Australasia*:

...The *Australasia* has probably the largest engine on the lakes.... It is a fore-and-aft compound, the high pressure cylinder being 30 inch bore and 45 inch stroke.... The boilers are made of Otis steel. They are two in number, 8 feet shell and 27 feet long...the wheel [propeller] [is] 12 1/2 feet in diameter.... She has one of the Providence steam windlasses, made by the American Windlass Company. It is the same as used on ocean steamships.... All capstans are on deck and are to be worked by steam. There is a strong hoisting engine on deck for raising sails, freight and for doing general heavy lifting. The two anchors are of the Boston patent make, each weighing about 3,000 pounds. The pilot house, captain's and officers' quarters are forward; the crew's between decks aft, and the engineers' and steward's aft. They are all large and commodious, conveniently arranged and handsomely furnished.... Her carrying capacity is estimated at 3,000 net tons, 100,000 bushels of corn, or 2,000,000 feet of lumber. The cost of the *Australasia* was between $140,000 and $150,000.... In her construction, 1,500,000 feet of oak timber and 300,000 feet of pine were consumed.

For the first two years of the *Australasia's* career, Capt. James Davidson himself owned and often proudly mastered the ship. In late September, 1886, he sold it with the schooner *Polynesia* to N. P. Huntington and J. C. Corrigan of Cleveland for $160,000 cash. In her first full season under these new owners, the *Australasia* encountered her first problem. In August, 1887, a Duluth newspaper published a detailed account of the pleasant time that a group of young ladies had on board the *Australasia* while crossing Lake Superior. In this way, the Supervising Inspector of Steamboats at Buffalo became aware of the fact that the *Australasia* was carrying passengers without a license. The *Australasia's* owners were fined $500. A much more tragic situation engulfed the *Australasia* a month later. On September 7, 1887, a storm arose off Lake Superior's Whitefish Point while the *Australasia* was towing the 204-foot-long barge, *Niagara*, both ships heavily laden with iron ore. The steamer lost the *Niagara* when the towline broke, and the barge ended up sinking with the loss of all nine hands on board.

In the spring of 1889, the *Australasia* ran aground, sustaining over $10,000 worth of damage.

The *Australasia's* final misfortune occurred at another Whitefish Bay, this one near Death's Door, on October 17, 1896. The ship, running alone, was bound from Cleveland to Milwaukee with a cargo of 2,200 tons of soft coal. Newspaper reports agree on that much, but the accounts of the loss vary widely. One stated that the fire on board was noticed at 6 PM, while others claimed 11 PM. One newspaper said the fire was discovered "beneath the texas [a pilot house level] on the main deck," while another claimed that the fire came from under the boilers in the firehold. One proclaimed that "the crew of the burning steamer, 17 men all told, were rescued from their burning boat by the life-saving crew from Baileys Harbor," while another reported that the crew rowed themselves to shore and made their

The steamer, AUSTRALASIA, *with a tow, quite likely the* NIAGARA, *which the* AUSTRALASIA *lost off Whitefish Point in Lake Superior in 1887 with the tragic loss of all nine lives on board.*
ARTIST UNKNOWN.
CRIS KOHL COLLECTION

way to a saloon in Jacksonport where they proceeded to get drunk and belligerent (definitely the more interesting story!). One thing was sure: the *Australasia* was beached and she burned to the water's edge, a total loss.

The wreck was sold to the Leathem & Smith Towing and Wrecking Company on October 23, 1896. Their plans were simple: "The cargo will be pumped out, after which the hull will be patched up and an effort made to raise it." To these ends, they were only partly successful.

By November 3, 1896, only 250 tons of the coal cargo had been recovered, and bad weather was setting in. One gloomy newspaper even wrote that "The whole outfit is not worth 10 cents, as the wreck is settling in quicksand." But good weather gave the company an unexpected break. The hull, however, was "too badly broken up to be saved," and much of the coal was washing ashore, to the delight of local residents who gathered it up quickly. On December 3, 1896, the *Detroit Free Press* gave this update:

> The *Australasia* wreck still holds out first rate, and at last reports was not so very badly used up. Considerable of her cargo has washed ashore and been picked up by people in the vicinity. The wrecking company had writs served on these people by the sheriff last week to prevent their using the fuel and compelling them to have the same delivered at the piers at Jacksonport. The beach was covered with the coal previous to the recent storms and piles several feet deep were nothing unusual in close proximity to the wreck, but the recent south-west gale has caused the sand to cover the coal and bury it out of sight.

Salvage continued for nearly a year. The *Marine Review* of Sept. 2, 1897, reported:

> Wreckers on the tug *Wright* have succeeded in raising and delivering at Sturgeon Bay both boilers from the burned and sunken wreck of the *Australasia* in Whitefish bay. They have also secured the steam steerer, fan and engine, steam capstan, boiler arches, steam fitting, coils, pumps, condenser, hawsepipes, iron

AUSTRALASIA BURNED

FLAMES SUPPOSED TO HAVE START- ED IN THE FIRE-HOLD.

SPREAD OVER THE ENTIRE BOAT IN SPITE OF THE CREW.

BOAT RUN ON THE BEACH NEAR BAILEY'S HARBOR AND SCUTTLED.

Crew Removed by Life-Savers With- out Loss of Life.

Sturgeon Bay, Wis., October 18.—The big wooden steamer Australasia, coal laden from Lake Erie to Milwaukee, burned in Lake Michigan last night and the wreck now lies sunk in Whitefish Bay. The crew

The large, wooden steamer, AUSTRALASIA, *burned and sank near Death's Door, as reported by the* DETROIT FREE PRESS *on October 19, 1896.*
CRIS KOHL COLLECTION

towposts and a score of other things. The wreckers are now removing the working parts of the engine, and propose also to recover the shaft and the wheel.

Finally, on Saturday, October 2, 1897, the salvage story wrapped up (again from the *Detroit Free Press*):

The Leathem & Smith Towing & Wrecking Company have about completed work on the wrecked steamer *Australasia*. The tug *Wright* visited the wreck Thursday, and all that remained that was of any value was brought up. The first of the week the shaft and wheel were recovered by blowing away the after-part of the wreck with dynamite. After getting the shaft wheel loose it was found that there was too much sea to hoist it up, so work was suspended until the following day. When the diver again visited the wreck it was found that in some manner one of the flukes to the wheel had been broken off, making the wheel valueless. It was brought in by the *Wright* Tuesday and placed on Leathem & Smith's dock, where it was broken up Friday with dynamite. The wheel was a 12-foot one.

One of the largest wooden steamers ever built on the Great Lakes was thus whittled away, piece by piece, by Nature and Man. In the summer of 2005, two jet-skiers found broken remains of a ship's bow and stern (the mid-section was completely covered by sand), and within a month, these were identified as the *Australasia*. This technical information, published at the time of the *Australasia's* launching in 1884, helped identify the wreck:

...Her main keelson is 16 by 16 inches, with assistant keelsons 14 by 16 inches on either side. There are five floor keelsons on either side 14 by 15 inches, making thirteen in all. These immense pieces of oak are thoroughly edge bolted with three bolts of 1 1/4 inch and 1 inch iron into every frame. There are five strakes of bilge keelsons on each side, three at the turn of the bilge 11 x 10 inches and two 9 x 10 inches.... The lower deck beams are 9 x 12 inches; upper deck beams 8 x 12 inches. [There is] a tamarack knee 8 inches in thickness under each beam of the upper and lower decks.... The boat has a double stern post 20 x 24 inches. The skeleton of the boat is inclosed [sic] in a complete network of iron bands, which the planking hides from view. A belt or girt of iron 10 inches wide and 3/4 of an inch thick extends from stem to stern on the outside near the top of the frames, and on the inside is another band of the same dimensions. To this the outside cord is thoroughly riveted. To the latter are riveted straps five inches wide and one-half inch thick, which take a diagonal course to the turn of the bilge, where they take hold of the long floor timbers. These diagonal straps commence at every opening of frame and cross twice, and are firmly riveted at each crossing....

The *Erie L. Hackley*
(October 3, 1903)

Death did its worst in the Death's Door region in late 1903 when a diminutive steamship sank in a tornado-accompanied storm on Green Bay, taking with it eleven of the nineteen persons on board. The small, wooden steamer, *Erie L. Hackley*, cleared Menominee, Michigan at 5:05 P.M., Saturday, October 3, 1903, and set course for her first stop, Egg Harbor, across Green Bay. The vessel, its seven crew and its twelve passengers were soon caught in a real blow, estimated at 60 miles an hour, and by 6 P.M., the ship was in serious trouble about one mile off Green Island. Reports indicate that the vessel broached-to several times before finally being engulfed in a trough and getting swamped by the waves. Within seconds, the ship sank, taking with it several people. Survivors found themselves bobbing in the cold waters, clutching at any debris which would keep them afloat. Six people took refuge atop a deck covering and floated on it for 14 hours before being rescued by the Goodrich steamer, *Sheboygan*, the next morning. Two others were also picked up alive, but eleven people lost their lives. Survivors recalled last seeing Capt. Vorous in the ship's pilot house, desperately trying to aim the ship into the forceful winds.

The seven crewmembers on board the *Erie L. Hackley* when it sank were: Capt. Joseph Vorous (lost, part owner, from Fish Creek),
Carl Pelkey (lost, cook, from Fish Creek),
Hugh Miller (lost, deckhand, from Charlevoix, Michigan),
Frank C. Blakefield (saved, purser, from Fish Creek),
Blaine McSweeney (saved, fireman, from Fish Creek),
Milton Hansen (saved, fireman, from Fish Creek),
Orin Rowin (saved, engineer, from Fish Creek).

The twelve passengers on board the *Erie L. Hackley* when it sank were:

> Henry Robertoy (lost, part owner, on board as a passenger),
> Freeman Thorp (lost, from Fish Creek),
> Lawrence Barringer (lost, from Fish Creek),
> Edna Barringer (lost, from Fish Creek),
> George LeClair (lost, from Jacksonport),
> Nels Nelson (lost, from Ellison Bay),
> Edna Vincent (lost, from Egg Harbor),
> Ethel Vincent (lost, from Egg Harbor),
> John Haltug (saved, from Fish Creek),
> F. Mathieson (saved, from Ellison Bay),
> Martin Olson (saved, from Ellison Bay),
> Milton Olson (saved, from Ellison Bay).

Eyewitness accounts left us with numerous dramatic details about each of these 19 individuals. Capt. Vorous, who could not swim, was last seen keeping tightly in place inside his pilot house as it was torn from the ship. Carl Pelkey, the cook, never escaped the sinking hull; neither did deckhand Hugh Miller. Their ends came fast. Purser Frank Blakefield was in the pilot house helping the captain hold the wheel, but decided that he was needed more at the stern to launch the yawlboat. No sooner did he leave the pilot house than the wind tore it away and, amidst a shower of debris, Blakefield leaped into the dark waters. He became one of seven people sitting on some floating upper works, but, realizing that it could not support so much weight, he tied several loose planks together and headed out on his own, thereby relieving some of the strain on the main raft.

Fireman Blaine McSweeney, when he realized that the ship was sinking, pulled 17-year-old Edna Barringer out of the cabin with help from her brother, Lawrence. All three found themselves plunged into the chilly bay waters. Edna held tightly to McSweeney's hand after they hit the water, but suction from the sinking ship tore them apart. Fortunately, both managed to pop back to the surface. McSweeney, seeing that he was swimming next to the yawlboat, which had somehow broken loose from the *Hackley*, struggled to climb into it. He then paddled towards the anxious Edna, who was frantically treading water nearby. As he reached out to her, a wave capsized the boat, throwing him once again into the cold waters. When he surfaced, Edna was gone. McSweeney and fellow fireman Milton Hansen swam to the sanctuary of that large piece of flotsam which already held several people.

Engineer Orin Rowin managed to climb out of his flooded engine room when the *Hackley* capsized and clung to the overturned hull. Deciding that his chances of survival were better on a floating plank than on a sinking ship, he made the leap to a piece of lumber. Spotting a section of rope and more floating debris, he was able to tie together a small raft, to which he

The small steamer, ERIE L. HACKLEY, *was heading from Menominee, Michigan, to Egg Harbor, Wisconsin, when it sank in a storm in 1903 with great loss of life. This photograph shows the ship when it worked in the Manitou Islands in 1902.* CRIS KOHL COLLECTION

eventually lashed himself, and he drifted eleven miles before he, suffering from severe hypothermia, was rescued the next day; he died a year later.

From among the passengers, Henry Robertoy (who was also a part-owner of the *Hackley*) managed to free himself from the sinking ship, but had trouble staying afloat. One survivor heard him screaming for a life preserver, but one never came his way, and soon he was silent.

Freeman Thorp's legs and ankles were badly cut during his escape from the sinking ship. He clung to some scattered wreckage while the storm pushed him eastward. His lifeless body was found at Hat Island, "laying across a plank" (as the Wreck Report stated).

Lawrence Barringer apparently never surfaced from the swirling waters into which he had jumped with his sister Edna and Blaine McSweeney.

George LeClair, whose wife was the older sister of Edna and Lawrence Barringer, for some time clung to the same debris which supported engineer Orin Rowin, but waves frequently washed both men from their frail life supports, and they struggled to regain their holds in the pounding waves. About six hours after the *Hackley* sank, in the darkness of the midnight hour, a fatigued George was swept off a final time, never to return.

Edna and Ethel Vincent, sisters who were teachers in Michigan's upper peninsula, leaped hand-in-hand into the tempestuous seas. Several people reportedly attempted to place them onto floating debris, but without success. These young women weakened quickly, then sank slowly beneath the dark waters. They had been on their way to visit their mother in Egg Harbor.

Nels Nelson reportedly was trying to sleep, or perhaps was actually asleep, when the ship went down, and he never escaped from the cabin. He carried over $400 on his person with him to the depths.

John Haltug survived the initial shock of the sinking ship and his plunge into the bay, and quickly swam to the large piece of floating superstructure. F. Mathieson soon swam over and joined him on this tiny island of safety.

Sixty-year-old Martin Olson and his young son, Milton, who had just been released from the hospital in Menominee and was not yet fully recovered from his ailment, fortunately found themselves in the water quite close to the miracle superstructure which ended up saving several people's lives. Their swim to this wooden raft was easier than the draining night they had to spend clinging desperately to it in the brutal, relentless waves.

The steamer, *Sheboygan*, was quickly steaming south into Green Bay from Washington Island early on Sunday morning, fortunately delayed by the night's severe storm. Capt. Asa Johnston's lookouts spotted shipwreck debris near the Strawberry Islands, and soon saw and saved the castaways.

A few days later, the *Hackley's* cabin floated ashore near Eagle Bluff. Inside were the ship's lifebelts still in place, indicating that the ship sank so fast that there was no time to remove them from storage. Also inside were the ship's wheel and papers. The ship's bell, still attached to the cabin roof, was used for many years afterwards as a dinner bell at an Ephraim resort.

The Sturgeon Bay Canal Life-Saving Station Wreck Report, dated "October, 1903," gave the following details about the work its members performed (original spelling retained):

> At 10 o'clock A.M. a message was received from the village of Fish Creek 30 miles N.N.W. of Station on the waters of Green Bay, saying that the steamer *Erie L. Hackley* had foundered off Green Island at 6 o'clock P.M. Oct. 3, and that eight of the crew and passengers had been picked up and one body found on a plank. The survivors were picked up by the Steamer *Sheboygan* and the body found by the citizens of Fish Creek at 8 o'clock A.M. Oct. 4th on pieces of wreckage 12 miles from the scene of disaster. The message was asking if this service would be so kind as to go and give a hand and search over the distance from Green Island to Fish Creek for either the dead or the dying that yet might be found. I thought it would be no more then right from this service to show a good will towards the people and I summoned the Tug *Sylvia* on account of the Great distance and went as fast as we could and were searching in a zig zag way over the distance untill dark, but nothing could be found of the missing ones, and went to the village of Fish Creek to stay over night. On the morning of Oct. 5 at break of

STEAMER HACKLEY FOUNDERS.

Goes Down Near Green Island During a Terrific Squall on Saturday Evening While on Her Way to Egg Harbor.

ELEVEN PERSONS LOSE THEIR LIVES.

All the Drowned Are Door County People Who Were Members of the Steamer's Crew and Passengers on The Way to Their Homes. Eight Persons Rescued by the Steamer Sheboygan After Floating About on the Wreckage All Night.

The most disastrous shipwreck with the accompanying loss of life in the | over shoal, near Chambers Island. When rescued life was nearly extinct, | Life-Savers Go Out. As soon as word was received here of

For the first time in its 41-year history, the DOOR COUNTY ADVOCATE *published and distributed, between the regular dates of its weekly newspaper, a special flyer with the disastrous news of the loss of the* ERIE L. HACKLEY. CRIS KOHL COLLECTION

day we started from Fish Creek and searched the whole distance again and on some small Islands on the way and then started grappling for the missing ones and the steamer but could not find any one or the foundered boat on account of the great depth of water and gave up and went back and arrived at the Station about midnight.

Carl Anderson, Keeper

The *Erie L. Hackley* was valued at $2,500, and her cargo at $500. Neither was insured. Needless to say, the loss of this ship, besides causing many families grief, put the Fish Creek Transportation Company out of business.

Searchers found the sunken *Hackley* on October 15, 1903, by sweeping a long cable between two boats. Grappling for bodies soon brought up the Vincent sisters, found only about 20 feet apart. They were later buried in Stephenson, Michigan. A buoy was left to mark the spot where the sisters were found, and when that line was pulled up the next day, Henry Robertoy's body came up with it. On October 31, the body of Capt. Vorous was grappled to the surface by the tug *Leona R.* Six of the 11 victims were never recovered.

Capt. Vorous reportedly had an ill feeling, or foreboding, about this trip. He would not permit his sister to accompany them, "and also an elderly lady who wanted to take passage. He told her to sit in the waiting room until the boat was ready to go, and then left port without her."

The captain and the *Hackley* were targeted for criticism. A government court of inquiry was convened, and after considerable testimony, the findings completely exonerated the captain's actions and the ship's suspect condition.

Launched on August 11, 1882, as a small steam yacht for Capt. Seth Lee and built by J. P. Arnold at Muskegon, Michigan, the 54.61-ton wooden *Erie L. Hackley* (79' x 17'4" x 5'2", and named after the adopted daughter of Muskegon's lumber tycoon and philanthropist, Charles H. Hackley), was purchased in late 1892 by Capt. Peter D. Campbell. He fitted the ship's cabin with 16 folding berths for excursionists to Chicago's Columbian Exposition in 1893. Then, for two years, he operated the ship between Muskegon and Whitehall. In 1896, he moved to Charlevoix and put her on the mail run to St. James on Beaver Island until 1901. In 1902, the *Hackley* operated on the Manitou Islands route, but was plagued with mechanical difficulties and was sold later that year to Benjamin Newhall of Chicago. He, in turn, sold the vessel in March, 1903, to a group of four men who had started the Fish Creek Transportation Company -- Capt. Joseph Vorous, his father, Levi, Henry Robertoy and E. T. Thorp. They ran the *Hackley* between Sturgeon Bay, Menominee and Washington Island, with several stops in between. The *Hackley's* loss was the worst loss-of-life sinking anywhere on the Great Lakes in 1903 (one ship sank with all hands, the schooner-barge, *Emerald*, in Lake Erie on November 29, 1903, but the crew numbered only six.)

The wreck of the *Erie L. Hackley* was located in 112 feet of water and first explored and identified by Richard & Susan Boyd, Gary Means and Bernie Bloom on the Memorial Day weekend, 1980. On November 1, 1981, well-known shipwreck hunter and diver, Frank Hoffman attempted to raise the *Hackley*. Hoffman had successfully raised the schooner, *Alvin Clark*, from deep Green Bay waters in the summer of 1969 (although earlier he succeeded only in breaking in two the wreck of the *Jennibell* which he had tried to raise in 1963). His efforts to raise the *Hackley* failed when a cable beneath the hull slipped, breaking the stern. Only the ship's rudder and a part of her stern railing surfaced. Small artifact recovery followed.

Also in 1981, divers brought up some bones from two of the victims of the *Hackley* disaster. Hoping that relatives of the deceased would step forward, the divers were placed in an awkward position when no one appeared. Returning the bones to the shipwreck would have been "polluting," and human remains, by law, had to be buried in a legal grave, which would have cost about $1,000. Davis Mortuary stored the bones at no charge. Finally, on May 10, 1986, the skeletal remains of two of the *Erie L. Hackley* victims were properly buried in Bayside Cemetery in Sturgeon Bay, with Davis Mortuary donating the wooden coffin and use of the hearse, and the cemetery providing the gravesite and its future care. Local firms paid for the digging, a burial vault, flowers and a tombstone, which was inscribed simply "Unknown sailors from the shipwrecked *Erie L. Hackley* --- 1903."

Thus the worst loss-of-life shipwreck in the Death's Door area saw some closure more than eighty years after the ship sank.

HORSESHOE
SHIPWRECKS

H orseshoe Bay, Horseshoe Point, Horseshoe Island, Horseshoe Reefs -- all of these places of geographic diversity on the Green Bay side of Death's Door share a common name, yet they defy the historic custom of having been given that name because of their close proximity to one another. Horseshoe Bay and Horseshoe Point lie logically together, as do Horseshoe Island and Horseshoe Reefs, but the two pairs are located approximately twelve miles apart from one another, a geographic disparity which has confused more than one mariner.

Horseshoe Island is probably the best known of the four horseshoes. It is certainly the most memorable due to the fact that the island is actually shaped like a horseshoe, something which cannot be said about the other three horseshoes. Located one-third of a mile off the nearest mainland, which is Peninsula State Park on the Door Peninsula, and two miles off the town of Ephraim at the mouth of Eagle Harbor, the island, formerly named Eagle Island, has played its role in local history. Its excellent natural harbor drew attention and praise early in the region's settlement. A pier was built in that harbor in 1850, and steamships stopped there regularly to replenish their supply of wood which they burned beneath the boilers of their steam engines. Norwegian pioneers used Horseshoe Island as a jumping off point, living there while building their permanent Moravian settlement on the mainland, today's town of Ephraim. But the small island ran out of timber by 1853, after which it was used by ships only as a harbor of refuge from foul weather -- a status which did not provide or ensure a stable economic incentive to foster permanent settlement.

The island was purchased by an individual in 1855 for the sum of $600. In 1882, Sturgeon Bay's Joseph Harris purchased the island at public auction for the amount of back taxes owed: $18.46! But in 1888, Frank Folda of the Omaha Bank paid $500 for it to fulfill his dream of owning a serene, island home. His children, Engelbert and Martha, inherited the island when their father died in 1892. Their ambitious plans for constructing a family lodge there were threatened in 1909 when the State of Wisconsin began buying up land on the mainland for the creation of Peninsula State Park -- and the state planned to include Horseshoe Island in the park! Historian Hjalmar Holand owned much mainland shoreline property there, including the cliff called Eagle Bluff, and he, extremely hostile to the state takeover, unsuccessfully fought to keep his property. The Foldas knew that they would lose their island through "eminent domain," a policy which gives a governing entity the right to pay a "fair" price for any property "deemed to be for the public good of all." Engelbert Folda, aware that his family's dream island was on the verge of no longer being theirs, offered the state this deal: the state could buy the island from them for $5,000 if it assured Engelbert, his wife and his sister the use of the island, free of any real estate taxes on the island or any buildings they would construct, for their lifetimes. On October 11, 1909, the state agreed. In 1912, the Foldas built a lodge-like home there called "Engelmar," complete with guest lodging, a boathouse and a dock, most of which, unfortunately, is gone today from this state park island.

Horseshoe Bay, about ten miles to the south, could also claim to be in the shape of a horseshoe, but one which has had its ends pulled wide apart; a stretch of one's imagination could picture that. However, this one is the horseshoe which has seen shipwrecks; the usual horseshoe luck failed them.

The first ship which wrecked at Horseshoe Bay was the small schooner, *Ellen Couture*. On August 4, 1885, a strong summer storm from the north tore the ship from her moorings and forced her ashore, where she broke up. Then the 44-ton schooner, *Willard A. Smith* (65' x 16'6" x 6'; built in 1875 at Charlevoix, Michigan), on October 14, 1893, was lumber-laden when a storm broke her from her pier dockage and pounded her on the rocks. The

The schooner, Farrand H. Williams, *on the right in the photograph, was one of several ships which was stranded and wrecked at Horseshoe Bay. The* Williams *went ashore there on September 11, 1900. This picture was taken in 1885 at Manitowoc.*

Courtesy of Henry Barkhausen

170

Viewed aerially, Horseshoe Island exhibits its unique shape which gave it its name. Once privately owned, the 38.2-acre island passed to state control through the process of eminent domain, and is today part of Peninsula State Park. PHOTO BY CRIS KOHL

Many schooners in the Death's Door area were not as fortunate as the one depicted above, pulling up to the dock at Horseshoe Island during a storm and thus reaching "Safe Harbor," the name of this artwork created by Charles Peterson. The artist was sailing his boat when a storm suddenly arose, forcing him to seek shelter at Horseshoe Island, an incident which inspired him to create this painting. Several sailing ships of old, like the IVER LAWSON, *were not as fortunate at Horseshoe Bay.* ART BY, AND COURTESY OF, CHARLES PETERSON. CONTACT: C. L. PETERSON STUDIO, BOX 81, EPHRAIM, WI 54211, TEL.: 920-854-4033

The same October, 1905 storm which sank ships and killed sailors in other lakes stranded the beautiful, but aging, three-masted schooner, Iver Lawson, *seen here ashore near Horseshoe Bay.* Door County Maritime Museum and Lighthouse Preservation Society, inc.

two sailors on board were saved, but not the uninsured vessel and cargo.

The three-masted, 95-ton scow-schooner, *Farrand H. Williams* (88'8" x 22'8" x 6'6"), built by Capt. Farrand H. Williams at Manitowoc in 1882, stranded and broke up at Horseshoe Bay on September 11, 1900.

The most dramatic of the Horseshoe shipwrecks was the *Iver Lawson,* which was one of the victims of the first of two life-destroying fall storms to hit the Great Lakes in 1905. After passing through Death's Door on her way north, the *Lawson's* sails were blown out by a sudden, 70-mile-an-hour wind change from the north, pushing her south. Stranded at Horseshoe Bay on October 19, 1905, this schooner ended so far ashore that curious, camera-toting spectators could walk completely around the high-and-dry vessel. But the *Lawson* and her four crew were lucky; many area fishermen had lost boats, sheds and docks in that gale. The *Iver Lawson's* Capt. Larson could not immediately free his vessel, and in the spring of 1906, he sold her. A couple of successive owners succeeded only in accumulating salvage debts, but failed to salvage the ship. In July, 1908, the still-beached *Lawson,* pulled by a tug, fell from her screwjacks and makeshift launchramp. Salvage work stopped, and the vessel was burned for her iron. The 170.15-ton *Iver Lawson* (117'8" x 25'7" x 9'5", and named after a Norwegian-born Chicago politician/businessman who lived from 1821 to 1872), launched at Chicago in 1869 as a two-master, was re-rigged as a three-master in 1888. Ironically, this fine ship seems to have been photographed only after becoming a wreck.

THE *R. J. HACKETT*
(NOVEMBER 12, 1905)

W hen a ship safely entered Green Bay from Lake Michigan by means of the dangerous Death's Door Passage, one more serious obstacle lay in wait near the middle of the bay. Far off shore and surrounded by water over one hundred feet deep, a long, narrow, snake-like barren rock, actually exposed in low-water years, lurks in a totally unexpected location. Because its smooth rock sometimes appears above the water's surface, imaginative sailors years ago thought it resembled the back of a whale, so they named it Whaleback Shoal.

Its danger to navigation being obvious, this shoal was the object of frequent clamors to have a lighthouse constructed there, for example:

The "Whale's Back."
The Menominee *Herald* says:
This rocky reef...lies in Green Bay midway between the "Door" and Cedar River and a few miles north of Chambers Island.... It is about six miles long, lying lengthwise of the Bay and at low water comes to the surface in many places. Every year adds one or more to the list of its victims, and lying as it does in the center of the channel, and under water is much more dangerous than the islands and other headlands upon which lighthouses have been erected. Petitions should be circulated before the close of the winter setting forth these facts and asking Congress to make a suitable appropriation for the construction of a lighthouse.
--- *Door County Advocate,* **October 17, 1872**

No lighthouse was ever constructed at Whaleback Shoal, but two buoys, one at each end, have warned sailors of this danger since the late 1800's.

173

One of the first wrecks on Whaleback Shoal was the 226-ton brig, *Sam Hale*, stranded there on September 22, 1868. The ship broke up, but the crew survived (the two mates just barely). The *Toledo Blade* wrote, "...The brig *Hale* was a very old vessel, and was of very little value. Her outfit was worth about $2,000; the hull was not worth more than $1,000."

A strange tale of this reef occurred in November, 1886. A ship arrived at Escanaba reporting a vessel ashore on Whaleback Shoal. The tug, *Delta*, immediately started to the rescue. Upon arrival, the tug's crew discovered the stranded schooner, *Ishpeming*, loaded with coal and her bow two feet out of the water, with colors at half-mast (a signal of distress), its union down, her canvas all right, and not a person on board. The clothing of the crew had been packed and lashed to the forecastle. The yawlboat was gone, but nothing else suggested the fate of the crew. Two hours of pulling released the *Ishpeming* uninjured, and the tug towed her to Escanaba. Days passed with no sign of the crew, and newspapers as far away as New York City began relating the unusual tale of "The Lost Crew of the *Ishpeming*." Then, seemingly out of nowhere, the eight sailors appeared at Baileys Harbor, took a stage to Sturgeon Bay and caught a train to Escanaba to rejoin their vessel. After they had abandoned their ship, they landed at Death's Door, then traveled by foot "twelve or fifteen miles." Other than that, they said nothing about their experiences, probably embarrassed because they had frantically left what old-time sailors called "their vessel in water in which hardly any wind could damage her." The 166-foot-long *Ishpeming*, built in 1872, worked for many more years on the Great Lakes, finally stranding and breaking up on Lake Huron's tiny Black River Island on Nov. 29, 1903.

CRIS KOHL COLLECTION

Whaleback Shoal Victim

The fine, three-masted schooner RED, WHITE AND BLUE *(157'3" x 30'7" x 13'), while in tow of the steamer,* OTEGO, *stranded with a cargo of coal at Whaleback Shoal on October 14, 1895. The vessel was undamaged, but the salvage team experienced a series of pump failures, and the onset of bad weather broke up the ship. The vessel was stripped of her "nautical paraphernalia." As much of the accessible coal cargo was scavenged by fishing tugs, only six of the 800 tons were recovered. Built as a bark by the Bailey Brothers at Madison Dock, Ohio, and launched in the spring of 1863 (in the middle of the Civil War, hence the patriotic name), the 447.34-ton* RED, WHITE AND BLUE *was rerigged as a schooner at Milwaukee in April, 1878. Coincidentally, her towing steamer, the 334-ton* OTEGO *(139' x 25'9" x13'7", built in 1874 as the* CITY OF ST. CATHARINES*), which also stranded at the shoal but only temporarily, burned to a total loss with one life lost a week later while at dock at Green Bay; cut loose, the flaming ship nearly destroyed the Mason Street bridge.*

The most significant shipwreck at Whaleback Shoal was that of the steamer, *R. J. Hackett*, on November 12, 1905. No lives were lost, no irreplaceable cargo went down, but on that day, the Great Lakes lost one of its most historic vessels.

Capt. Robert Jerome Hackett (1827-1879) was co-designer (along with E. Peck) of, and chief investor in, this ship which became the forerunner in the design of modern Great Lakes freighters. This was the first steamship specially produced to carry bulk cargo, particularly iron ore. It was the first ship to have 24-foot hatch centers (aligning with the spacing of the iron ore loading chutes at Marquette, Michigan) in a long row of cargo holds uninterrupted by cabins or propulsion machinery. It was the first ship to have the pilot house positioned at the extreme bow, and the crew's cabin, engine and other large machinery at the extreme stern, with nothing but wide open cargo space in between. It was the first steamer designed to tow another vessel carrying a cargo equal to its own. It was the first steamship to carry a cargo of iron ore to Cleveland when it delivered 648 tons from Lake Superior on August 14, 1871. Before that, sailing ships monopolized the bulk cargo trade, but this new steamship helped put an end to the golden age of sail on the Great Lakes. This ship was named after Capt. R. J. Hackett.

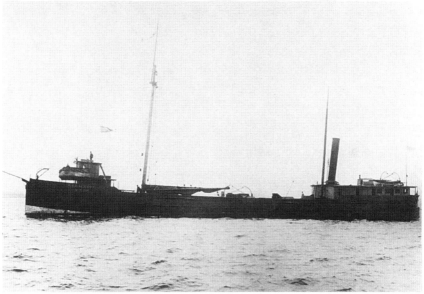

The revolutionary 1869 wooden steamer, the **R. J. HACKETT,** *was the trendsetting ship which established the unique design of Great Lakes bulk freighters. With the pilot house at the bow, and the engine room and crew's quarters at the stern, the large, open deck space in between facilitated access to the several cargo hatches. Its boxy shape allowed maximum size cargoes. After 36 years of service, the* **HACKETT** *burned to a complete loss in 1905 at Whaleback Shoal in Green Bay just west of Death's Door.* CRIS KOHL COLLECTION

175

Above: *Because it stranded right on the seemingly seamless, solid rock and broke its back at Whaleback Shoal, the steamer,* **R. J. H**ACKETT, *took quite a beating and lies in many pieces in shallow depths up to 25 feet. The boiler sits in 18 feet.* PHOTO BY CRIS KOHL

Inset: *The historic* **R. J. H**ACKETT'S *propeller at Whaleback Shoal.*   PHOTO BY CRIS KOHL

Above: *Unlike the boiler, which sits off to one side by itself, the* **R. J. HACKETT'S** *broken steam engine and propulsion system form a massive debris field.* PHOTO BY CRIS KOHL

Inset: *Joan Forsberg explores the site and attempts to identify the many large and small pieces of steel which were once the power behind the* **R. J. HACKETT.** PHOTO BY CRIS KOHL

Built by Cleveland's Elihu Peck and launched on November 16, 1869, the 1,129-ton wooden steamer measured 211'2" x 32'5" x 19'2". Since the 1970's, Great Lakes ship design, unfortunately, has been gradually returning to the saltwater style of placing the pilot house astern or midship, but many of the uniquely-designed Great Lakes vessels remain. Today, any time you spot a freighter on the freshwater seas with that classic profile of its pilot house on the bow, you will know that it was modeled after the *R. J. Hackett*.

The steamer, *R. J. Hackett*, toiled for many years on the inland seas, encountering very few difficulties, but shortly after 6 A.M., Sunday, November 12, 1905, the ship was completely destroyed by fire at Whaleback Shoal in the middle of Green Bay. The steamer, in command of its owner, Capt. Henry C. McCallum of Detroit, was on its way from Cleveland to Marinette, Wisconsin, with 1,200 tons of coal. Thought to have been caused by an overturned lamp, the fire broke out just aft of the engine room. While the captain ran the ship onto Whaleback Shoal, crewmembers quickly aimed two streams of water at the flames. Before long, the smoke inside the engine room drove the firefighters out of there. Two large oil tanks in the engine room, plus one in the lower hold, exploded, blowing the stern cabin sky high. But by then, fortunately, all the men were safely away.

Lifesavers from the Plum Island Life-Saving Station eleven miles away, seeing the smoke, rowed their boat with great difficulty against the strong wind as they raced to the rescue of the crew. It took them four hours to get there, and by that time, the ship was doomed and the 13 people on board the *R. J. Hackett* had safely launched their two yawlboats. They tossed about in the heavy seas for about an hour before being picked up by the fish tug, *Steward Edwards*, from Washington Island, and taken to Menominee.

The lifesavers' exhausting trip to the *Hackett*, however, was not in vain. The steamer's stern had completely burned away, and its crew had abandoned the vessel two hours earlier, but Capt. Egin and several of his lifesaving crew boarded the bow and secured the captain's and mate's papers from the pilot house, items which had been forgotten in the hasty departure.

The *R. J. Hackett*, valued at $16,000, was insured for $12,000, while the coal cargo was insured for its full value of $4,000.

Just the year before, on June 5, 1904, the *R. J. Hackett's* near-sister ship, the *Forest City*, had stranded heavily, bow on, a total loss, at Bear's Rump Island near Tobermory, Ontario, in Lake Huron's Georgian Bay, and sank down a steep slope in deep water, its stern end reaching a depth of 150 feet. Today that shipwreck is part of the first underwater park in the Great Lakes, established at Tobermory in 1972. The *R. J. Hackett* lies broken up in 12 to 20 feet of water on Whaleback Shoal. This historic shipwreck at this remote site was the subject of a State Historical Society of Wisconsin underwater survey in 1988.

The *C. C. Hand*
(October 6, 1913)

C aptain Francis Hackett, of Amherstburg, Ontario, had sailed the lakes since he was a boy and had always dreamed of one day owning a boat of his own. By May of 1913, he had saved enough money to purchase the steamer *C. C. Hand*, a 2,122-gross-ton vessel in liquidation from the Gilchrist Transportation Company. He immediately put her into drydock, spending $18,000 for necessary repairs. Answering an urgent call for fuel to abate the growing chill of autumn in Chicago, the captain set out from Cleveland on the 265-foot-long, 41-foot-wide wooden steamer with a huge cargo of 2,400 tons of coal. Even though he had put practically every penny he had into the boat, in his haste to get underway, he postponed insuring the *Hand*. He was realizing the dream of his life as he made his first voyage as owner and master. That dream would become a nightmare only three days later when the 23-year-old, oak-hulled steamer, with its holds loaded with volatile soft coal, would meet a fiery death in the dense fog of Poverty Passage.

Captain Hackett must not have been a superstitious man because he disregarded two of the most notable superstitions among sailors. The *Hand* had been originally named the *R. E. Schuck* when it had been built in Cleveland by Thomas Quayle's Sons for J. C. Gilchrist in 1890. In 1904, the ship was renamed the *C. C. Hand* for Chester Cummer Hand who had been the popular manager of the coal-loaders in Sandusky, Ohio. Although changing a ship's name is considered unlucky, Capt. Hackett purchased her anyway. But the captain was really pushing his luck by choosing to leave Cleveland bound for Chicago on Friday, October 3, 1913. Leaving

STEAMER IS DESTROYED BY FIRE

FREIGHT STEAMER C. C. HAND BURNS TO THE WATER'S EDGE

Freighter Ladened With Coal Enroute From Cleveland to Chicago is Destroyed

SINKS IN 30 FEET OF WATER

Captain and Crew of Sixteen Manage to Reach Summer Island in a Single Lifeboat

SIX NARROWLY ESCAPE DEATH

The steamer "C. C. Hand," bound from Cleveland, Ohio, to Chicago, with a cargo of coal, lies just east of Poverty Passage to the northeast of Big

FIGHT TO THE DEATH

Green Bay Men Engage in Terrific Struggle—One Dead, The Other Dying

(By Associated Press.)

Green Bay, Oct. 7.—Margo Walowitz of Milwaukee is dead and Mike Janic seriously wounded and Miss Milka Conkoviz and Mrs. Janic, slashed, as the result of a knife battle in a small room in the Janic house.

Walowitz tried to force an entrance to the house early in the morning and would not leave when told to do so. Forcing an entrance he was met inside of the door by Janic. Each of the men was armed with a sharp jagged beet topping knife, which was used by them in the beet fields. The men

CITY OF NOME IS DESTROYED

STORM THAT HAS RAGED FOR TWENTY-FOUR HOURS SHOWS SIGNS OF ABATING

BODIES ARE WASHED ASHORE

Two Miles of Water Front is Wrecked and Fire Completes the Devastation

APPLES TO SPARE? SEND THEM TO GOOD WILL FARM

Freight Will Gladly be Paid—Seven Year Old Child Given Home at Ford River

Mrs. Donaldson, superintendent of the Good Will Farm at Houghton arrived in Escanaba last evening. She brought a seven year old boy from the home and placed him at the home of William Van Enkevort at Ford River.

Mrs. Donaldson states that because of the strike the Good Will Farm is having a rather hard row to hoe at

BOAT BURNS; CREW MAROONED

Sailors of Steamer C. C. Hand Spend Night on Barren Island.

[SPECIAL TO THE RECORD-HERALD.]

ESCANABA, Mich., Oct. 7.—The steamer C. C. Hand, one of the oldest boats in service on the lakes in the coal trade, was burned to the water's edge off Big Sum-

The wooden steamer, C.C. Hand, was bound for Chicago with her coal cargo when she experienced her final, unfortunate accident, as reported by the The Escanaba Daily Press of Oct. 7, 1913 and (inset) the Oct 8, 1913 Chicago Record-Herald.

Cris Kohl Collection

port on a Friday was considered so unlucky that it was rarely ever done.

By late Monday afternoon, October 6th, the *Hand* was fighting her way through thick fog, trying to make Poverty Passage. The ship grounded twice on Big Summer Island, was backed off each time, and the captain finally ordered the anchors dropped to wait until the fog lifted. Then the luck of the *C. C. Hand* really ran out. At about 6:00 PM, while the crew was at mess, smoke suddenly began filling the mess room. The men raced up to the deck as flames burst from the aft bunkers into the engine room. The crew's efforts with the hand extinguishers and even the steam extinguisher were to no avail. Fire on board a ship carrying volatile soft coal is certain disaster, and it took only minutes for the vessel to be engulfed in flames. Sensing that his boat was doomed, Capt. Hackett ordered the men to abandon ship. The rapidly-spreading fire prevented the crew from launching the port lifeboat, but with some difficulty, they were able to clear the starboard boat. With Mate MacLean at the rudder, the first boatload

Lying in only thirty feet of water alongside Summer Island, the wreck of the wooden steamer, C. C. Hand, which burned to a total loss in October, 1913, fortunately with no loss of life, usually offers very clear water, easy scuba diving at a shallow depth and many exploratory and photographic opportunities. The huge, four-bladed propeller resting upright on the sandy lake bottom is one of this shipwreck site's highlights.

PHOTO BY
KIM BRUNGRABER

carrying seven men came within 50 feet of Big Summer Island and the men waded ashore in waist-deep water so that the boat could return to the *Hand* as quickly as possible for the next group. Six men boarded the lifeboat for the second shift to be taken the quarter mile to the island. Mate MacLean again ordered the sailors to jump over early and wade ashore, knowing that the five brave men still on the *Hand* were in grave peril. With two men on the sculling oar, he made the final trip back to the ship, which by then was almost entirely ablaze. Their backs to the encroaching fire, the captain and remaining crew huddled in the small space at the bow which was not yet burning. Capt. Hackett had to restrain some of the men from jumping overboard to escape the intense heat. The captain, the last one off, had scarcely made it into the boat when the blaze swept across the entire ship. From the safety of the island, the men watched as the steamer burned to the waterline and sank in thirty feet of water shortly after 8:00 PM, with only its bow remaining above the water.

The crew erected a primitive shelter using a boat cover and built a fire,

181

trying to get dry and warm as best they could. At 1:00 AM, seeing a blaze about three miles distant, Capt. Casey of the small community of Fairport set off in his fishing launch toward the burning ship. Spotting the crew's fire on the island, he took them all aboard and by 2:00 had brought them to Fairport. In the morning when the fog lifted, the sailors were taken to Escanaba so the captain could arrange for their transportation back to Cleveland. With the loss of the *Hand*, Capt. Hackett had lost practically everything he had, but he hoped to salvage the fine engine from the wreck.

Thomas H. Smith purchased the coal cargo from the underwriters and arranged for Capt. Peter Batchelder with the tug *Hunsader* and barge *Advance* to salvage the coal. By the time the salvagers reached the wreck of the *Hand* five days later, some of the coal was still burning. Since it was too hot and dangerous for the salvagers to board the ship, operating the clam shovel was made more difficult. In addition, a storm blew in and caused the *Advance* to flee to the safety of Washington Harbor with four feet of water in her holds. Only 400 tons of the coal had been recovered by October 15th when the *Hunsader* returned to port and reported that fishing boats were doing their own recovery of the coal cargo. In due course, the *Hunsader* and the *Advance* did return to do more cargo salvage work. Several years later, in May, 1920, the two scotch boilers, built by the Cleveland Shipbuilding Company in 1890, were removed from the wreck.

The *C. C. Hand* had stranded in the past, even before the ship's name change. In September, 1903, in her earlier life as the *R. E. Schuck*, she ran aground in the Chicago River. The 3,000 tons of coal she was carrying caused her draft to be 18 feet, which was six inches too deep for the crown of the LaSalle Street tunnel. When the tugs attempted to pull the *Schuck* off the obstruction, the direction of the wind changed suddenly and caused the level of the river to drop even further. The heavy ship was pinned for more than sixteen hours until the wind changed course into the east and the water level rose enough for the tugs to pull the steamer off.

Near the end of the shipping season in early December, 1905, the *C. C. Hand*, carrying a cargo of oats, had stranded near Port Hope, Michigan, in Lake Huron. The wrecker *Huron City* happened by and offered assistance to the grounded steamer. The crews of both boats shovelled oats overboard until the *Hand* was light enough for the *Huron City* to free her.

The cause of the fire that destroyed the *C. C. Hand*, one of the oldest lake boats in service in the coal trade, was never determined. Those who are superstitious would say that the captain had been tempting fate. However, one can be certain that, on his maiden voyage as owner and master of his own ship, Captain Hackett's heart broke as he watched his dream go down in flames.

THE GREAT STORM SHIPWRECKS
(NOVEMBER 8-10, 1913)

Death's Door was hit hard by the worst storm in Great Lakes recorded history. Referred to simply as "The Great Storm," it lasted from November 8th until the 10th, 1913, and although it severely damaged dozens of ships, totally destroyed eighteen others and killed more than 250 sailors in all four of the westernmost Great Lakes, the area hit the hardest was lower Lake Huron, where eight steel freighters went missing with all hands. All around Great Lakes' shorelines, deep, drifting snow closed roads and paralyzed traffic, while downed telephone lines interrupted communications. In the twelve hours between Friday evening, November 7th, and Saturday morning, November 8th, the temperatures at Oshkosh, Wisconsin, dropped from 60 to 20 degrees, and four inches of snow fell. Death's Door was not spared, and these severe gales did considerable damage to small boats, fishing nets, docks and shoreline buildings. Of the four vessels which bore the brunt of the storm in this area (*Louisiana, Halsted, Thistle* and *Plymouth*), the results were dramatically different for each ship.

The first vessel to feel the furious wrath of the Great Storm at Death's Door, the old, wooden steamer, *Louisiana*, was bound light (that is, without any cargo, having just delivered a full load of coal from Lorain, Ohio, to Milwaukee) for Escanaba to pick up a heavy cargo of iron ore. Shortly after the ship successfully steamed through Death's Door Passage, there was an awkward stillness before the winds shifted from the southwest. Soon fifty-five-mile-an-hour northwest gales stung the face of Capt. Frederick MacDonald and compelled him to seek shelter for his vessel in Washington Harbor at the top of Washington Island. It was then around midnight. Inside the bay, however, too much open water on the northwest side exposed the

Several ships sought refuge from the Great Storm of 1913 at Washington Island, but the intense winds not only lasted longer than anticipated, they also changed directions. Bucking the fury of those gales in Washington Harbor were the anchored schooners J. H. STEVENS (left) and the MINERVA. The Plum Island Life-Saving team arrived at this harbor to rescue the crews of the LOUISIANA and the HALSTED, but finding that neither crew needed their assistance, remained at the scene of the two anchored schooners "prepared to save the crews if the hooks would not hold." But both old sailing ships survived the bouncing. The J. H. STEVENS (100' x 21'3" x 6'6"), built as a small sloop in 1860 at Milan, Ohio, and enlarged into a schooner in 1891, burned to a total loss at Presque Isle, Michigan, on Lake Huron years later, June 10, 1927. The MINERVA (125'5" x 26'7" x 9'8"), launched at Black River (Lorain), Ohio, in 1863, transferred to salt water in 1916, stranding to become a total loss on Anastasia Island, Florida, on June 25, 1920. CRIS KOHL COLLECTION

steamer to increasingly severe winds. At 2:00 A.M., Saturday, November 8, 1913, the *Louisiana's* anchor failed to hold, and the ship stranded just off the eastern shore. The 17-member crew managed to get one of their men safely ashore to hike about three miles across the island to the southern end where the Plum Island Life-Saving Station could be summoned for help.

Waiting out the storm while on a stranded ship would not have been much of a problem for the *Louisiana's* remaining crewmembers had their vessel not caught on fire. As if the ship bashing on the rocks were not enough, flames in the after hold, discovered at about 8 A.M., intimidated the men further. They fought the wind-fanned flames for an hour when the *Louisiana's* captain took stock of the situation, then ordered the lifeboat launched into the heavy seas. Threatened with swamping in the huge, crashing waves, the boat, crammed tight with sixteen men, fortunately made

The wooden steamer, Louisiana, *was bound light from Milwaukee to Escanaba to pick up an iron ore cargo. After making it through Death's Door Passage, the ship sought shelter from the swelling storm in Washington Island Harbor, little realizing that this would be the worst storm ever in Great Lakes recorded history.* CRIS KOHL COLLECTION

it to shore safely. As the shivering crewmen watched, their ship burned to the water's edge, a total loss.

The *Louisiana's* First Mate, Finley McLean, gave his account:

> ...We tried to drop the anchor to escape being blown on the beach, but the wind was too much for us. It blew us back faster and faster and all this time the engines were going full steam ahead. By 1:00 A.M., the wind had increased to seventy miles an hour and we were really scared. We were fighting helplessly to keep off the beach. We just couldn't do a damn thing. At 2:00 A.M., we struck the shore on Washington Island.
>
> Our situation then was even more terrible. The wind and seas were breaking over the entire ship. Six hours later, we finally managed to get a man ashore to take the news of the wreck to the lifesavers at Plum Island.
>
> Before he even reached there, we were placed in deadly peril and were forced to face the icy breakers. How it happened we never knew for certain, but the old *Louisiana* caught fire. Probably the wrecked engines started it, but we never had a chance to find out. The old craft was made of wood and burned like tinder.

> Fighting the blaze was hopeless. We launched a lifeboat as fast as possible into the roaring breakers and floundered [sic] through them safely to shore, half drowned, two-thirds frozen, and just blamed scared. We were smart to start so promptly. In fifteen minutes from the start of the blaze, the whole ship was wrapped in flames. She burned clear to the water as we watched. There was nothing left of her but her red-hot engines, which hissed like a volcano and sent off clouds of steam as the seas rushed over them.

Mate McLean then claimed that the nearest farmhouse was five miles away, which was an exaggeration; the first farmhouse the desperate crew found in the severe storm probably only felt like it was five miles from the wreck! The extreme opposite end of Washington Island from the wreck of the *Louisiana* in Washington Harbor is 5.8 miles, with many farmhouses creating a formidable obstacle course along that route.

The storm was, however, worsening, as Mate McLean discovered when he attempted to contact the outside world:

> I was anxious to notify my wife, so that if she got news of the wreck from other sources she wouldn't worry about me. At the first opportunity I made my way to a telegraph station on the island where I managed to get a message started. I wasn't quick enough, however, for the wire went down as my message was being transmitted, breaking all contact with the outside world. All the receiving end ever got were the words "LOUISIANA WRECKED ON WASHINGTON ISLAND." Fortunately the operator knew or guessed the purpose of the message and mercifully added the word "SAVED." It was Tuesday [three days

What remained of the old steamer, LOUISIANA, *after the Great Storm of 1913, mainly part of the burned-out wooden hull enmeshed with twisted pipes and fallen decking, provided an adventurous setting and years of exploration for local children.* CRIS KOHL COLLECTION

later] before we could get to the first town on the mainland, Escanaba. Until I sent her further word from there, my wife hardly slept at all...."

What the outside world incorrectly learned initially about the *Louisiana's* fate was the word which accompanied "Washington." A geographically-challenged reporter hastily interpreted the ship as stranding at Port Washington, Wisconsin, a town just north of Milwaukee, and not Washington Island. This misinformation spread quickly. Two tugboats with lifesaving crews on board searched the shorelines at Port Washington and Sheboygan without locating the *Louisiana*, concluding that "the steamer struck the rocks and sank with all men on board." Newspapers in Detroit, Toledo, Chicago and elsewhere reported that the *Louisiana* was lost at Port Washington. Vessel-men shook their heads in disbelief that this ship had taken nearly two days to steam just 25 miles from where she had unloaded her cargo at Milwaukee! In reality, the *Louisiana* was about 180 miles north, burned to a total loss at Washington Island. Within two days, this geographical error was corrected.

Launched on Thursday, May 12, 1887, at Marine City, Michigan, on the shores of the St. Clair River, the 1,929-ton *Louisiana* (267' x 39' x 20') carried one smokestack and, originally, four masts, which were later cut down to two masts, the configuration at her demise. Her fore and aft compound steam engine could produce 450 horsepower. The new ship was rated A1 by insurance companies and valued at $110,000, but by the time of her loss 26 years later, the vessel was appraised at $15,000.

The 171-foot-long, unpowered barge, *Halsted*, towed by the steamer, *James H. Prentice* (180' x 31'6" x 13'6", built in 1885 at Trenton, Michigan), was in trouble while sheltering at Washington Island, coincidentally just behind the burning *Louisiana*. Both oak-hulled vessels, the *Halsted* and the *Prentice*, were sailing without cargoes, and both had sought shelter in Washington Harbor when the towline broke. The

The wooden barge, HALSTED, *built at Little Sturgeon Bay in 1873, and seen here in the Soo (Sault Ste. Marie) Canal Locks, stranded near the* LOUISIANA. CRIS KOHL COLLECTION

Above: *Washington Harbor provides protection against storms, but not from those with a north wind, such as the Great Storm of 1913. The* LOUISIANA *and the* HALSTED *both stranded on the far shore.*

Left: *Artifacts from the* LOUISIANA *are displayed at the Jacobsen Museum on Washington Island.*

Below: *The shoreline remains of the* LOUISIANA. PHOTOS BY CRIS KOHL

188

Above: *Although much of the wreck of the wooden steamer,* Louisiana, *disappeared when the ship burned and broke up in late 1913, enough of the hull remained above water to make it an exciting place for children to explore. Today, about 100 years later, what is left rests completely underwater, lying in two to twenty-five feet.* Inset: *Much hull planking and many bolts remain at this large shipwreck site.* Photos by Cris Kohl

189

Halsted ashore at Washington Harbor

Above: *Not long before 1913, newspaper technology reached the point where photographs could be published, replacing the line drawings which had featured so strikingly in newspapers of the 1880's and 1890's (and also putting hundreds of artists out of work!). This photo of the* HALSTED *was published on the front page of the* DOOR COUNTY ADVOCATE *on January 1, 1914.* DOOR COUNTY MARITIME MUSEUM AND LIGHTHOUSE PRESERVATION SOCIETY, INC.

Below: *The newspaper reported about the* HALSTED, *"The craft was not injured, even though she came near being thrown up into the woods."*
DOOR COUNTY MARITIME MUSEUM AND LIGHTHOUSE PRESERVATION SOCIETY, INC.

Above: *Over the course of the winter of 1913-1914, the schooner-barge,* HALSTED, *helplessly stranded at Washington Island Harbor, endured icings and other punishing forms of weather.* DOOR COUNTY MARITIME MUSEUM AND LIGHTHOUSE PRESERVATION SOCIETY, INC.

Below: *In the spring of 1914, salvage work on the solid, 40-year-old* HALSTED *commenced and occupied several weeks. The* DOOR COUNTY ADVOCATE *reported on Thursday, July 16, 1914: "Work on the barge* HALSTED, *which has been at the shipyard since she was rescued from the beach at Washington Harbor, was completed Monday and the day following, the tug* TORRENT *transferred her to the Leathem & Smith wharf. The* HALSTED *was taken across to the Green quarry after having some coal put on her, and will be taken to Green Bay when the* TORRENT *goes up there." The* HALSTED *worked for another two decades, attesting to her sound oak construction and rebuilds.* CRIS KOHL COLLLECTION

Halsted's anchor could not plant its hook, and the ship was slowly being pushed towards shore by the gales. The frozen lifesaving crew, disappointed at having arrived too late to help the *Louisiana's* sailors, remained at the scene, ready to rescue the *Halsted's*. Anticipation increased as the severe winds drove the *Halsted* closer and closer towards shore over the next 20 hours, while the dutiful Plum Island Life-Savers kept miserable watch in the bitter cold from the snow-covered shoreline. At 5:00 Sunday morning, the *Halsted* pounded onto a huge rock only 60 feet from shore, sending the lifesavers into action. Every man did his job in setting up the breeches buoy, and a whipline was shot aboard the *Halsted*.

But fate cheated the lifesavers from completing their rescue. A powerful wave lifted the *Halsted* and deposited the ship far up on the pebbly beach. Capt. Rudolph Peterson, his wife, and five sailors clambered down the side of the ship on a rope ladder and safely reached the island.

Bad news sells better than good news. Initial newspaper accounts told the tragic tale of six *Halsted* sailors freezing to death after their ship stranded on Washington Island. Fortunately, the truth was reported by the time the towing steamer, the *James H. Prentice*, conveyed the *Halsted's* and the *Louisiana's* crews safely to Escanaba on Tuesday, November 12, 1913. The *Halsted* was recovered in 1914 and worked for many more years, as did the *Prentice*. Both ships were abandoned due to old age in the 1930's.

The Great Storm tore the small Hart Transportation Company passenger and freight steamer, *Thistle*, from her winter moorings on the east side of Sturgeon Bay. The ruthless winds blew the 80-foot-long ship across the bay and deposited it on the western side, specifically upon the slab dock of the Washburn Company at Sawyer. The Sturgeon Bay Canal Life-Saving personnel came to the rescue of the crew, while the tug, *N. Boutin*, easily recovered the damaged steamer. The 26-year-old *Thistle* was repaired and returned to service the following year.

The only truly tragic maritime loss at Death's Door during the Great Storm of 1913 was the lumber barge, *Plymouth*. The tug, *James H. Martin*, towed the *Plymouth* out of Menominee (Michigan) harbor on Thursday, November 7, 1913, heading for northern Lake Huron. Encountering huge seas, both ships remained behind St. Martin Island until Saturday morning, when, realizing that the storm was building and that they were in a bad position, they raised anchors and proceeded to Gull Island, where the helpless barge anchored and the tug steamed to shelter at Summer Island.

Two days later, the tug, *James H. Martin*, returned to pick up its tow, only to find that the *Plymouth*, with the seven crewmembers who had been on board, had disappeared.

A few days later, wreckage from the *Plymouth*, consisting of a broken

Above: *The tug,* JAMES H. MARTIN *(left), frequently towed the barge,* PLYMOUTH, *seen here heavily loaded with lumber.*   CRIS KOHL COLLECTION

Above: *The barge,* PLYMOUTH, *built in 1854, almost ended her career near Marquette, Michigan, on Lake Superior, on Oct. 24, 1887, when the ship stranded and was forced to spend the winter in this precarious setting. Teams of horses pulled wagons loaded with the ship's recovered coal cargo across the ice. The vessel was pulled off in the spring of 1888 and returned to service.*   CRIS KOHL COLLECTION

MENOMINEE HERALD-LE

VOL. XVII. NO. 130.   MENOMINEE, MICHIGAN, WEDNESDAY EVENING, NOVEMBER 12, 1913.

SEVEN MEN DROWNED
ON BARGE PLYMOUTH

Terrible Gale Which Swept Great Lakes Believed to Have Destroyed Barge Plymouth --- Seven Men on Board Probably Drowned---Six of Them Lived in Twin Cities, Including Deputy United States Marshal Christ Keenan --- Eager Search Brings no News from Missing Men---Story of Storm told by Survivors on Tug Martin, Which Arrived Last Night from Disaster.

WOODS FIRE
AROUSES IRE

Originals Accuse National Committeeman Woods of Heading Corrupt Political Machine.

"GANG" TO USE WILSON

Allege That Purpose is to Build Up Tammany in Michigan—Job Seekers They Say Haven't Reformed Yet.

Detroit, Mich., Nov. 12.—"Charges that National Committeeman E. G. Wood, Congressman Frank E. Doremus and Judge Connolly are trying to enlist the aid of President Wilson in building up 'a Michigan Tammany' were made by Arthur D. Maguire, of the Michigan Wilson organization Sunday.

Maguire's statement was made in reply to a report from Washington, quoting Mr. Wood as saying that Maguire is associated with "some queer people." If as Maguire says, he is a friend of Governor Ferris.

"It seems we have earned the title—henchmen," said Maguire.

"I notice that Mr. Wood claims that Governor Ferris by my speech at Bay City last winter, if telling the governor some homely truths was in-

Left at anchor to fend for itself, the unpowered barge, PLYMOUTH, *disappeared with all seven hands. Several bodies washed up across Lake Michigan.*

CRIS KOHL COLLECTION

The barge Plymouth, owned by the McKinnon & Scott Transportation company, with seven men aboard, is believed to have gone down last Saturday or Sunday with all hands shortly and Captain Setrucks declare that it was impossible for the men aboard the Plymouth to make shore in the lifeboats, as no boat could live in a sea so terrific as the one that lashed the

193

lifeboat, hatch covers and other debris, was blown ashore by the powerful western gales near Ludington on the other side of Lake Michigan.

On November 20, 1913, a bottle containing an undated, hand-scrawled message was picked up on shore five miles from Pentwater, Michigan. It had been written by Christopher Keenan, a deputy U.S. Marshall from Menominee who had been placed on board the *Plymouth* because that vessel had been taken into custody. The emotional message in the bottle, written by a doomed man, was published in nearly every newspaper in the inland seas, and it burned itself into the minds and memories of everyone in Menominee and many other parts of the Great Lakes:

MESSAGE OF DEATH

Bottle Washed Ashore Brings Word to Mrs. Chris Keenan of Husband's Death.

PICKED UP AT PENTWATER, MICH.

Note Sent to Menominee Business Firm on Whose Stationery it Was Written.

TELLS OF TERRIBLE FATE

Forty Hours in Storm, Keenan Bids Family Good Bye—With Six Others on Plymouth Drowns.

"Dear Wife and Children:
We were left up here in Lake Michigan, captain of the James H. Martin tug, at anchor. He went away and never said good-bye or anything to us. Lost one man last night. We have been out in the storm 40 hours. Good-bye, dear ones, I might see you in heaven. Pray for me— CHRIST K.
I felt so bad I had another man write for me. $35.00, so you can get it. Good-bye forever."

When F. P. Smith, manager of the Central West Coal company opend his mail shortly after 1 o'clock yesterday afternoon, after being absent from his office—

Reports of the message found in a bottle from the doomed PLYMOUTH *made front-page news in many Great Lakes newspapers.*
CRIS KOHL COLLECTION

Dear Wife and Children:

We were left up here in Lake Michigan by McKinnon, captain of the *James H. Martin* tug, at anchor. He went away and never said good-bye or anything to us. Lost one man last night. We have been out in the storm 40 hours. Good-bye dear ones, I might see you in heaven. Pray for me--- CHRIST K.

I felt so bad I had another man write for me. Huebel owes $35.00, so you can get it. Good-bye forever.

If ever a message condemned a ship's officer, it was this one. Investigations followed, along with several delays and considerable intrigue (e.g. the controversial tug, *James H. Martin,* was purposely scuttled by parties unknown). In the end, Capt. Donald I. McKinnon's pilot license was revoked, while tug engineer Capt. Louis Setunsky had his license suspended for one year.

Besides Keenan, the men lost with the *Plymouth* were Capt. Axel Larson of Marinette, cedar inspector for the C. J. Huebel Lumber Company; Edward Johnson of Marinette; Clyde Jessup of Grayling, Michigan; James Sabata of Menominee; Clifford DuChaine of Marinette; and Henry Kosak of Menominee. Some of the unfortunate crew were located. Keenan's body, after drifting 75 miles, washed ashore near Manistee, Michigan, on Sunday, November 16th; 17-year-old Edward Johnson was found half-buried in the sand just south of Empire, Michigan, on November 30th

Presque Isle & Partridge Island. Marquette, Mich.

Above: *The barge,* PLYMOUTH *(213'1" x 35'2" x 13'6", built in 1854 at Cleveland), often required a tugboat to pull it off a rock or a shoal where it had ground itself, a common event for commercial ships on the Great Lakes. Here, the setting was once again near Marquette, Michigan, on mighty Lake Superior, depicted in the colorized photograph on this postcard printed in Germany in about 1904.* CRIS KOHL COLLECTION

Below: *In late 1913, the tug,* JAMES H. MARTIN, *plowed headstrong into the severe seas churned up by the worst storm in recorded history while towing the helpless barge,* PLYMOUTH, *with seven men on board. The* MARTIN *released the towline, forcing the* PLYMOUTH *to drop anchor and fend for herself.* ARTWORK BY, AND COURTESY OF, MARINE ART OF JAMES CLARY. **Tel.: 810-987-0767, e-mail: marineart@jclary.com, website: www.jclary.com**

195

(his location, 60 miles north of where Keenan's body was found, suggests that he was the first of the *Plymouth* crew to die, the "lost one man last night" in Keenan's message); Axel Larson's body, found on Sunday, December 14th, at Little Sable Point near Shelby, Michigan, had drifted 130 miles.

Until the month of November, losses on the Great Lakes for the year 1913 had been astonishingly small: only about a dozen lives had been lost, mostly from the exploding of the steamer, *E. M. Peck*, at Racine on June 11th, with seven lives lost, and the sinking of the barge, *Annabelle Wilson*, on Lake Erie on July 12th, where two men perished. But the devastation in the month of November shot the year's total upwards by more than 2000%.

A month after the Great Storm of 1913, despite the fact that it was December, most ships on the Great Lakes went about their business as usual. The steamer, *Sailor Boy*, made her final trip of the season to Marinette, while the *Bon Ami* returned from her last trip north. The tug, *N. Boutin*, made one more crossing to Ludington, Michigan, with the stone-laden barge, *Ida Corning*, in tow. The stone barge, *Empire State*, which had lain submerged next to the upper mill wharf in Sturgeon Bay for the past year, was pumped out by the *I. N. Foster* in anticipation of returning the old vessel to service in 1914. The Sturgeon Bay Life-Saving Station planned to close for the season at midnight on Saturday, December 20th.

Normal routine had resumed and the navigation season was winding down, but the nightmares and the fears over the gales of November stayed for the remainder of their lives with those sailors who had been picked by fate to survive its fury in the Great Storm of 1913.

The barge *Plymouth* could have been swept out into the deep, midlake waters of Lake Michigan. In the 1960's, scuba divers claimed to have found the *Plymouth* in water about seventy feet deep off Poverty Island, but no positive proof of identification has been made.

The *Louisiana* is a different story. During the 1920's, the very visible wreck of the *Louisiana* held strong appeal to adventurous boys. But as boys are wont, their imaginations ran rampant trying to explain how this shipwreck met its fate. One of the "tall tales" of these young explorers is told in *A Gleam Across the Wave* by Arthur and Evelyn Knudsen:

> Once, when this ship was trying to come around Bowyer's Bluff, a big wind came up and whizzed her, faster than the fastest airplane, down to the end of the harbor and smashed her all up and killed all her crew. And us kids don't like to go in swimmin' near her, because the heads of the dead men are still rollin' and floatin' and bumpin' around down there underneath her.

Swimmers! Scuba divers! Beware of those rollin' heads on this shipwreck!

THE *CITY OF GLASGOW*
(OCTOBER 6, 1917)

T he life of the steamer, *City of Glasgow*, is a tribute to, and shining example of, the never-say-die spirit of the enterprising vesselmen of the Great Lakes. She grounded (so often that she could have been called the "Queen of the Beach"), she foundered, she burned and she sank in her career, but time after time, she was raised, repaired and returned to service. In today's "disposable" society, one wonders if she might have been abandoned to the elements the first time she "broke" by modern-day owners unwilling to invest the time, effort and money to restore her to working condition. The shipowners, builders, masters and seamen of a hundred years ago were fired with the conviction that to "give up" was unworthy.

Launched amid great fanfare at West Bay City, Michigan, in 1891, the *City of Glasgow* was built by James Davidson, the iconic Great Lakes builder of great wooden ships. She and her sister ship, the *City of London*, were wooden steamers 297 feet long and 41 feet wide, and they boasted a gross tonnage of 2,002. Together with the 298-foot-long *City of Paris* and *City of Berlin*, launched in the same year, they were called "The Big Four."

The *City of Glasgow* was also one of the fastest ships on the lakes in 1892; she made the Duluth-to-Buffalo round trip, with wheat downbound and coal upbound, in less than eleven and a half days. The year 1892 would also see the construction of three more Davidson wooden behemoths: the *City of Genoa*, the *City of Venice* and the *City of Naples* (later to become the *Frank O'Connor*; see chapter 26, pages 201 to 218). Proud of his *"City"* ships, Davidson retained ownership of the *City of Glasgow* until 1895, when she became the first ship of the fledgling Buckeye Steamship Company, newly formed by Charles Hutchinson.

One of those ships with the proverbial nine lives, the 297-foot-long steamer, CITY OF GLASGOW, *was converted into a stone barge in 1911.*   CRIS KOHL COLLECTION

Despite her speed, size and staunch construction, the *City of Glasgow* suffered many accidents in her career. Beginning a run of grain downbound to Buffalo and coal upbound to Milwaukee, she went ashore at Whitefish Point in Lake Superior. Leaking slightly but not seriously damaged, she continued this December, 1896 trip after a brief stop at Sault Ste. Marie to wait for better weather. Heading for Midland, Ontario, in Georgian Bay with a cargo of wheat from Duluth, the *City of Glasgow* went aground at Saw Log Point on June 17, 1899. Wreckers lightered 30,000 bushels of wheat before being able to release her and she reportedly had a considerable amount of water in her hold. The entire process took nearly a week.

Barely three weeks later, the *Glasgow* was aground again, this time in the St. Clair River and carrying a cargo of iron ore downbound. Released by the wrecking tug, *Saginaw*, she completed her journey. On October 14, 1904, the *City of Glasgow*, towing the *Abyssinia* and carrying iron ore for Buffalo, stranded off La Pointe, Madeline Island in Lake Superior. After jettisoning 300 tons of the ore, the tugs *B. B. Inman* and *Crosby* were able to free her and she continued on her way without serious damage. A final minor mishap occurred on November 29, 1907. In a snow storm, the *Glasgow*, carrying coal for the city of Green Bay, ran up on Peshtigo Reef, whose light had been removed two weeks earlier. She was released by the tugs *O. M. Field* and *W. S. Taylor* after lightering some of her cargo, and

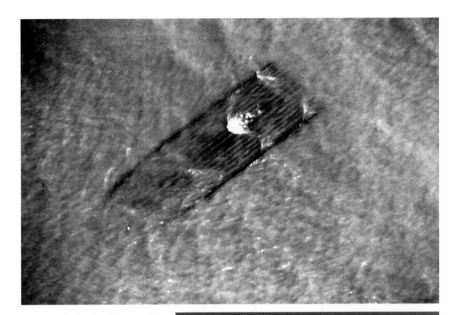

Above: *Only the bow section of the wooden steamer,* CITY OF GLASGOW, *remains visible in shallow water a few hundred feet off shore in Lily Bay, Lake Michigan, south of Death's Door. The straight break in midship indicates that the hull came apart at the seam created in 1911 when the vessel was shortened.*

PHOTO BY CRIS KOHL

Right: *The enormous rudder and rudder post were recovered from the wreck site of the* CITY OF GLASGOW *and stand outside the Gills Rock branch of the Door County Maritime Museum.* PHOTO BY CRIS KOHL

continued on to her destination. The stage was now set for a distinct change for the worse in the life of the steamer *City of Glasgow*. She had barely cleared the port of Green Bay when she ran aground and again had to be towed off by the *W. S. Taylor*. Her final act as a proud steamer was about to come to an end. Fire broke out on the ship and, once more, the tug *Taylor* came to the rescue, but this time to no avail. The strong north wind fanned the flames, and the crew, after a futile battle with the fire, escaped in the yawl boat.

It was a total loss for Hutchinson and the Buckeye Steamship Company, but Thomas Smith of the Leathem and Smith Towing and Wrecking Company, had an idea. The *Glasgow* lay blocking the entrance to the port of Green Bay, but rather than let her be dynamited, Smith, after considerable time, effort and expense, managed to get the burned hull to Sturgeon Bay. He salvaged the machinery, cut 100 feet off her, rebuilt her and enrolled her as a stone barge in 1911. The once-mighty *City of Glasgow* was humbled, but still alive.

Enroute light from Milwaukee, the *City of Glasgow*, in tow of the tug *John Hunsader*, was joined by her old consort, the schooner-barge *Adriatic*, in Manitowoc, also cargo-less. As the trio passed Two Rivers, the wind freshened and the seas built. But about two miles out of the Sturgeon Bay Ship Canal on October 6, 1917, the tow line between the tug and the *Glasgow* parted. Leaving the propulsion-less barges at the mercy of the now-ferocious lake, the *Hunsader* ducked into the canal to signal the Coast Guard for help. The Coast Guard set out immediately and found that the helpless barges had dropped their anchors, but the *Glasgow's* was not holding. The stricken ships piled up on the beach at Lily Bay. With great difficulty, the life-savers were able to rescue the two men from the *Glasgow*, Charles Wilman and Tom Torstenson, but could not get near enough to the *Adriatic* to take off her crew until the next day. A few days later, the *Adriatic* was pulled off the reef, but the *Glasgow* was far up on the beach.

It probably never occurred to the vesselmen involved in this maritime accident to give up on these ships without a fight. Indeed, Thomas Smith continued the battle to save the *City of Glasgow* for a year and a half. Not willing to give up easily, he did not declare her officially abandoned until 1922 -- a full five years after the *City of Glasgow*, the ship with nine lives, stranded in Lily Bay.

THE *FRANK O'CONNOR*
(OCTOBER 2, 1919)

A red glow dominated the afternoon and night-time sky over Lake Michigan along Door County's eastern shoreline on October 2, 1919. The wooden steamer, *Frank O'Connor*, was ablaze.

Launched amidst great fanfare at West Bay City, Michigan, on Saturday, September 17, 1892, the 301-foot-long *City of Naples* (later to be renamed the *Frank O'Connor*), was the last of an "Italian" trio of huge (2,109 gross tons), wooden bulk freighters, the other two being the *City of Genoa* and the *City of Venice*. Davidson had earlier launched another "City of" series of four slightly shorter ships named after London, Paris, Berlin and Glasgow. The successful Davidson, who had been in the business for many years, rallied against a new shipbuilding material -- steel -- which was then beginning to see extensive use in the construction of Great Lakes freighters, and he planned to show the world that wooden vessels, particularly huge ones over 300 feet in length, still had a competitive place in the world.

It was a losing battle against progress, of course, just as old-timers a few years earlier had unsuccessfully rallied to maintain the use of sailing ships in commerce. By the time the final wooden freighter was launched on the Great Lakes in 1902, steel ships had proven their worth for over a decade already on the inland seas, and by 1906, steel freighters constructed to a breathtaking length of 600 feet had become the norm. The era of wooden shipbuilding had ended completely, and one by one, the existing smaller, wooden freighters succumbed to the ravages of time and use, and were not replaced by similar vessels.

The *City of Naples* was owned by her builder, James Davidson for the first two years of the ship's life. During that short time, the vessel provided her builder/owner with more than the usual number of negative experiences associated with any new ship.

For example, in April, 1893, a few months after her launching, the brand new steamer, *City of Naples*, lay tied to a dock on the north side of the Chicago River awaiting her turn to take on a cargo, when sudden gusts of wind from a storm blew from the east off Lake Michigan. These gusts created waves in the river strong enough to separate the *City of Naples* from the lines holding her to the dock. Just as suddenly, ebb waves carried the huge steamer in the opposite direction, downstream, causing the ship to violently strike the docked schooner, *City of Sheboygan*, which had just taken on 17,000 bushels of corn. The schooner gave a roll and sank within a minute. Fortunately, no lives were lost and no one was injured, and eventually the schooner was raised and returned to service, but the *City of Naples* was found liable and steamship owner James Davidson paid heftily for the damage his new ship had done.

On September 22, 1893, a year after the *City of Naples* had been launched, the steamer lost her towbarge, the 271-foot-long, iron-ore-laden *Michigan*, after that ship sprang a leak in heavy seas and sank in 30 fathoms of Lake Superior water seven miles above Point au Sable. Fortunately again, no lives were lost in this incident. The *City of Naples* was still owned by James Davidson, while the barge *Michigan* had belonged to shipping company president Joseph C. Gilchrist (1850-1919) of Cleveland.

Davidson, anxious to be rid of his problem-plagued steamer, sold the *City of Naples* to none other than J. C. Gilchrist in 1894, and for the next 19 years, the ship faithfully served as part of the growing Gilchrist fleet, which numbered 70 ships by 1907. A rebuild in the winter of 1904-05 extended the life of the *City of Naples*, as well as raising her deck by 18 inches for increased cargo carrying capacity, but by 1913, the 21-year-old vessel was starting to show her age. Owner Gilchrist had had an incapacitating stroke in 1907, a year of economic depression, and his company had also run into financial difficulties due to its too-rapid expansion and the aging of its large, wooden-hulled fleet. The company went into receivership in 1913.

The court sold the *City of Naples* in 1913 to Norris & Co. of Chicago, which in turn sold the ship a year later to the Tonawanda Iron & Steel Co., but the vessel was not in commission the following year, 1915, as there was little work to be had for comparatively small, aging wooden steamers.

However, in 1916, a ship chandler named James O'Connor from Tonawanda, New York, a man who had started a transportation company more than a decade earlier, purchased the *City of Naples* and renamed the steamer after his 15-year-old youngest son, Frank. In less than a year, the

United States found itself actively engaged in World War One, and the ship named the *Frank O'Connor* began making money again for the first time in years.

        *   *   *

By late 1919, the country was changing rapidly. World War I had ended, and captured German U-boats were exhibited to a fascinated public. The nation was bracing itself for the introduction of Prohibition, and thousands of beer steins manufactured in Milwaukee and Chicago were hastily disposed of by cheap sale to the inhabitants of Java, Borneo and other Pacific Ocean islands. But the sudden transport of beer mugs did not buoy the merchant marine of the inland seas, whose workhorses continued to carry the usual bulk cargoes of iron ore, coal, grain and lumber.

At the outset of her final voyage, the *Frank O'Connor* had loaded 3,000 tons of coal at Buffalo, New York, on September 29, 1919, and headed for Milwaukee, Wisconsin, almost 1,000 water miles away. Four days later, the steamer cruised abeam of Cana Island, Wisconsin, close to her destination, when the dreaded cry of "FIRE!" accompanied by the sudden, frightful, non-stop clanging of bells, startled everyone on board into action.

The watchman had discovered smoke streaming from one of the aft hatches. Hatch covers were quickly removed in an attempt to locate the source of the fire, but thick, billowing smoke drove back the men on deck. Air currents wafted into the open hatchways, and soon, soaring flames replaced the smoke. The water hoses seemed like Davids battling Goliaths.

Captain William J. Hayes of Tonawanda, who happened to be the ship owner James O'Connor's son-in-law and, hence, brother-in-law to the ship's namesake, immediately steered his desperate vessel towards the western shoreline about ten miles away, soon realizing that his ship would burn to the waterline. When the flames cut through the vessel's steering mechanism, Hayes ordered the sea cocks opened to hasten the *O'Connor's* sinking, thinking that the unburned portion of the ship might be raised in the future (he was later exonerated by government officers of any blame in the vessel's loss at a trial in Milwaukee in March, 1920; unfortunately, he passed away from unrelated causes in 1923). Then all hands were ordered to abandon ship. They quickly began to row towards nearby Cana Island Lighthouse in two lifeboats, but long before they reached their destination, lighthouse keeper Oscar H. Knudsen and his assistant, Louis Picor (who had just started working there a week earlier, and quit three months later!), met them in their powerboat and took them under tow. Soon, the Baileys Harbor Coast Guard Station crew picked up the tows and safely removed the 21 tired and shaken crewmembers, none of whom was injured.

Capt. James O'Connor

JAMES O'CONNOR
COURTESY OF KEVIN J. O'CONNOR

Born in County Cork, Ireland, on Oct. 27, 1855, James O'Connor came to America with his family in 1867 when he was 12 years old, settling in Oswego, New York.

On Dec. 24, 1879, James married Mary Elizabeth Flynn, who was born at Oswego on Dec. 13, 1858, and they then proceeded to have 13 children over the next 22 years. In 1890, they moved to Tonawanda, New York, where James' eventual business successes made him "for many years a leading citizen."

He worked on Great Lakes ships for several years before establishing a ship chandlery and general contractor supply store (which earned him the humorous nickname of "Jimmy Junk") at 24 North Niagara St., as well as the O'Connor Transportation Company of Tonawanda.

The first ship which he owned was the *P. H. Birckhead*, a 168-foot-long wooden steamer built in 1870 and which O'Connor used in the lumber trade until that vessel burned at Alpena, Michigan, on September 30, 1905. The local newspaper reported that "the ill-fated boat was insured." The captain, James Heffernan, married one of James O'Connor's daughters three months later.

The P. H. BIRCKHEAD *burned to a total loss at Alpena, Michigan, on Sept. 30, 1905.* CRIS KOHL COLLECTION

Within a few months, on February 22, 1906, O'Connor closed a deal for the purchase of the 259-foot-long steamer, *Lycoming*, which he converted into a lumber carrier. That ship burned four years later, again with insurance and with no lives lost. Her captain was William Hayes, James O'Connor's son-in-law since 1903.

Within a year, O'Connor bought the 213-foot-long, iron-hulled *Alaska*, which, fortunately, did not burn.

In late 1919, after his largest ship, the wooden-hulled *Frank O'Connor*, which he had purchased in 1916, burned to a total loss, he sold the *Alaska* and devoted himself totally to his ship chandlery business.

Active in city politics for many years, he retired from his chandlery business due to ill health when he was 71 years old.

James O'Connor died at the age of 72 on April 7, 1928. His wife, Mary Elizabeth, passed away many years later on November 11, 1950, at the age of 91. They lie side-by-side in the family plot in Mount Olivet Cemetery, Tonawanda, NY.

INFORMATION COURTESY OF KEVIN J. O'CONNOR AND NED SCHIMMINGER/HISTORICAL SOCIETY OF THE TONAWANDAS

O'Connor owned the old barge EMMA C. HUTCHINSON, *which was abandoned by 1913.* CRIS KOHL COLLECTION

The iron-hulled ALASKA, *built in 1871, was scrapped in 1946 after a long career.* CRIS KOHL COLLECTION

The steamer LYCOMING *burned to a total loss at Erieau, Ontario, on Oct. 21, 1910.* CRIS KOHL COLLECTION

Above: This 1908 photograph shows the original O'Connor Ship Chandlery store at 24 N. Niagara Street in Tonawanda, NY, eight years before James O'Connor owned the Frank O'Connor. *Standing, left to right: Capt. William Hayes (who was married to James O'Connor's oldest daughter, Helene "Nellie" Veronica, and was master of the steamship* Frank O'Connor *when it sank), Julia O'Connor, Paul O'Connor, Irene O'Connor Draddy, and James O'Connor (all children of James O'Connor). "Tonawanda was a rootin' tootin' town back then when it was the break-bulk of Midwest lumber ships down to Erie Canal packets bound for New York and beyond. I'm very proud of my family's role in it. They had the guts to do what it took to get by comfortably, and probably had fun doing it!" stated Kevin J. O'Connor, great-grandson of James O'Connor. "We all have the Great Lakes in our blood."* Photo courtesy of Kevin J. O'Connor

Below: An O'Connor invoice. Courtesy of Ned Schimminger/Historical Society of the Tonawandas

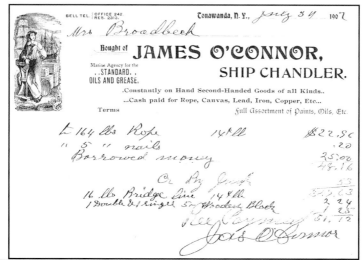

Above: *Launched on September 17, 1892, the enormous steamer,* City of Naples, *was part of a small fleet of ships constructed by shipbuilding giant James Davidson to prove that wooden vessels still held viable positions in commercial shipping.* Cris Kohl Collection

Below: *On August 14, 1917, the* City of Naples, *by now renamed the* Frank O'Connor, *sat in a Buffalo drydock for some maintenance work.* Cris Kohl Collection

Above: *After the* City of Naples *was purchased in 1916 by the O'Connor Transportation Company of Tonawanda, New York, James O'Connor defied superstition, for the first time in his 12 years of owning several ships, and changed the ship's name, tagging it after his youngest son, 15-year-old Frank O'Connor.* Cris Kohl Collection

Below: *Fortunately, the* Frank O'Connor *carried a pair of lifeboats.* Cris Kohl Collection

The crew had seen the illumination of the burning vessel grow smaller as they had rowed away from their doomed ship, but no witness was present that night when the *Frank O'Connor* finally hissed in extinguishing anguish as it plunged to the dark, cold bottom of the lake. Although no cause of the fire was officially determined, a carelessly discarded match or cigarette butt coming into contact with the tinder-dry grain dust lining the holds from the many grain cargoes carried that season was the main suspect.

The press reported that the ship went down in 17 fathoms (102 feet) of water, but revealed neither the source of this (mis)information, nor too many details surrounding this event.

There was a local man working on board the *Frank O'Connor.* Gardner Karker of Sturgeon Bay had hired on as a fireman, despite the fact that he had survived a shipwreck just the year before! He had been on board the 166-foot-long wooden steamer, *Cream City,* when it stranded in dense fog on July 1, 1918, in northern Lake Huron near False Detour Passage. All were rescued. In fact, the *Cream City* still had salvage crews and ships attempting to free her from her impalement when the *Frank O'Connor* burned and sank 15 months later (after two years of futile salvage attempts, the *Cream City* was abandoned and, in 1925, she burned to the waterline). Mr. Karker reportedly found it very convenient this time to land "directly in his old hometown upon being rescued."

At the *Frank O'Connor's* home port of Tonawanda, New York, the local press (*The Evening News*, Oct. 6, 1919) gave this account of the loss, perhaps the most detailed given by any newspaper:

STEAMER FRANK O'CONNOR
IS DESTROYED BY FIRE
Crew Fights Flames Until Forced to Flee in Lifeboats
-- Vessel and Cargo Total Loss.

Captain William J. Hayes of the steamer *Frank O'Connor*, owned by the O'Connor Transportation Company of Tonawanda, accompanied by his chief engineer, George Bacon, of Tonawanda arrived at his home here Saturday night with reports of the destruction of the steamer on Lake Michigan, eight miles off Canny [sic] Island Thursday night.

The *O'Connor* was on its way from Buffalo to Milwaukee with a cargo of coal when fire broke out in the hold of the vessel. The crew under the direction of Captain Hayes made efforts to put out the fire but was finally forced by the dense smoke to give up the fight. Distress signals were blown for a long time before the fight to save the vessel was given up.

After the crew had launched boats and started towards shore, they were picked up by the life saving crew from Canny [sic] Island. The steamer burned to the water's edge and then went to the bottom of the lake.

The vessel was value [sic] at $65,000 and was partly covered by insurance.

Right: *The Cana Island Lighthouse keeper, Oscar H. Knudsen (on the right in photo) and his assistant quickly moved in their small, outboard-engine-driven boat to the rescue of the burning* FRANK O'CONNOR'S *crew. Knudsen (1862-1960) worked as lighthouse keeper at Cana Island from 1918 until 1924, when he transferred to Grosse Point Light in Evanston, Illinois, reportedly to be closer to his son who went to school there.*

THE DOOR COUNTY MARITIME MUSEUM AND LIGHTHOUSE PRESERVATION SOCIETY, INC.

Members of the Baileys Harbor Coast Guard crew, stationed a few miles to the southwest of Cana Island, used this boat to rush to the assistance of the FRANK O'CONNOR'S *large crew, which had already safely left the blazing vessel in their own pair of lifeboats.*

THE DOOR COUNTY MARITIME MUSEUM AND LIGHTHOUSE PRESERVATION SOCIETY, INC.

Frank O'Connor -- 50 years after his "demise"

Three Great Lakes maritime history books and a state website claim that the name-sake of the steamer _Frank O'Connor_ died at age 24 on a World War I battlefield in Europe in May, 1918. Apparently those authors received some serious misinformation.

The authors of this book were very fortunate to have been granted unparalleled access to the archives of this notable, extraordinary family, foremostly by Kevin J. O'Connor, the great-grandson of James O'Connor, who owned the _Frank O'Connor._

The above photo shows Mr. Frank O'Connor, after whom the steamer _Frank O'Connor_ had been named back when he was only 15, enjoying a beer on the stoop of his home in the late 1960's when he was in his late 60's. He was still very much alive.

Born Francis Xavier O'Connor in Tonawanda, New York, on Oct. 20, 1901, the youngest of 13 children, he was affectionately considered by family members, a "spoiled brat," a condition which likely worsened after his father, James, named a 301-foot-long ship after him. In high school, Frank's nickname was "Fink," his "Favorite Occupation" was listed as "Smoking his daddy's cigars," and the words "The young millionaire" appeared under the heading, "As Seen by Others," in _The Scholastica,_ a student publication.

At the tail end of World War I, young Frank worked towards becoming a medical technician, training which he parlayed into a lifelong medical career with the Veterans' Administration. When he was 19, Frank was involved in an automobile accident in which he possibly saved the life of his 17-year-old niece. It was on June 11, 1921, that Frank, driving his Buick roadster, lost control of the vehicle after it broke a steering knuckle. He hurriedly opened the door and, just before the vehicle rolled twice, pushed out his niece, Mary Cherubum Hayes (the daughter of Frank's oldest sister, Nellie, 21 years his senior, and her husband, Captain William J. Hayes, who had mastered the _Frank O'Connor_ when that ship sank; Hayes was also Frank's godfather, a title be received in 1901 two years before he married into the O'Connor family). Thirteen stitches closed the gash on Frank's head, while Mary escaped with some scrapes.

Frank O'Connor, who never married, died unexpectedly on Sunday, May 26, 1974. Buried in the O'Connor family plot in Mount Olivet Cemetery in Tonawanda, he never revealed what thoughts he may have had about his namesake ship and its loss in the month that he turned 18.

PHOTOS AND INFORMATION COURTESY OF KEVIN J. O'CONNOR, MARY DOINO AND NED SCHIMMINGER/ HISTORICAL SOCIETY OF THE TONAWANDAS

The only consolation over losing the steamer *Frank O'Connor* could be found in that last line in the newspaper article about the ship having been partly covered by insurance. James O'Connor had fortunately seen to it in the past that his ships were insured, and such was the case with this latest loss to fire. However, when the underwriters examined his filed claim, they could find no proof of vessel inspection for the year 1919. A winter or spring inspection of his ship prior to the shipping season was mandatory for an owner to be able to purchase insurance, yet somehow, in early 1919, the *Frank O'Connor* had managed to receive insurance coverage without having gone through an inspection! The underwriters refused to pay anything on the *O'Connor's* loss, and James took the matter to court. Unfortunately, he lost the case. He returned to court to try to recover the premiums which he had paid to the insurance company. He lost that case, too.

Clearly, James O'Connor had to think long and hard about his shipping business. He had lost three of his five ships to fire over a 14-year span, but Fortune had smiled upon him because no one had been killed or injured in those burnings. Yet James must have felt the "luck of the Irish" running out, particularly after the financially deadly *O'Connor* fire and its four-year-long insurance battle, so he left the transportation business and focused upon his already successful chandlery shop in Tonawanda, New York.

However, in the world beyond Tonawanda, the loss of the *Frank O'Connor* and the demise of a shipping company was almost non-news. In 1919, when there were no such things yet as commercial radio, television or the internet, newspapers were basking in the luxury of their golden age, virtually free from competition except that which existed among themselves. Getting the "scoop" on their rival newspapers was the main goal of reporters, and they were constantly sniffing out exciting news stories which would help sell more of their newspapers than their competition could sell. However, the burning and sinking of an old, wooden ship on Lake Michigan with no casualties was just not considered very newsworthy by 1919. Old hulks were towed out regularly at this time into deep waters of all of the Great Lakes and purposely sunk just to get rid of them. Only one of the four daily newspapers in Chicago reported the *Frank O'Connor's* demise, and that in a mere eleven-line story on a secluded page. So it appeared that the *Frank*

COAL SHIP BURNS ON LAKE

Steamer Takes Fire Off Wisconsin Peninsula; Crew Flees in Boats.

[By The Associated Press.]

Sturgeon Bay, Wis., Oct. 3.—The steamer Frank O'Connor of the O'Connor Transportation company, North Tonawanda, N. Y., bound down on its way from Buffalo to Milwaukee with 3,000 tons of hard coal, was completely destroyed by fire last evening while five miles off Taylor island, in the vicinity of Bailey's Harbor.

Capt. William J. Hayes ordered the crew to the boats and the men reached Sturgeon Bay late Thursday night.

Newspapers generally expended very little ink in reporting the loss of the old steamer, FRANK O'CONNOR, *in October, 1919.* CRIS KOHL COLLECTION

O'Connor fizzled out of existence, much quieter than when the ship began its life nearly three decades earlier.

*   *   *

The public may have viewed the *Frank O'Connor* as being old and expendable when it sank, but its 3,000-ton anthracite coal cargo was considered a treasure. It had a reported value of $50,000 at that time, or the equivalent of more than 25 years' worth of average salary. It was definitely worth recovering!

Several months after the *Frank O'Connor* sank, the "roaring" 1920's officially started, along with the beginning of America's gradual love affair with cars, airplanes, speedboats, wireless, the Charleston, filmmaker Mack Sennett's Bathing Beauties – indeed, anything which moved fast or appeared to do so – and it took little time for one imaginative adventurer/entrepreneur to conjure up a modern means of locating an old shipwreck: the *Frank O'Connor* and its valuable cargo could be found from the air!

Clarence Labeau of the Labeau Wrecking Company of Toledo was determined to locate the wreck of the *Frank O'Connor* in the summer of 1920. He had purchased the rights to the wreck and its cargo for $1,100 from the insurance company which had underwritten it, but he had failed to find the shipwreck using the wrecking steamer, *Philetus Sawyer.* Deciding to innovate with the newest technology available in 1920, Labeau became the first person to search for a Great Lakes shipwreck using an airplane.

The Green Bay Aero Club, formed in late 1918, took great pride in its one and only aircraft, a Curtiss Jenny biplane, which each of the five investors took turns flying. In the summer of 1920, one of them flew shipwreck hunter Clarence Labeau over the waters north of Cana Island.

Unfortunately, they failed to find the shipwreck.

Following reports that the ship had drifted north after being abandoned by its crew, Labeau ended up searching closer to Spider Island, which is seven miles north of Cana Island where the fire on the *Frank O'Connor* broke out. He should have remained further south.

Three years later, in June, 1923, local resident Charles Innis and Chester Smith of Milwaukee tied 1,000 feet of rope between two small gasoline-powered boats and dragged the bottom for the *Frank O'Connor*, locating the wreck within half an hour (few modern-day shipwreck hunters have experienced such fast fortune using their costly, state-of-the-art electronic technology!) Innis and Smith decided to keep the location their secret "until some definite settlement is made with the owners of the cargo." Business transactions apparently took place, as the Marine Salvage and Wrecking Company of Milwaukee, using centrifugal pumps, their barge,

212

AIRPLANE TO FIND TREASURE

Wreck of Steamer O'Connor With $50,000 Cargo of Coal To Be Located From the Air.

Sunken treasure in the lake off North Bay will be located by the use of an airplane according to the plans of the Leathem Smith company of this city. The treasure consists of 3,000 tons of hard coal, the cargo of the steamer O'Connor which sunk after burning last fall. At the prevailing market price the coal has a value of approximately $50,000.

When World War I ended in 1918, many military pilots turned to the adventurous life of "barnstorming," entertaining crowds and taking paying customers for short rides. These daredevils flew mostly 90-horsepower, water-cooled, two-seater Curtiss Jenny JN-4D's, the prime training biplane during the war and, consequently, the most readily available for private purchase after 1918, obtainable for as little as $600. Of the 6,000 built, only about 12 remain today. The Green Bay Aero Club procured one in late 1918. In 1920, it and a pilot were hired to find the FRANK O'CONNOR, *the first time that an airplane was used to search for a Great Lakes shipwreck.*

CRIS KOHL COLLECTION

Liberty, and the tug, *Smith,* spent more than a month over August and September that year recovering about 700 tons of coal from the shipwreck, which the press described as sitting in 60 feet of water. Not only was the company hampered by bad weather in its salvage efforts, it also claimed that most of the coal cargo must have been strewn along the lake bottom as the flames burned holes through the hull, since they claimed that only a small fraction of the entire cargo was found at the site.

In the Depression year 1935, a dozen years after the salvage of part of the *O'Connor's* coal, Charles Innis still believed that the Milwaukee salvage company was wrong and that sufficient coal could still be recovered from the site to make salvage efforts worthwhile. Innis successfully lured noted Chicago hardhat diver Frank P. Blair into project partnership before he had his son-in-law spend three weeks on the water relocating the shipwreck (no one told him that TWO boats worked better when you used a sweep or drag line!) Reportedly about 100 tons of coal were recovered in 1935, and another 200 tons in 1936, the latter being offered for sale at Sault Ste. Marie off the barge *Michigan* at $6.00 a ton.

Further disturbances of the *Frank O'Connor* ceased for several decades until well into the modern scuba diving era. Reportedly relocated and immediately lost again by a scuba diver in the late 1970's, the wreck of

Above: *The Cana Island Lighthouse keeper, Oscar H. Knudsen, and his assistant, Louis Picor, motored their small boat towards the burning* Frank O'Connor. *By this time, the imperiled ship's entire crew had loaded and launched their two lifeboats and were hastily rowing towards shore.* Specially commissioned oil painting by Robert McGreevy. Telephone **989-479-9592** or see **www.mcgreevy.com** for more art and information.

Above: *The waters around Cana Island, bright, gorgeous blue on some days, black like foul weather on others, have witnessed much maritime drama.* PHOTO BY CRIS KOHL

Right: *The historic and restored Cana Island Lighthouse is an excellent place to visit when it is open to the public between May and October. Springtime offers myriads of blooming lilacs to add color and scent to this island location.* PHOTO BY CRIS KOHL

Left: *On the Cana Island lighthouse grounds, co-author Joan Forsberg examines the controversial anchor initially removed by scuba divers from a location not far from the wreck of the* FRANK O'CONNOR.

PHOTO BY CRIS KOHL

215

Above left: *Rising to within 45 feet of the surface of Lake Michigan, the* FRANK O'CONNOR'S *enormous, upright triple expansion steam engine serves as the solid anchor for a modern shipwreck-marking buoy.* PHOTO BY CRIS KOHL

Above right: *Diver Joan Forsberg swims to an ensemble of ship's tools, including a large wrench, placed by early divers on top of the ship's engine for unobscured viewing.* PHOTO BY CRIS KOHL

Below: *A school of whitefish serenely passes the* O'CONNOR'S *engine.* PHOTO BY CRIS KOHL

Above left: *Schools of silvery baitfish are often seen here, attracted by the protective habitat offered by such an unusual item as a shipwreck.* PHOTO BY CRIS KOHL

Above right: *A scuba diver examines the burned stern section.* PHOTO BY CRIS KOHL

Below: *At the extreme stern of the* FRANK O'CONNOR *shipwreck, the fallen rudder, post and steering quadrant offer a unique opportunity for detailed study, with the enormous, four-bladed propeller visible just to the right.* PHOTO BY CRIS KOHL

the *Frank O'Connor* was relocated once and for all in late 1990 by Sam Mareci and Tom Beaudwin, who had been searching for the wreck of the schooner, *F. J. King* (see chapter 13). However, within a year, Chicago scuba divers had illegally removed what appeared to be one of the ship's anchors. Several outraged Wisconsin divers, recognizing the anchor's historical and recreational value, reported the offenders to the police, and, after charges were laid, an out-of-court settlement drafted by the Door County (WI) District Attorney was accepted. The defendant had to surrender the anchor, which he had placed as ornamentation at his cottage, and move it to the Cana Island Lighthouse, where it was put on public display overlooking the waters where its ship met its end. One controversial aspect of this episode is that the anchor was reportedly found away from the shipwreck itself, and may not actually have come from the *Frank O'Connor.*

In the last two decades, local Great Lakes divers have become increasingly protective of the non-renewable, historic shipwreck sites in their areas, willing to back up the protective laws which have been enacted in each of the eight states and the large Canadian province bordering our freshwater seas. Unfamiliar divers are often watched closely to ensure that they remove nothing from the shipwreck. Unlike depleted fish life on coral reefs, stripped shipwrecks cannot replenish themselves over time.

The *Frank O'Connor* sits upright in 67 feet of water with most of her artifacts and much machinery, including the 20-foot-tall, 1,100 horsepower triple expansion steam engine and two 13-foot Scotch boilers, still in place. There are also a steam windlass, a capstan, a steering quadrant, a 12-foot diameter, four-bladed propeller and long stretches of wooden hull at the site. Portions of the coal cargo lie scattered around the wreck site, visible evidence of the several salvage efforts. Underwater visibility can range from 20 to 50 feet, and the slight current is negligible.

Ships which sank due to fire are usually low on any shipwreck hunter's priority list because of the anticipated poor condition of the wreck once it is found. However, the steamer *Frank O'Connor* is in a surprisingly favorable state – the early opening of the seacocks and the resultant scuttling undoubtedly did much to maintain the good condition of the wreck – and this site has been described as "a mini-museum of nautical engineering."

The wreck of the *Frank O'Connor* is like a phoenix springing back to life after rising from the ashes, with greater public awareness about it existing today than when it sank in 1919. The *O'Connor* has strong historic value as one of the best examples viewable today of a transitional (from that era between wooden and steel hulls) Great Lakes freighter. It certainly has proven to be one of the more interesting and frequently visited wrecks along the shipwreck-rich western shoreline of Lake Michigan.

THE *LAKELAND*
(DECEMBER 3, 1924)

Deep sea divers, diving gas experiments, charges of insurance fraud, court cases, a fifty-five-year-old automobile enigma and the Roaring '20's are part of the controversial and mysterious events surrounding the sinking of the *Lakeland*. Ending her career in dramatic fashion and leaving many questions unanswered, the *Lakeland* remains today one of the most notorious of the Death's Door area shipwrecks.

Built as the *Cambria* in 1887 by the Globe Iron Works in Cleveland for the Mutual Transportation Company, the steel bulk freighter had to carry three masts for insurance reasons (the middle mast was removed in 1897). She was one of the first three steamers on the lake to have a triple expansion engine and she carried bulk cargoes of ore and coal. Overshadowed by the enormous, 600-foot-long freighters being constructed in the early 1900's, the 280-foot-long *Cambria* was sold in 1910. A second deck with luxurious cabins was added, the cargo hold was rearranged, side gangways were installed, and, with a change of name, the *Lakeland* began a new career as a passenger and package freight carrier.

The Roaring '20's saw a growing demand for cars during this era of increased prosperity, and so the *Lakeland* carried new automobiles in addition to the passengers and package freight between Cleveland, Detroit, Milwaukee and Chicago. But by 1924, the aging steamer, experiencing minor difficulties with leakage, was limited to running during calm weather. The *Lakeland*, setting out from Chicago to Detroit, attempted a final run of the season carrying a smaller-than-usual load of 40 Nash and Kissell cars. Capt. John McNeely, warned by means of wireless (radio) of a southwest storm brewing, ducked his ship into the Sturgeon Bay Canal and waited all day Tuesday, December 2, 1924, for better weather. Wednesday morning at 7:10, Capt. McNeely steered the *Lakeland* out into Lake Michigan. Discovering that the hull was leaking, the captain engaged the pumps and turned back towards shore. About five miles out, seeing that the pumps were losing the battle, he ordered the engines shut off so that full steam could be applied to the pumps, but it proved hopeless. Capt. McNeely wired an SOS message, ordered a distress signal flown, and sent 23 of his crew into the lifeboats. He and three officers stayed aboard in case something could be done to save her.

The *Ann Arbor #6*, a car ferry enroute to Menominee, came alongside the *Lakeland*, which was sinking by the stern, and picked up the men from the lifeboats. A Coast Guard cutter, mastered by Capt. R. Anderson, and another freighter, the *Cygnus*, had arrived and stood by, ready to rescue the remaining men. When Capt. Anderson saw the *Lakeland* listing at a dangerous angle, he ordered the ship vacated and took Capt. McNeely and his officers aboard the cutter.

As the ship began its final plunge to the depths, her last gasp blew the cabins and hatches forty feet into the air, and her electric lights went out.

The 37-year-old *Lakeland* was dead, but the battle over her remains went on for years. The insurance underwriters, with $350,000 in claims pending, suspected that Capt. McNeely, in collusion with the owner, the Thompson Transit Company of Cleveland, had scuttled the ship. Their suspicions were based on the facts that the *Lakeland* had sunk in calm seas,

Photographs were taken of the steamer, LAKELAND, *as she sank.* CRIS KOHL COLLECTION

Above: *The wreck of the excursion steamer,* LAKELAND, *lies off the Sturgeon Bay Ship Canal in 210 feet of water, with the deck rising to about 185 feet. No lives were lost when this popular cruise ship sank, but numerous automobiles went down with the ship.* **Below:** *A close-up and lighted view of the 1924 automobile pictured above, lower right.*

VIDEO FREEZE-FRAME IMAGES (ABOVE) AND PHOTO (BELOW) BY KIM BRUNGRABER

was carrying only a light load, and that Thompson was in financial difficulties. The insurance companies brought in a team of Atlantic coast underwater salvagers and Navy deep sea divers, under the command of Capt. Alfred Tooker, to examine the sunken vessel for signs of foul play. Because the divers would be working at depths of about 200 feet, the Navy decided this would be a good opportunity to test a new breathing gas mixture of helium and oxygen (which had been tried only on guinea pigs in a chamber before) and a new decompression table, in hopes of eliminating the "bends," or decompression sickness, which had claimed the lives of so many divers in the past. The work of examining the *Lakeland's* submerged remains went on for three weeks in August of 1925, and all five divers by the last day were treated in the recompression chamber on board the diving barge, *Chittenden*, which had been conveyed from New York. However, all members of the dive team, which included world deep (305 feet) diving record holder S. J. Drillishak, recovered quickly and none suffered a serious case of the bends.

The *Lakeland* case was heard in the federal court in Cleveland in late October/early November, 1925, where three of the divers testified that the seacocks were open, which would lend credence to the scuttling theory. On the side of the Thompson Company, the *Lakeland's* chief engineer stated that the valves were open only to take in water for the boilers and the ballast tanks. The captains of the *Ann Arbor #6* and the *Cygnus* testified that the *Lakeland* was pumping out water when it sank, another point for the shipping company. The trial resulted in a hung jury.

The court found in favor of Thompson Transit in a second trial in February, 1926. Not satisfied with the judgment, the insurance companies sought a third trial, hoping that a "submarine camera," newly invented by O. A. Tesch of Milwaukee, could take pictures of the *Lakeland* to bolster their case. However, the circuit court of appeals denied the bid for a third trial.

Fifty-five years after she sank, the *Lakeland* made news again. Well-known Wisconsin shipwreck hunter, historian and diver Kent Bellrichard, in the summer of 1979, raised one of the cars from the shipwreck. The nylon line attached to the automobile broke, and the car crashed to the lake floor 100 feet below, suffering considerable damage. When the car, a 1924 Rollins, was finally brought to the surface, it showed 22 miles on the odometer and created another mystery. According to historian Jon Paul Van Harpen, there was no Rollins on the *Lakeland's* manifest. The car's body and the frame separated in the crash, but many parts of the vehicle were in excellent condition. In 1980, Bellrichard recovered the ship's steam whistle.

Today the *Lakeland* lies peacefully in 210 feet of cold, fresh, Lake Michigan water. Visiting divers are able to see dozens of 1924 automobiles still there, looking as though they could be dusted off and driven away.

THE *MICHAEL J. BARTELME*
(OCTOBER 4, 1928)

Few people in the shipping business had heard of the *Michael J. Bartelme* before October of 1928. She had sailed under that name only a few months and it was the third name of her career. There was really nothing remarkable about this ship; she was one of the many steel steamships that hauled bulk cargoes, like coal and iron ore, throughout the Great Lakes.

Built by F. W. Wheeler in West Bay City in 1895 for Mitchell and Company of Cleveland, at 352 feet long, 44 feet wide and 3,400 gross tons, she was not the largest or the first or the fastest of the early steel steamers. Under her original name, the *John J. McWilliams*, she was already eclipsed by the 380-foot-long *Merida*, built in 1890, and only eleven years later would be dwarfed by behemoths like the *Daniel J. Morrell*, a 600-footer constructed in 1906. New owners in 1916, the Paisely Steamship Company, renamed her the *Central West*, which lasted until 1928, which saw her final owner, the Valley Camp Coal Company, and her final name, *Michael J. Bartelme*. In short, the *Bartelme* was one of the ordinary, near-modern workhorses of the inland seas, sailing from port to port without drama or excitement.

That is, until coming to an ignoble end on the rocks of Cana Island, she would become the "rock star" of Door County shipwrecks.

Making one of her customary "triangle" runs, Ashtabula to Milwaukee with a load of coal, Milwaukee to Escanaba light, and Escanaba back to Ashtabula with iron ore, the *Bartelme* never completed that second stage towards Escanaba. Northbound along the eastern shore of the Door Peninsula, the vessel was heading for Death's Door Passage in thick fog on

The steel steamer, MICHAEL J. BARTELME, *launched at West Bay City, Michigan, in 1895 as the* JOHN J. McWILLIAMS *and renamed the* CENTRAL WEST *in 1916, received its final name -- and the one by which the shipwreck is known -- only a few months before the vessel's demise. The* BARTELME'S *namesake, a dock superintendent reportedly born in 1881, lived until 1970, 42 years after the ship was lost.* CRIS KOHL COLLECTION

Thursday, October 4, 1928. Her steel bow ground against the rocks off the southern end of Cana Island at about 1:00 in the afternoon. Lighthouse keeper Clifford Sanderson noted in his log that he didn't know for certain that the boat was stranded until 3:00, when the fog lifted. At that point, he telephoned the Baileys Harbor Coast Guard Station. Arriving at 4:00, the Coast Guard stood by, ready to assist the crew if needed.

Attempting to back the vessel off the shoal, the crew tried to lighten the boat by pumping out the water ballast and throwing the anchors and chain overboard to rest on the bottom, but a strong southeasterly wind and heavy sea running from the south caused the ship to slam broadside against the rocks. That evening, the wind blew fresh out of the south and the rough waves pounded the steamer so hard that the rocks punctured her steel plates.

The tug, *Leathem D. Smith*, of Sturgeon Bay arrived on Friday and tried to pull the *Bartelme* off the rocks, but she was stuck fast. Summoned from St. Ignace, the big wrecking tug, *Favorite*, arrived on Saturday morning at 9:00. Capt. Cummings tried to maneuver his tug close enough to the stricken steamer to install pumps aboard so she would remain afloat in case the tug released her. This attempt also failed. The *Smith* returned to its home port. Bringing a lighter from Manitowoc, the tug, *Arctic*, added its expertise to the effort on Sunday night, but a south gale blew in, bringing thunderstorms and heavy seas and another failed recovery. The storm increased ferociously overnight so that the tugs had to flee for their own

The steamer, MICHAEL J. BARTELME, *stranded on Cana Island in a heavy fog on October 4, 1928.* DOOR COUNTY MARITIME MUSEUM AND LIGHTHOUSE PRESERVATION SOCIETY, INC.

safety: the *Arctic* took shelter in Baileys Harbor and the *Favorite* took refuge behind Plum Island in Death's Door Passage. The tugs did not return to the wreck site.

By Sunday afternoon, a crowd of about 30 visitors had gathered on the island to see the big shipwreck-in-progress, which was very visible lying like a beached whale only about 300 feet from shore -- a conveniently close, impromptu tourist attraction! Word spread about the stranded steamship, a sight which one did not see every day.

Monday afternoon, with the seas still running high and the ship pounding on the rocks, the Coast Guard decided it was advisable to remove the crew from the *Bartelme*. Making four trips through the raging surf, the Coast Guard brought the 26 men and their belongings to the mainland west of the island. The *Bartelme's* master, Capt. Crockett, and chief engineer, Wally Ives, returned to the steamer and stayed on board Tuesday and Wednesday.

John Smith, a Detroit marine architect, was summoned to inspect the wreck to determine if the cost of salvage would exceed the amount of insurance on the vessel. The famous Capt. Tom Reid of the Reid Wrecking Company of Port Huron, Michigan, arrived to take soundings and survey the boat to determine if he could save it. Before he made his inspection, the

Tourists were quickly attracted to the wreck of the steel steamer, MICHAEL J. BARTELME, *on the shores of easily reached Cana Island. It took scrappers years to remove enough of this shipwreck so that nothing remained above the water, giving uncountable families many opportunities to pose with this unfortunate vessel turned celebrity.*
CRIS KOHL COLLECTION

ever-confident Reid stated that she could probably be refloated if they had several days of good weather. The Reid Wrecking Company was well-known throughout the Great Lakes as the shipwreck salvage company. If it were possible to save a ship, the Reids would find a way. In spite of the dangers of their work, they had lost only one diver in their company's history. Installing enormous pontoons to raise the steel steamer, *Cayuga*, which had gone to the bottom of northern Lake Michigan near the Straits of Mackinac after a collision with the *Joseph L. Hurd* in 1895, a hardhat diver descended rapidly in the deep water, had a problem with his air supply and was killed. The wooden steamer, *Joseph L. Hurd*, survived until 1913, when it was scuttled in Sturgeon Bay.

Having completed their investigation of the stricken ship, Capt. Reid and John Smith left Cana Island on Friday, October 12, 1928, bound for Cleveland to meet with the *Bartelme's* owners. Facing high salvage costs of $150,000 for a thirty-three-year-old steel vessel valued at $200,000, the

A few nimble tourists with boat access explored the wrecked BARTELME *early in its scrapping stage directly from the vessel's high deck, gaining an unparalleled view of the Cana Island Lighthouse.* DOOR COUNTY MARITIME MUSEUM AND LIGHTHOUSE PRESERVATION SOCIETY, INC.

Above: *To this day, debris left over from the long scrapping work on the* Michael J. Bartelme *lies scattered along the rocky shoreline of Cana Island.*   Photo by Cris Kohl

Below: *Artifacts from the wrecked steel steamer,* Michael J. Bartelme, *can be seen on exhibit at Cana Island.*   Photo by Cris Kohl

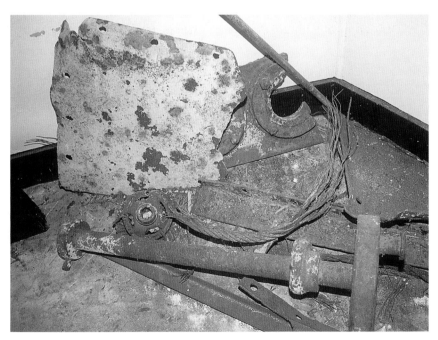

Valley Camp Coal Company could not justify recovering the ship. The rule of thumb in the industry at the time was that if the cost of repairing a vessel was more than three-fourths of the insured value, then the vessel would be abandoned. Such was the case for the *Bartelme*; she would never again sail the lakes.

The Valley Camp Coal Company, a few days later, ordered Capt. Crockett to strip the steamer and abandon her. Over the next week, with the help of the Assistant Lighthouse Keeper, the *Bartelme's* crew began to remove anything of value from the ship. Lake Michigan, however, had not finished with the *Bartelme*. Lashed by a violent southeast wind on November 5th, she broke in two. The November 9, 1928, *Door County Advocate* wrote,

> The continual pounding that the steamer has received since going aground gradually weakened the steel plates forward of the engine house and in the heavy sea Monday the hull parted and the stern dropped several feet, flooding the engine room, putting out the fires.

Fifteen truckloads of salvaged material worth more than $20,000 were hauled away to Sturgeon Bay.

For five years, tourists came by the thousands to see their local shipwreck and to have their photograph taken on the shoreline with the wreck behind them. Some even managed to board and explore the ship. The hundreds of cars carrying the *Bartelme* fans were becoming a problem for the lighthouse keepers, who reported traffic jams on the road leading to the island. Even Herman Runge, who would become one of the most famous Great Lakes ship historians and the creator of the Runge File held at the Milwaukee Public Library, "...saw her there July 13, 1933, and the break in her side was about 6 or 8 ft. wide -- straight up and down amidships."

By July, 1933, the famous shipwreck's days were numbered. In August, the scrappers began to cut her up into six-foot by 18-inch-wide sections which were taken to Sturgeon Bay on scows. The engine and boilers had already been removed in June of 1930. Little by little, the *Bartelme* disappeared from view, and so did the tourists who had been attracted by the bold sight of a helpless shipwreck. The stripping work continued, and by August of 1934, the iron and steel was being freighted to Milwaukee. Nothing remained visible above water, and soon, even the keel was taken away.

All that remains today is some braided steel cable on shore, a few artifacts at the Cana Island Lighthouse, some valves and steel rigging in fifteen feet of water, some black-and-white photographs, and the memory of the *Michael J. Bartelme*, to remind us of the days when Cana Island, for a little while, had its own "rock star."

THE LEGEND OF THE
POVERTY ISLAND TREASURE

We like to think that, as extensive and as illustrious as Great Lakes Maritime History is, it simply has to include exciting tales of adventurous pirates and fortunes to be found in the form of gold and silver treasures lost when ships sank. Indeed, when people learn that we are scuba divers who explore shipwrecks, we are often asked if we have ever found any treasure.

The five Great Lakes, alas, were a bit out of the way of the Spanish trade routes upon which sailed galleons groaning under their heavy loads of precious metals and shimmering jewels. The inland seas lacked pirate-infested cities such as Port Royal and Hispaniola in the Caribbean. By far the majority of the ships on the freshwater seas were common workhorses hauling bulk cargoes, mainly lumber, grain, coal and iron ore, bland cargoes which did little to stimulate the swashbuckling imaginations of the men, and perhaps of the few women, working upon them.

Treasure tales of the Great Lakes have been few and far between, so when the chance for a good yarn presented itself, some wide-eyed people embraced it like a first-time lover, and then, like some lovers, spread word of that experience enthusiastically to others. Sailors, regardless of whether the spray which strikes them tastes salty or fresh, share certain character traits, including a penchant for gullibility and excitability when it comes to treasure stories.

A book called *Directory of Shipwrecks of the Great Lakes* by Karl E. Heden was published in Boston in 1966, with these opening words to the Introduction:

> There is a legend that a mysterious ship foundered near Poverty Island in Lake Michigan, with $4,500,000 in her safe. It is doubtful that this legend would persist without foundation, but it is just as doubtful that the vessel will ever be found without proper research and planning....

Unfortunately, nowhere else in his 116-page book does Mr. Heden make any further mention of this fabulously wealthy treasure ship. We will take a look at the "foundation" which has allowed the Legend of the Poverty Island Treasure to "persist."

The legend of the Poverty Island treasure has variations in its tellings. The most common one relates the tale of a ship in 1863 secretly loaded with five chests of gold, supposedly from the French government, to back the Confederate States of America during the Civil War. (France depended upon the South's cotton then the same way we depend upon foreign oil today.) Departing Escanaba for the open lake to head south, this ship was intercepted by Union authorities, but not before the chests were hauled on deck, chained together and dropped overboard off Poverty Island for later recovery. One variation tells of British (others say French) sailors putting the treasure overboard prior to a pirate raid during the War of 1812. Another version has a band of Canadians attacking the treasure-laden ship in 1863 (despite the fact that this occurred on Lake Michigan, the only Great Lake which shares no shoreline with Canada). One more story variation has the five chests of gold coming from the dying Confederacy in 1865, bound for Canada, to be kept in safekeeping until the South could rise again.

Accounts exist of roving bands of pirates terrorizing northern Lake Michigan in the latter half of the 1800's, and it is perhaps from their imaginative, tavern-bred stories that this legend started and spread. There is, however, one front-page newspaper story about an event which gave the legend some credibility. It appeared in the *Gladstone* (Michigan) *Delta* on Saturday, July 9, 1904. Gladstone is a harbor town eight miles north of Escanaba:

> The steamer, *Etruria,* came in Monday with 7,000 tons of coal, and cleared Friday. Capt. Green reports a singular occurrence which took place Monday. He came by Poverty island at 12:05 that morning and let go anchor at 12:55 on account of thick weather, in about ten fathoms [60 feet] of water. At 1:30 he heaved anchor, and found that it had caught the cable chain of a vessel, as well as some wreckage and a chest, which sank as soon as it appeared on the surface. Attached to the chain was an old fashioned "Swedish" anchor, with rotted stock. The anchor by some means broke loose, but the chain was saved. It is a hand made chain of seven-eights inch iron and links about five inches long. There was about thirty-two fathoms [192 feet] in the piece. The captain estimated from the size anchor and chain that it had belonged to a vessel of four or five hundred tons burden. From the spot where the anchor was found, Peninsula point light bore N. W. and Rock Island due south. This brings the place about seven miles E. S. E. of the Eleven

Foot Shoal. Captain Green is of opinion, from the surrounding circumstances, that he dropped his anchor on the hulk of a vessel that had been sunk years ago, from some cause or other. Captain Green would like to know what vessel of this description was sunk inside Poverty Passage.

Nothing more, apparently, occurred regarding the Poverty Island treasure until the 1930's. Surprisingly, the innovative 1920's, known for adventurous feats of daring, produced no treasure hunts. It took the Great Depression of the 1930's, with its shortage of money, to compel someone to organize a quest for this treasure.

In the summer of 1933, Wilfred Behrens equipped a small, 35-year-old schooner named the *Captain Lawrence* (formerly the *Alice*), for a treasure hunting expedition to Poverty Island.

The *Alice*, built as a schooner yacht in 1898 at Green Bay by Horace J. Conley, was rebuilt in 1919 with a small gasoline engine installed for auxiliary power. Contrary to some romanticized reports, the *Alice* was not built for Chicago merchandise magnate Marshall Field, nor named after his wife, nor used in the Spanish-American War. In November, 1923, Douglas Van Dyke paid $3,200 for the *Alice* and donated the vessel to the Milwaukee Boy Scouts, who were "bubbling over with gratitude." They renamed the ship the *Captain Lawrence* on May 19, 1924, and used it as a training vessel for several years. But by 1931, the worst years of the Great Depression had started, and the *Captain Lawrence* was laid up and idle at Milwaukee. Apparently there were no funds available for the maintenance of this aging, wooden boat.

Wilfred Behrens bought the vessel from the Boy Scouts for $150 in May, 1932, fixed it up a little bit, loaded it with diving equipment and friends Alfred Graham and his son Immanuel of Milwaukee, and Walter Hartman of Muskegon, Michigan, and on August 26, 1933, departed Milwaukee headed to Poverty Island in quest of riches.

The *Captain Lawrence* stranded in a storm on Poverty Island at 3:00 A.M. on September 19, 1933, broke up and sank. The four men on board

The small, 43-ton schooner, Alice *(60'8" x 16'2" x 9'), in Milwaukee just prior to being renamed the* Captain Lawrence *in the 1920's.*   Cris Kohl Collection

made it safely to shore but lost everything on the ship: hardhat diving equipment (scuba had not yet been invented), a large diving bell, and all their personal belongings which they had brought with them. *The Great Lakes News* of October, 1933, reported that

> ...The "Captain Lawrence" was seeking treasure lost years ago between Poverty Island and Middle Gull Island. The content of the treasure and its location were kept secret [by the *Captain Lawrence's* crew]. Four members of the crew saved themselves when the vessel struck. They had been diving for the treasure....

A young boy had been watching the anchored *Captain Lawrence* from Poverty Island prior to the storm which destroyed the ship. His name was Karle Jessen, and he was the lighthouse keeper's son. His eyewitness account popped up on numerous occasions over the years. When he worked in a saloon on Washington Island, he often recounted the tale. How much it varied with each telling is not known, but the gist of it was recounted by Special Assignments Editor Bill Barada in the March, 1969, issue of *Skin Diver* Magazine, in an article titled "The Treasure of Poverty Island":

> ...one day when the [diving] bell came up from a dive, he saw the men grab each other and go into ecstatic dances all over the deck. They were so close to shore he could hear their shouts and yells. Their celebration lasted all day, and Karly [sic] is sure they found something because he had never seen them so excited. However, fate stepped in and snatched the treasure from their grasp. That same night a storm hit so suddenly and violently that the men were lucky to escape with their lives. It smashed their ship to pieces and destroyed their equipment....

Barada's article listed some of the other shipwrecks in the Death's Door area and concluded, "The treasure is made to order for sport divers...." Nearly four decades later, despite extensive scuba diving activity in this area, the treasure has not yet been located.

By the early 1980's, the legend of the Poverty Island treasure had been retold in a number of sensationalistic accounts in newspapers and magazines around the Great Lakes, all of them repeating the same old story. William Ratigan's 1960 book, *Great Lakes Shipwrecks and Survivals*, told the tale in a single sentence:

> If legend holds true, the most fabulous sunken treasure on the Great Lakes is still begging discovery off Poverty island, near Escanaba, at the top of Lake Michigan, where a nameless vessel 'sailed away' with five million dollars in her strongbox.

In the summer of 1985, interest in treasure hunting was renewed after Mel Fisher found the fabulous riches of the Spanish galleon, the *Atocha*, off the Florida Keys. That year, 47-year-old diver Richard Bennett of Wau-

Left: *The Poverty Island Lighthouse is where the young son of the light-keeper was staying when he saw the men on board the small schooner,* CAPTAIN LAWRENCE, *rejoicing over an apparent discovery in 1933. Did they locate the longlost treasure?*
PHOTO BY CRIS KOHL

Right: *As pretty as it looks on some days, Poverty Island received its name for a reason. Ironically, the Great Lakes' greatest treasure reputedly lies off its rough shores.*
PHOTO BY CRIS KOHL

watosa, Wisconsin, talked about pursuing "$300 million worth of glittering coins...sitting in five steel-banded chests." He and his team had reportedly been diving for the Poverty Island treasure for 18 years, even going to the point of building a 14-foot-long, $25,000 submarine to help with the search, all to no avail. Imbued with a sense of humor, Bennett claimed that he had one big advantage over other divers: he knew where the treasure was not.

In 1994, one source related that a latter day diver had located at least a portion of the treasure in Poverty Island Passage, hidden it in a crate of car engines, secretly retrieved it later, and retired to a life of luxury in Hawaii.

In the 1980's, Virginia treasure hunter Steve Libert, President of Fairport International Exploration, Inc., believing that the 1933 wreck of the *Captain Lawrence* would yield clues to the Poverty Island treasure, located what appeared to be that shipwreck and made a salvage claim and excavation request from the State of Michigan. After much legal wrangling, the court denied the requests. The 1995 Order of Dismissal declared that the wreck had been abandoned by the owner, and it was embedded in the lake bottom, hence falling under the jurisdiction of the State of Michigan:

> ...Libert has been diving around Poverty Island since 1983. He has identified a debris scatter in 40-60 feet of water, adjacent to the shore of Poverty Island, which includes planks, a cable, barrels, and several areas of magnetic declination. In 1984 he found an anchor. In 1985 he located a propeller blade wedged in the rocks off the north shore of Poverty Island.... Libert is certain these objects belong to the *Captain Lawrence*.... the diving equipment on the *Captain Lawrence* included a compressor, hard hat diving apparel, and a diving bell. A diving bell washed ashore on the north side of Big Summer Island in 1942.... Libert...needed to dredge 3 to 12 feet of silt in a football field sized area.... In 1994, John Halsey, State Archaeologist with the Bureau of History, Michigan Department of State, dove in the area identified by Libert as the site of the *Captain Lawrence*. The visibility around the area was only 5 to 10 feet and silt was easily stirred up, reducing visibility to 0 feet. Halsey observed scattered wooden planks, bricks, a tire, cable, crushed barrels, pails, a metal strainer from a gas engine, and a hanging knee. Most of the observable cultural materials were embedded within the bottom sediments.... The State does not consider any of the artifacts to be significant for purposes of the National Register of Historic Places.... The evidence is too sparse and generic to be able to say with any certainty that it comes from one vessel, much less to say that it comes from the specific vessel, the *Captain Lawrence*.... the evidence, although circumstantial, clearly demonstrates Wilfred Behrens' intent to abandon the vessel. He valued the vessel at only $200, had no insurance on it, and wrote it off as a "total loss." Had he wanted to salvage the vessel, the best time would have been immediately after it was stranded on the beach. Yet there is no evidence that he attempted any salvage operations immediately after the wreck. The evidence shows that Behrens was offered assistance from the Coast Guard immediately after the storm, but declined it. The evidence shows that Behrens was an experienced salvager, and continued his salvage diving for over ten years after the shipwreck. Yet there is no evidence that he ever attempted to salvage the *Captain Lawrence* in the years after the wreck. Behrens did not discuss the location of the *Captain Lawrence* with his family. He died intestate. He did not leave his interest in the vessel to his family or to anyone else. There is no evidence that his crew showed any interest in returning to the *Captain Lawrence*. Behrens' family did not seek out salvage divers to help locate the remains of the *Captain Lawrence*. They showed no interest in finding the *Captain Lawrence* until Libert told them of the possibility of a link between the *Captain Lawrence* and the legendary gold treasure....

Does Poverty Island still hide the secret to a great treasure? So far, it appears as likely as the compatibility of the words "poverty" and "treasure," but that's not to say that future (or even today's) technological advances capable of locating submerged and buried riches won't continue to make this region a hotspot of interest.

30

THE BONEYARD SHIPS

B oneyard ships usually had long, productive careers, but when these
faithful oldtimers reached the point where regular maintenance
could no longer keep up with all of the splits and leaks in the hulls,
these vessels were often, in a most disloyal display of unappreciation, towed
to an out-of-the-way part of the harbor, bay or river and left there to rot.

Boneyard ships had become such eyesores that often municipal, and
sometimes even federal, funds were provided to eliminate them in the 1920's
and 1930's. Sometimes the above water portions of these old ships were
purposely set ablaze to sweep them beyond visibility. Occasionally the old,
sunken vessels were uprooted from their shallow graves and dismantled.
Often the remains were used for firewood. Sometimes the hull of an old
ship was sunk as a dock or in front of a harbor for use as a breakwater. Old
wooden ships on occasion were, as their truly dramatic swansong, turned
into public spectacles by being set on fire and allowed to sink while hundreds
of paying customers thrilled to the unusual sight. Most frequently, however,
in the Great Lakes, abandoned ships in harbors were raised from the mud
in which they were mired, at times with such difficulty that dynamite was
required to dislodge them, then towed out (in pieces on barges or sometimes
even on their own old hulls) into adequately deep waters of a lake and
scuttled. In those environmentally worry-free days, out of sight was out of
mind. Dozens of ships whose glory days were long gone were raised and
towed out of harbors such as Kingston (Ontario), Chicago, Sarnia Bay/Port
Huron, and Port Arthur, Ontario (present-day Thunder Bay), then purposely
sunk in a lake's open waters in anywhere from 60 to 250 feet of water.

A hardhat diver examines the hull of an aged, wooden ship in Sturgeon Bay, circa 1920. These tired vessels were minimally maintained, yet every year there was hope that they would last for at least one more season. When they were finally abandoned, they often became a nautical nuisance. In the summer of 1910, the DOOR COUNTY ADVOCATE *warned that "These sunken hulks are a serious menace to the navigation of small boats in this bay and it is a wonder no serious accidents have occurred," and in April, 1913, wrote, "Some of the old wrecks that lay in the mud between the Leathem & Smith property and the shipyard were cut up during the past winter for firewood by beachcombers. Pity the hulks could not be towed out in the lake and sunk." The man in the power boat has been tentatively identified by maritime historian Jon Paul Van Harpen as Mr. Leathem D. Smith.* DOOR COUNTY MARITIME MUSEUM AND LIGHTHOUSE PRESERVATION SOCIETY, INC.

When the old, wooden vessels in Sturgeon Bay sank at dock, they were usually quickly pumped out, refloated, repaired and returned to service. People of a century ago were not as helpless as we in this modern era may suspect. In fact, the opposite is true, as resourcefulness and hard work raised most sunken ships and quickly had them working again (today, they would simply be replaced). But when the leaks grew worse and the sinkings did not end, those vessels were abandoned in out-of-the-way "boneyards." Sturgeon Bay is full of sunken boats. DOOR COUNTY MARITIME MUSEUM AND LIGHTHOUSE PRESERVATION SOCIETY, INC.

The wooden steamer, FOUNTAIN CITY, *new in 1857 (left) and wrecked in 1896 (above).*   CRIS KOHL COLLECTION

Ben Drake (June 22, 1882)

Sunk in the Peshtigo River, then raised and taken to Sturgeon Bay, this 47-ton wooden tug, built in 1864 in Brooklyn, NY, was stripped and the hull abandoned.

Home (late 1882)

After her engine and boiler were transplanted into the tug, *Thomas Spear,* the wooden hull of this 84-ton tug was abandoned at Sturgeon Bay.

Ira Chaffee (September 13, 1892)

This 193-ton wooden steamer (127'6" x 25'6" x 8'1"), built in 1867 at Allegan, Michigan, burned to a complete loss with no lives lost at Sault Ste. Marie, Michigan on July 11, 1891. The remains were towed to Sturgeon Bay where the engine and boiler were removed, and the hull was abandoned on the north side of Dunlap Reef. The ship's enrollment was surrendered at Detroit on September 13, 1892.

Fountain City (May 5, 1896)

Partially burned at the coal dock in Sturgeon Bay on May 5, 1896, the 630.12-ton steamer, *Fountain City* (210' x 30'4" x 12'), was declared a total loss and abandoned. The ship had been built at Cleveland by Peck & Masters in 1857.

The steamer, JOYS, *was wrecked by a Christmas Day fire in 1898 with no lives lost.* DOOR COUNTY MARITIME MUSEUM AND LIGHTHOUSE PRESERVATION SOCIETY, INC.

The steamer, MARY MILLS, *two years before she burned.* CRIS KOHL COLLECTION

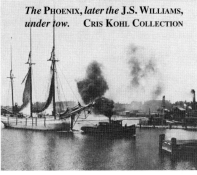

The PHOENIX, *later the* J.S. WILLIAMS, *under tow.* CRIS KOHL COLLECTION

Alfred Mosher (May 16, 1897)

This 37.34-ton tug (70'8" x 15' x 7'4"), built at Chicago in 1863, burned and sank east of the old mill slip on May 16, 1897. In 1912, her intact boiler was recovered from deep in the mud with plans to put it into the *City of New Baltimore.*

Joys (December 24, 1898)

Built at Milwaukee in 1884, the steam barge, *Joys* (131' x 28'2" x 9'9"), burned at her moorings at the west end of the Sturgeon Bay Ship Canal.

Mary Mills (December 12, 1900)

Launched on July 3, 1872, at Vicksburg, Michigan, this lumber steamer (117'9" x 24'8" x 8'6") burned at the head of Sturgeon Bay on December 12, 1900. The metal equipment was salvaged and the stern was dynamited in 1902.

J. S. Williams (May, 1902)

Built as the lumber schooner *Phoenix* in 1868 at Henderson, NY (Lake Ontario), and renamed the *J. S. Williams* (121' x 26' x 8') in 1896, she was partially sunk as a dock at the Graef & Nebel quarry at the mouth of Sturgeon Bay. She later burned.

Cleveland (June, 1902)

The old steamer, *Cleveland* (135' x 25'9" x 11'6"), built in 1860 at Cleveland, Ohio, was sunk as a dock next to the *J. S. Williams* at the Graef & Nebel quarry.

Bay State (April, 1903)

This 249-ton schooner, built in 1855 at Buffalo, New York, was towed to the mouth of Sturgeon Bay and sunk by Thomas Smith at his quarry for use as a dock.

Kate Hinchman (Spring, 1903)

This aging schooner (116' x 26' x 11') joined previous ships as a dock at Thomas Smith's quarry near the mouth of Sturgeon Bay.

Leo (1904)

This 94-ton schooner, built at Sheboygan, Wisconsin, in 1861 and abandoned near the bridge in Sturgeon Bay in 1904, was dynamited in 1919.

Dan Hayes (1905)

This three-masted, 146-ton scow schooner (112' x 24'2" x 7'), built at Fairport, Ohio, in 1868, was dismasted in a storm in 1898 off Milwaukee. In 1900, the Graef & Nebel quarry bought the vessel for $226 for hauling stone, but the ship, needing

The two-masted schooner, CHARLEY J. SMITH (left), is seen broadside while docked with three other schooners. HENRY BARKHAUSEN COLLECTION

constant maintenance, was abandoned in Sturgeon Bay.

Charley J. Smith (October 10, 1905)

This small, 42.94-ton, twin-masted schooner (60' x 16'8" x 4'9"), built at South Haven, Michigan, in 1879, was left in a sunken condition at the Stevenson dock at the head of Little Sturgeon Bay. Her final enrollment was surrendered at Milwaukee on October 10, 1905, and endorsed as "abandoned."

The 1,936-ton wooden steamer, GEORGE PRESLEY. CRIS KOHL COLLECTION

George Presley (June 18, 1906)

This steamer (265' x 41' x 23'7"), launched at Cleveland on May 22, 1889, burned at Death's Door on July 26, 1905. The burned-out hull was towed to the Sturgeon Bay boneyard on June 18, 1906.

Cecilia Hill (1906)

Built at Fish Creek, Wisconsin, in 1896, and burned there on April 7, 1906, the remains of this 44-ton, wooden steamer (93' x 19' x 7'5") were towed to Sturgeon Bay in the summer of 1906, placed next to the *George Presley*, stripped and abandoned.

German (November 28, 1908)

This two-masted, 79.78-ton scow schooner (80'8" x 20'7" x 5'9"), built by Henry D. Root at Black River (Lorain), Ohio, launched in mid-1868, was stripped and abandoned south of one of the shipyards in Sturgeon Bay. Her final enrollment, surrendered in Milwaukee on November 28, 1908, stated the ship was "abandoned."

Sanilac (December, 1911)

This old, wooden steamer (161'5" x 27'5" x 10'; 310.31 tons) quietly sank along the dock north of the Sturgeon Bay shipyard. Built in Algonac, Michigan, in 1867, the ship's final enrollment indicated that the vessel had been abandoned.

Mishicott (January 26, 1912)

This twin-masted, 73.49-ton scow schooner (79'2" x 21'5" x 6'), built by George Jorgenson at Manitowoc, Wisconsin, in 1882, lay inactive in the shoreline mud on the east side of the Leathem Smith shipyard from 1905 until January 26, 1912, when the decaying vessel's final enrollment was endorsed as "abandoned."

D. F. Rose (September, 1912)

Dismantled of anything useful, this old, wooden steamer (140' x 26'3" x 10'9", built in 1868 at Marine City, Michigan) was abandoned at Sturgeon Bay.

Minnie Warren (November, 1912)

This 13-ton fish tug (47' x 12'4" x 5'4"), built at Buffalo in 1869, had her machinery removed before being abandoned north of the Pankratz Lumber Mill.

Above, left: *The steamer,* PEWAUKEE, *formerly the Canadian bark,* TWO FRIENDS, *stranded at Baileys Harbor in 1880 but recovered, was abandoned due to age in Sturgeon Bay in 1913.* CRIS KOHL COLLECTION.   **Above, right:** *The steamer,* PEWAUKEE, *abandoned in the foreground, with the then-still-active barge,* ADRIATIC, *self-loading stone in the background.* DOOR COUNTY MARITIME MUSEUM AND LIGHTHOUSE PRESERVATION SOCIETY, INC.

Pewaukee (November 10, 1913)

Launched as the bark, *Two Friends*, in 1873 at Port Burwell, Ontario, the ship was nearly destroyed several times, particularly in the Big Blow of 1880, but was recovered in 1881 and renamed *Pewaukee* (141' x 26' x 11'), converted to a

The steamer, JOSEPH L. HURD.
CRIS KOHL COLLECTION

steambarge in 1888, into a tow barge in 1905, and formally abandoned due to age on the same day as the *Joseph L. Hurd*.

Joseph L. Hurd (November 10, 1913)

The *Hurd* (171' x 29'2" x 10'9"), launched at Detroit on September 1, 1869, was formally abandoned the same day as the *Pewaukee* after spending her final years as a stone barge and stranding north of the Ship Canal on September 25, 1913; it was removed and sunk off the end of the Leathem Smith quarry dock.

James H. Martin (April, 1914)

This tug (72' x 15' x 8'2"), built in 1869 at Cleveland, and notorious for having abandoned the *Plymouth* (see Chapter 24), sank while wintering at Sturgeon Bay.

Emma Bloeker (April, 1914)

This tug (56'2" x 13'9" x 4'7"; 31 tons), built at Grand Haven, MI, in 1889, was sunk by ice near the Sturgeon Bay south dock, her machinery already removed.

Oneida (April, 1914)

Built in Ashtabula, Ohio, in 1857, this 201-ton schooner (134' x 24') was sunk by late-winter ice at her Sturgeon Bay dock near the canal, and was abandoned.

Myron Butman (November 19, 1914)

Launched as a schooner in 1885 at Gibraltar, Michigan, and later converted to a barge (164'3" x 31'2" x 10'2"), this 424-ton ship stranded in a storm near the bridge in Sturgeon Bay and was abandoned.

Robert Holland (May 11, 1915)

Launched in Marine City, Michigan, in 1872, as the *Robert Holland*, and burned

The ROBERT HOLLAND, *burned to a total loss in Sturgeon Bay in 1915, sank once before in 1881 while named the* NORTHERN QUEEN.
CRIS KOHL COLLECTION

The schooner, LIBBIE NAU, *surrendered her final document at Milwaukee on June 30, 1918, endorsed "abandoned."*
CRIS KOHL COLLECTION

at Sturgeon Bay on May 11, 1915, as the *Robert Holland* (156' x 30' x 11'4"), this wooden steamer was named the *Northern Queen* from 1878 to 1882, and as such, sank at Manistique (see Chapter 12). The ship was reportedly filled with stone and sunk as a dock.

Peter Coates (June 17, 1915)

This 32-ton tug (61'5" x 15'2" x 6'8"), built at Grand Haven, MI, in 1886, sank at her dock on Sturgeon Bay's west side, was pulled onto shore and abandoned.

Eddie (April, 1918)

A small 30-ton schooner built in Mount Clemens, Michigan, in 1892, the *Eddie* (59'6" x 17'6" x 3'6") was purposely sunk at the Leathem & Smith quarry dock.

Libby Nau (June, 1918)

This schooner (129' x 26'6" x 10'), built at Green Bay in 1867, was filled with stone and sunk at the Leathem & Smith shipyard next to the sunken *Robert Holland*.

Advance (Oct. 19, 1921)

Built in 1871 at Trenton, Michigan, this 438-ton lumber schooner-turned-barge (139' x 28'7" x 11'5"), stranded on the north point of Sand Bay and was abandoned.

W. H. Meyer (August, 1922)

This 94-ton tugboat (89' x 24' x 11'2"), built in 1898 at Benton Harbor, Michigan, was changed to a barge in 1922, the same year she went to the boneyard.

Vermillion (August, 1922)

Launched as the *J. C. Gilchrist* in 1887 at Trenton, Michigan, this wooden steamer (252' x 42' x 20'4") had her name changed in 1904. This old ship was sunk as a breakwater at the Leathem & Smith quarry.

G. M. A. Herrmann (September, 1922)

Built at Milwaukee in 1891, this 34-ton fish tug (61'6" x 14'6" x 6'5") was dynamited to make way for a Sturgeon Bay Dry Dock Company launching.

I. N. Foster (1927)

Launched on April 6, 1872, at Port Huron, MI, this schooner-then-steamer (1893)-then-barge (134'9" x 26'2" x 11'5") was abandoned in Sturgeon Bay.

Adriatic (1930)

Abandoned just northwest of the old railroad bridge, this 915-ton schooner-changed-to-barge-in-1924 (202' x 34'7" x 16'6") was built at West Bay City, Michigan, by James Davidson in 1889. (See also page 200.)

Above: *The abandoned* JOSEPH L. HURD *remains today where she was towed and scuttled in late 1913. The wooden* HURD, *is perhaps most notoriously remembered for having collided with the larger, newer steel steamer,* CAYUGA, *in northern Lake Michigan on May 10, 1895; surprisingly, the* CAYUGA *sank! The* HURD *lies today off the old Leathem Smith stone quarry dock in 15 to 30 feet of water, filled with stones, and considerably deteriorated.*
PHOTO BY CRIS KOHL

Left: *The steamer,* MUELLER, *was, for a while, abandoned just off the Leathem Smith quarry dock. Recent research indicates that the* MUELLER *was likely removed and scrapped. If that is the case, then all that remains of this ship is its propeller, shaft and wooden stern section, exhibited in the waterfront park across the street from the old, open-faced quarry (background).* PHOTO BY CRIS KOHL

The Bullhead Point Wrecks

WHERE IS THE IDA CORNING?

Chicago, November 20.—A dispatch from Charlevoix, Mich., to-night stated that fishermen at the point two miles north of there reported wreckage coming ashore. One jacket lifepreserver

The schooner-barge, IDA CORNING (1881-1928), was named after an East Saginaw lumber mill owner's baby daughter who lived from 1880 until 1947.

CRIS KOHL COLLECTION

The IDA CORNING was feared lost in late 1895 when a lifejacket with her name on it washed ashore. The printed name, however, turned out to be LYCOMING (with some letters obscured), and that steamer was not in peril -- it had simply lost an old lifejacket.

CRIS KOHL COLLECTION

The steamer, EMPIRE STATE (1862-1929), was the sister ship of another boneyard resident, the FOUNTAIN CITY. CRIS KOHL COLLECTION

The schooner-barge, OAK LEAF (1866-1928), and the other two ships were all destroyed by fire on June 21, 1931.

CRIS KOHL COLLECTION

Oak Leaf (1928)

This three-masted schooner, launched at Cleveland on April 14, 1866, was rebuilt in 1891 and converted to a barge in 1917 (160' x 31'2" x 10'7"). Used extensively in the stone trade, the *Oak Leaf* was abandoned in 1928, and lies sunk in the shallows off the southernmost part of Sturgeon Bay's Bullhead Point.

Ida Corning (1928)

For the first 27 years of her career, the 444-ton schooner-barge *Ida Corning* (168' x 31'3" x 10' 9") worked as a lumber hooker. Launched at East Saginaw, Michigan, in 1881 for Mr. G. Corning, a local lumber mill and ship chandlery owner, the ship was bought for the stone trade in 1908 and spent the remainder of her working days crossing Lake Michigan to Ludington and Holland with stone cargoes. This vessel was abandoned at Bullhead Point in 1928.

Empire State (1929)

Of the three shallow water wrecks at Bullhead Point, the wooden steamer, *Empire State* has the most notorious reputation. Built by Bidwell & Mason of Buffalo, New York, and launched on April 5, 1862, within the first decade of its existence, this ship collided with and sank two others, both on Lake Huron: the

Above: *The distinct shape of tiny Bullhead Point can be seen clearly from the air as it juts out into Sturgeon Bay. The "boneyard" ships, the* EMPIRE STATE, *the* IDA CORNING *and the* OAK LEAF, *lie in the shallows just beyond and to the right of the large tree standing on the peninsula's tip. Further distant, in the upper right corner, can be seen the northern end of Dunlap Reef.* PHOTO BY CRIS KOHL

Below: *The three abandoned vessels lying alongside Bullhead Point have inspired additional maritime displays. This wooden stock anchor, discovered by scuba divers in 1960 off Baileys Harbor and recovered by them, was moved here in 2003 from the nearby airport as part of the Wisconsin Historical Society's Maritime Trails program.* PHOTO BY CRIS KOHL

Above: *Three ship eras and styles are represented in this photo taken from Bullhead Point: in the background, the 1960 freighter,* Edward L. Ryerson *(with a length of 730 feet, this ship is one foot longer than the Great Lakes' legendary* Edmund Fitzgerald*); a small pleasure craft with anglers in pursuit of bass; and the visible remains of the former three-masted schooner named the* Oak Leaf. Photo by Cris Kohl

Below left: *Joan Forsberg, along the shoreline at the Bullhead Point wrecks, takes a look at the remains of the former steamer,* Empire State. Photo by Cris Kohl

Below right: *Joan makes a closer examination of the hull framing and planking of the abandoned schooner-barge,* Ida Corning. Photo by Cris Kohl

As evidenced in these photographs, the three abandoned ships at Bullhead Point can be enjoyed from the surface without getting wet, or they can be appreciated closer by snorkeling (mainly surface swimming) around the various timbers. Scuba diving these shallow sites provides the advantage of extended and detailed examination of the remains of each ship from the bay bottom up, with little concern for running out of air. In high water years, what is left of these ships lies completely submerged. PHOTOS BY CRIS KOHL

The steamer, MUELLER.
CRIS KOHL COLLECTION

schooner, *Dunderberg*, on August 13, 1868, and the steamer, *Wabash*, on June 5, 1870. An engine room fire at Chicago on Christmas Day, 1906, nearly destroyed the *Empire State*; it was rebuilt as a 637-ton stone barge (212' x 33' x 18'6"). The ship was abandoned at Bullhead Point after a 1929 fire on board.

Mueller (September, 1933)

Launched as the *Edwin S. Tice* in 1887 at Manitowoc, Wisconsin, this wooden steamer was renamed in 1901 (after William Mueller [1866-1944] of Chicago's Mueller Cedar Company). The ship burned in 1933. Recent research by Maritime Historian Jon Paul Van Harpen suggests that the wreck called the *Mueller* may really be the *Vermillion*, the *Mueller* having been removed and dismantled.

North Shore (1934)

Named the *Bon Ami* when first launched in 1894 at Saugatuck, Michigan, this

The steamer, NORTH SHORE.
CRIS KOHL COLLECTION

Victims of the December 3, 1935 Fire

Plus the Lucia A. Simpson, *next page...*

The E. G. Crosby *(1903-1935), the largest ship destroyed in the 1935 fire, had a dozen different owners in her 32-year career. She had been renamed in 1923 after a Great Lakes captain who was a* Titanic *victim.*
Cris Kohl Collection

The Swift *(1893-1935) worked as a lumber steamer.* Cris Kohl Collection

The tug, Beaver *(1892-1935), in foreground, burned twice: in 1915 and in 1935.* Cris Kohl Collection

The steamer, Petoskey *(1888-1935), defied sailors' superstitions regarding Fridays, with tragic results. When she burned, it was a Tuesday.* Cris Kohl Collection

The oak-hulled steamer, Waukegan *(1919-1935), was one of newest ships (along with the* Kenosha*) destroyed in the 1935 fire. Both vessels had been built for World War I, but saw no service.* Cris Kohl Collection

The wooden steamer, Kenosha *(1919-1935), was one of the two newest ships destroyed.* Cris Kohl Collection

Old Schooner To Be Used In Hunt For Lost Lake Treasures Springs Leak And Nearly Goes To Bottom

MANITOWOC, Wis., July 8—(AP)—
The schooner, Lucia A. Simpson, with seven men aboard on a cruise to seek adventure and possible riches

Jones, of Hancock; Helver Erickson, and Nelson and Martin Mathieson, all of Milwaukee.
The schooner was built in 1875 and

The last of the original Great Lakes topmast schooners plying the freshwater seas, the LUCIA A. SIMPSON, *was to be used as a treasure hunting ship in 1929 when she experienced her final, unfortunate accident (as reported by the* DAILY MINING JOURNAL *of Marquette, Michigan). She was photographed in a damaged condition while being towed to what became her final resting place in Sturgeon Bay. Plans to use her as a Chicago yacht club in 1932 and as a maritime museum at Manitowoc in 1934 failed. She received the most newspaper coverage when the Dec., 1935 fire destroyed seven ships.* CRIS KOHL COLLECTION

98-ton steamer (114' x 21'8" x 6'4") spent her first 24 years servicing Lakes Michigan and Superior until a fire on October 24, 1918, severely damaged her. Rebuilt, renamed and removed to Chicago, the *North Shore* worked for several years as an excursion ship running between downtown Chicago and north shore ports like Waukegan. The ship was abandoned at Sturgeon Bay by 1934.

Halsted (**1934**)

This schooner-barge (171' x 33'4" x 12'4"), built at Little Sturgeon Bay in 1873, was stranded in the Great Storm of 1913 (See Chapter 24), but was recovered and worked another 20 years before being abandoned in the Sturgeon Bay boneyard.

Mary Ellen Cook (**February 27, 1934**)

This 126-ton, three-masted schooner (118' x 25' x 7'), built at Grand Haven, Michigan, in 1875, was used as a pier in front of the Leathem Smith Lodge in Sturgeon Bay from 1922. The disintegrating ship was set on fire on Feb. 27, 1934.

Lucia A. Simpson (**December 3, 1935**)

This fine, 227.04-ton, three-masted schooner (127' x 28' x 8'7"), launched on November 21, 1874, by builders Rand & Burger at Manitowoc, Wisconsin, worked mostly hauling huge lumber cargoes. She was destroyed in the 1935 fire.

E. G. Crosby (**December 3, 1935**)

Launched as the *City of South Haven* on March 21, 1903, at Toledo, Ohio, this 1,918-ton, steel ship was renamed *City of Miami* in 1920 and *E. G. Crosby* (247'7" x 40'3" x 21'7") in 1923. The fire which destroyed this vessel and six others started here from a welder's torch, cutting the ship down to a barge. The hull was scrapped.

Swift (**December 3, 1935**)

Launched as the *Wotan* in 1893 at Marine City, Michigan, and renamed *Swift*

(191'5" x 36'5" x 13'6") in 1929, this wooden ship was destroyed in the 1935 fire.

Petoskey (December 3, 1935)

This 770.96-ton wooden steamer (171'3" x 30'4" x 12'2"), launched in 1888, by Burger & Burger at Manitowoc, Wisconsin, defied superstition, as seen by this *Chicago Tribune* article from October, 1888:

> Mariners, and there is no class of people more prone to superstition, are talking of the important part Friday has played with the passenger steamer *Petoskey*.... The *Petoskey's* keel was laid on a Friday, she was launched a Friday, and she made her first [run] a Friday. [The *Petoskey's*] Capt. Seymour was taken ill with typhoid fever a Friday, and died a Friday. His brother who served as clerk [on the *Petoskey*] is now ill with the same disease.... He took to his bed a Friday.

The defiant *Petoskey* was totally destroyed at Sturgeon Bay in the 1935 fire.

Beaver (December 3, 1935)

Launched as the *Oval Agitator* in 1892 at Grand Haven, Michigan, and renamed *Beaver* (98'4" x 19'6" x 8'6") in 1902, this 99-ton tug burned at Sturgeon Bay.

Waukegan (December 3, 1935)

Named the *Commodore* when built in 1919 at Sturgeon Bay (initially for saltwater use in World War I, then sold for private use) and renamed *Waukegan* (142'5" x 30'5" x 15'2") in 1920, this large tug and its sister ship, the *Kenosha* (same size) were so badly damaged by the 1935 fire that they never sailed again.

Kenosha (December 3, 1935) -- See *Waukegan* above.

Leathem D. Smith (1942)

Built at Toledo, Ohio, in 1893 as *Lightship No. 059* (which served at Lake Erie's Bar Point and Lake Huron's Poe Reef) and renamed in 1918, the tug, *Leathem D. Smith* (80' x 21'6" x 8'6"), inactive for years, was formally abandoned in 1942.

Wrecked or abandoned ships at Sturgeon Bay were not the exclusive playgrounds of adventurous youngsters! On any given Sunday, young-at-heart ladies would take a leisurely stroll along rotting decks while their boatman snapped a photograph of them. DOOR COUNTY MARITIME MUSEUM AND LIGHTHOUSE PRESERVATION SOCIETY, INC.

A Chronological Listing of Shipwrecks at Death's Door

N ewspapers, those massive and regular sources of reported information, particularly the *Door County Advocate* of Sturgeon Bay, Wisconsin, plus a large number of "Wreck Reports" from the National Archives (the Great Lakes branch at Chicago) provided most of the facts for this chapter. The other newspapers (available on microfilm) which proved to be of great assistance were the *Chicago Tribune*, the Chicago *Daily Inter Ocean*, the *Detroit Free Press*, the *Toledo Blade*, the Escanaba and Menominee (Michigan) and the Duluth (Minnesota) papers, plus a Great Lakes potpourri of newspaper miscellany. Keep in mind, however, that not all shipwrecks in any given area were reported by local newspapers, and that some which were reported as total losses were later recovered and returned to service, events which were sometimes not reported by newspapers. We have tried to include in our listing only the permanent ship losses.

Most of the natural shipwrecks which have dramatic stories behind them, or those which have been located to date and are regularly visited by scuba divers at or near the place called Death's Door, were given their own chapters in the preceding pages. What follows in this chapter is a listing with thumbnail histories which will hopefully give the reader some idea of the number of shipwrecks lying in these waters, a bit of information about each one, and a hint of the extent of the maritime traffic utilizing the passages connecting Lake Michigan and Green Bay.

Griffon **(September, 1679)** -- See Chapter 2, pages 71 to 74.

Dolphin **(October 17, 1841)** -- See Chapter 4, pages 79 to 92.

Eclipse **(November, 1843)**
This small schooner stranded on a reef near Rock Island; cargo was saved, ship, lost.

Wisconsin **(September, 1847)** -- See Chapter 4, pages 79 to 92.

Margaret Allen **(November, 1847)** -- See Chapter 3, pages 75 to 78.

Janette (May 1, 1851)
A late snowstorm stranded this schooner at Baileys Harbor, where she broke up.

E. H. Scott (November 11, 1852)
Built at St. Joseph in 1843, this 200-ton brig stranded and wrecked at Washington Harbor. No lives were lost.

George C. Smalley (September 5, 1853)
This schooner, sailing from St. Martin Island to Washington Harbor, capsized with the loss of three passengers from the eight people on board. It stranded on the northern beach of Washington Island and broke up.

Windham (December 3, 1855) -- See Chapter 3, pages 75 to 78.

Etta (August 1, 1856)
This small sloop, loaded with stone, foundered in 60 feet off Sturgeon Bay Bluff.

Homes (September 15, 1856)
This schooner, damaged in a collision with another ship, was towed to Baileys Harbor, but gales blew the vessel into Lily Bay. Stripped of cargo and hardware, she was abandoned.

Maria Hilliard (October, 1856) -- See Chapter 3, pages 75 to 78.

Shakespeare (June, 1858)
According to Mansfield's (1899) chronological listing, this brig, built in Cleveland in 1848, "wrecked on Pilot Island, Lake Michigan," but his index in the same volume suggests that the vessel was recovered and "afterward called *Empire State*."

Columbia (June 7, 1859) -- See Chapter 3, pages 75 to 78.

Minnesota (September 26, 1861)
Built in 1851 at Maumee, Ohio, this 749-ton, wooden sidewheel steamer (235' x 31' x 11') began leaking and was stranded at Summer Island, where she broke up in gales.

Agnes Willie (November 4, 1862)
This small, wooden vessel capsized off Baileys Harbor, drifted to shore and broke up.

Henry Norton (October, 1863) -- See Chapter 4, pages 79 to 92.

Cairo (October 18, 1863) -- See Chapter 3, pages 75 to 78.

Daniel Slauson (October 22, 1863) -- See Chapter 4, pages 79 to 92.

Alvin Clark (June 29, 1864)
Foundered in a gale off Chambers Island in Green Bay with the loss of three lives, this 218-ton brig (105'8" x 25'4" x 9'4") built at Trenton, Michigan in 1846, became famous after the intact shipwreck was successfully raised from 110 feet of water by Frank Hoffman in the summer of 1969 and turned into a popular tourist attraction at Menominee, Michigan. Unfortunately, funding could not be found to conserve this huge, wooden artifact, and by the mid-1990's, the ship's crumbled remains were hauled to the dump. For more detailed information about the *Alvin Clark*, read *Shipwreck Tales of the Great Lakes* by Cris Kohl.

J. (John) C. Fremont (June 26, 1865)
This twin-masted scow schooner (111' x 24' x 9'), built at Milan, Ohio, in 1856, sank fast after colliding with the much larger bark, *American Union*, off Baileys Harbor. The *Fremont* hailed from Chicago and her crew was rescued by the bark.

Lewis Cass (October 30, 1865)
This 191-ton schooner (98' x 24' x 9'), built at Vermilion, Ohio, in 1846, stranded in a

storm near Baileys Harbor and became a total loss.

Grapeshot **(November 1, 1867)** -- See Chapter 5, pages 93 to 98.

Maple Leaf **(November 1, 1867)** -- See Chapter 4, pages 79 to 92.

Hanover **(November 7, 1867)**

This 237-ton schooner, built in 1832 at Irving, NY, on Lake Erie, reportedly stranded "on Strawberry reef near Fish Creek," a total loss. She had sailed light (without a cargo), and was stripped before she broke up. The long, narrow reef running off Chambers Island's southeast point may have been named Hanover Shoal because the ship wrecked there.

Sam Hale **(September 22, 1868)** -- See Chapter 22, pages 173 to 178.

William M. Arbuckle **(November 23, 1868)**

Purposely stranded in a storm at Sister Bay to prevent her from sinking in deep water, the 126-ton schooner, *W. M. Arbuckle* (97' x 23' x 9'), built in 1853 at Erie, Pennsylvania, could not be released later, and was abandoned as a total loss.

Gray Eagle **(July 10, 1869)**

This 287-ton schooner (167' x 26' x 11'), built in 1857 by Bidwell & Banta of Buffalo, stranded in a storm on Whitefish Bay's north point. The pummeling seas soon broke up the ship; arsonists desirous of the ship's spikes and other iron burned her on September 20th.

Ocean Wave **(September 23, 1869)** -- See Chapter 6, pages 99-110.

Fairfield **(September 29, 1869)**

Built by famous Canadian shipbuilder Louis Shickluna at St. Catharines, Canada West (later Ontario), in 1846, this 199-ton schooner (128' x 26' x 11'), sailing light, struck a reef off the north point just outside Baileys Harbor and broke up shortly thereafter.

Sunshine **(September 29, 1869)**

Stranded in a gale on the north point of North Bay with a cargo of lumber, this 115-ton schooner, built in 1856 at Mt. Clemens, Michigan, slowly pounded apart, a total loss.

D. (Daniel) O. Dickinson **(October 8, 1869)**

This 15-year-old, 242-ton schooner (built in Milwaukee in 1854) stranded on "Strawberry Reef" (that southeast point of Chambers Island which is today called Hanover Shoal) in Green Bay with a cargo of lumber bound for Chicago, and broke up, a total loss.

Joseph Cochrane **(October 23, 1870)**

Bound for Chicago from Cheboygan, Michigan, with a lumber cargo, this 326-ton, three-masted schooner (136' x 26' 10') stranded and broke up on Baileys Harbor's north reef. This vessel had been built as a bark in Charlotte, New York, in 1856.

Carrington **(October 30, 1870)** -- See Chapter 7, pages 111-112.

Dauntless **(December, 1870)**

Built at Buffalo, New York, in 1857, this large, 299-ton schooner carrying 525 tons of iron ore stranded on St. Martin Island. She was stripped of her rigging, etc., and abandoned.

General Winfield Scott **(August 28, 1871)**

This 213-ton, twin-masted schooner (114' x 25' x 10'), built at Cleveland in 1852 and bound with lumber from Menominee to Chicago, capsized and went ashore on Hog Island (which lies about 1/3 mile east of Washington Island). Her cargo was recovered by locals.

Iron City **(September, 1872)**

Built in Cleveland by Quayle & Martin and launched in June, 1856, this large steamer-turned-barge (184'2" x 29'3" x 11'10"; # 12092) sank at Sturgeon Bay with iron ore.

Lydia Case **(late September, 1872)** -- See Chapter 4, pages 79 to 92.

Cherubusco **(November 10, 1872)**

This bark-rigged scow (114' x 27' x 9'4"), built at Milwaukee in 1848, was driven ashore in a gale in North Bay. The *Manitowoc Tribune* of November 14, 1872, wrote,

> The barque *Cherubusco* which left our dry dock here only a few weeks ago has had to be beached again to save her being entirely lost. Her Capt. W. T. Feltis found her getting waterlogged in spite of all he could do, off North Bay, and to save property and lives, made for the bay which he reached safely in spite of the dark night and the gale blowing at the time. The Capt. and crew staid on board for twelve hours after she got beached and then all got ashore safe and sound after a hard pull. The Capt. thinks that the repairs on her were not done thoroughly enough while in dry dock, and that thus she sprung a leak again so soon after she had left it.

Unfortunately, the *Cherubusco* was so badly damaged that she was abandoned.

Hampton **(September 20, 1873)** -- See Chapter 3, pages 75 to 78.

Meridian **(October 23, 1873)** -- See Chapter 8, pages 113-116.

Illinois **(October 29, 1873)**

Driven ashore near Smith's Pier in Baileys Harbor, this 85.6-ton, twin-masted schooner (95' x 21' x 7'), built in 1848 at St. Joseph, Michigan, broke up, a total loss.

Denmark **(November 1, 1873)** -- See Chapter 3, pages 75 to 78.

Cleveland **(June 13, 1875)** -- See Chapter 4, pages 79 to 92.

Ella Doak **(August 5, 1875)**

The *Door County Advocate*, on August 19, 1875, reported the following about a shipwreck, which actually revealed more about the owner than the vessel:

> The schooner *Ella Doak*, owned by Capt. John Doak, of Ahnapee, and sailed by O. P. Conger, was totally wrecked during the severe gale of Thursday night, the 5th inst., at Hedge Hog Harbor, in "Death's Door." There was no insurance on the vessel, and her loss will prove a severe blow to Capt. Doak, who has the sympathy of a large circle of friends in his misfortune. We shouldn't be surprised though but what he may have the *Doak* out again ere long if there are any pieces of her left. Hope so, at any rate.

Several weeks after the *Ella Doak* stranded, the *Green Bay Gazette* printed this item, which was reprinted in the *Door County Advocate* on September 23, 1875, and which revealed the personalities of both the ship and its owner:

> Those who keep track of marine matters will remember that some little time ago, the scow *Ella Doak* went upon the beach at Hedgehog harbor, just inside the Door. While she lay on the beach in an ugly position to handle, and while her captain was querying as to how he might get her afloat, the elements came to his rescue and put her in the best shape possible. A heavy north-easter came up and the waves hoisted her high and dry in such a position that all damage to her bottom could be readily repaired and timbers placed beneath her for the smoothest

kind of launch. She will be slid into the water some time this week and resume her profitable job of carrying stone for cribbing purposes to the east shore of Lake Michigan. This same craft, familiarly known among the sailing fraternity as "Queen of the beach," has had more narrow escapes from total wreck than any we have heard of. Less than a year ago she capsized; on one trip she went upon the beach four times, and during the time she has run she has each season gone through the toughest kind of experience. She was originally built by Capt. Jack Doak, who still sails her,.... She is a three-master, carries plenty of canvas, never shirks any kind of weather, and has thus far never failed, whether bottom side up in the Lake, or reposing on the beach, to come out in good shape. Capt. Doak has plenty of pluck, and isn't to be put down by trifles.

Unfortunately, the 75-ton *Ella Doak* (85' x 21' x 5', and launched in May, 1868, at Pentwater, Michigan) had sustained greater injuries than were first diagnosed. Although attempts were made for over a year to repair and recover this ship from the stony beach at Hedgehog Harbor, the *Doak* finally broke up in place. The press summarized this vessel's legacy:

> ...Her loss is not only felt by the owner, but her demise will be most severely felt by the entire newspaper press of this section of the State, and the whole western shore of Lake Michigan. Where will they find another object that will furnish as many first class items as the "Queen of the Beach" has furnished within the last few years? It is hard to tell.

Sea Bird (October 26, 1875)

This 284-ton schooner carrying 18,000 bushels of wheat sprang a leak, dropped anchor at Horn's Pier (immediately south of the Lake Michigan side of the Sturgeon Bay Ship Canal), but went ashore after her anchor dragged. The crew escaped; the ship was a total loss.

G. R. Roberts (September 25, 1876)

Valued at $1,000 at the time of loss, this small, 82-ton schooner was blown ashore at the head of Big Sister Bay after her anchor fouled in its chain. Sails and rigging were removed before the ship broke to pieces.

Dick Somers (November 19, 1877)

Strong gales during a storm forced this 332-ton schooner (built in 1863 at Milwaukee) carrying 550 tons of iron ore ashore just off the south end of Poverty Island. At $6 a ton, hardhat divers from Chicago recovered most of the cargo in 1878, as well as the ship's anchors, chains, windlass, capstan, pumps, blocks, and other marine items. This wreck reportedly lay in 14 feet of water about 100 feet from the Poverty Island lighthouse.

Dan Sickles (May 4, 1878)

When this 65-ton scow schooner (77'5" x 19'3" x 5'3") sprang a leak and capsized reportedly off Sherman Point, her crew reached shore in their yawl boat. Then the *Sickles* drifted, finally sinking in 16 feet of water half a mile from shore, "five miles north of the Sturgeon Bay Canal." This ship was built in 1866 at Elba Isle, Michigan.

Hunting Boy (October 12, 1878)

This 56-ton, sand-laden schooner stranded between the harbor piers at the Sturgeon Bay Canal (lake end). Her sails were recovered, and the wreck was dynamited in July, 1880.

Two Kates, or Two Katies (October 25, 1878)

This 73-ton, three-masted scow schooner collided with another ship during a storm and sank about four miles off the Ship Canal. The top-masts were seen above the water.

E. M. Davidson (October 18, 1879) -- See Chapter 4, pages 79 to 92.

Mariner (November 11, 1879)

Built in 1852 at Milwaukee, this 113-ton schooner hailing from Chicago was stranded by strong winds in Sherman Bay near the then-new Horn & Joseph Pier. The seven men on board reached shore safely, the cargo of ties and posts were recovered, but the ship was a total loss. Anchors and chains were salvaged and sold as "junk" for three cents a pound.

Warren (November 21, 1879)

This 77-ton schooner with a lumber cargo was blown ashore by gales while attempting to set sail out of Baileys Harbor. Unwilling to pay the tug captain's fee, the ship was abandoned in place. The cargo was recovered and the ship was stripped by late December.

Free Democrat (December 13, 1879)

This 63-foot-long, 40-ton schooner, loaded with lumber just salvaged from the wreck of the *Warren*, struck a rock on the east side of Baileys Harbor, holed her hull, and sank. She was built in 1853 at Port Huron, Michigan, and due to her age, she was of little value.

William Livingstone, Jr. (October 4, 1880)

This wooden tug (132' x 26' x 13'4") was built in 1874 at Port Huron, Michigan; the *Chicago Inter Ocean* described her on April 25, 1874: "...Aside from being the largest tug on the lakes, she is elaborately finished and elegantly furnished, and will no doubt create a sensation when she comes out to show herself, which will be in a few days." This lumber barge towship sank after breaking a shaft and before she could be towed into shallow water. The official "Wreck Report" says she sank "10 miles from shore off Baileys Harbor, foundered in 250 feet of water." This would be an impressive, historic find for technical scuba divers.

Ardent (October 12, 1880) -- See Chapter 3, pages 75-78.

Ebenezer (October 16, 1880) -- See Chapter 9, pages 117-120.

Perry Hannah (October 16, 1880) -- See Chapter 9, pages 117-120.

Josephine Lawrence (October 16, 1880) -- See Chapter 9, pages 117-120.

E. C. L. (October 20, 1880)

This three-masted, 248.92-ton schooner, built in Chicago in 1855 as a bark, was driven ashore during a storm while at anchor at Sister Bay, Wisconsin, and was wrecked. Purchased for $800, the wreck failed to be released, but was stripped of her rigging and other parts. A year later, a Norwegian family of nine removed the deck house and used it as their residence.

Ebenezer (June, 1881)

This small, old coastal schooner, not to be confused with one of the other "*Ebenezers*" which ran here, was stranded in fog at Sherman Bay. Only the sails and rigging were saved.

D. A. Van Valkenburg (September 16, 1881) -- See Chapter 10, pages 121-128.

Jennibell (September 17, 1881) -- See Chapter 11, pages 129-130.

Lewis Day (October 23, 1881) -- See Chapter 5, pages 93 to 98.

Pierrepont (November 26, 1881)

This 153-ton schooner, built at Sackett's Harbor on Lake Ontario in 1853, sank after being holed while moored at an outside pier at the lake entrance of the Ship Canal. Heavy seas destroyed the vessel before she could be salvaged, but spars and rigging were saved. In April, 1882, a tug towed the broken wreckage into shallows two miles from the canal.

Lake Erie **(November 24, 1881)** -- See Chapter 12, pages 131-134.

Ben Drake **(June 22, 1882)** -- See Chapter 30, pages 235 to 250.

Home **(late 1882)** -- See Chapter 30, pages 235 to 250.

Banner (November 4, 1883)

On her first trip under new owners who had paid $1,200 for her, this 72-ton scow schooner, built in 1864, stranded and broke up just south of the lake side Ship Canal breakwall.

Maria **(November 5, 1883)** -- See Chapter 3, pages 75 to 78.

H. Witbeck (December 26, 1883)

Built in 1869 at Oshkosh, Wisconsin, this tug foundered after a storm broke the ship away from her mooring at the Sturgeon Bay Ship Canal. The engine and boiler were salvaged and installed in a Forestville flour mill.

Christina Nilsson (October 24, 1884)

Built by Hanson & Scove at Manitowoc in 1871 for Chicago's C. M. Lindgren, and valued then at $19,000, this 295.8-ton, three-masted schooner (139' x 26'2" x 11'3") was badly damaged in the Chicago Fire at the end of her first season afloat. Thirteen years later, carrying a cargo of 575 tons of pig iron, she was wrecked after hitting a rock during an autumn storm ("Heavy weather, gale, snowstorm, high sea," according to the Wreck Report) at Baileys Harbor near the old lighthouse, and sinking in 15 feet of water. All eight men reached safety. The $2,000 cargo was fully insured, yet half of it was salvaged. The $10,000 vessel, insured for $8,000, was destroyed by subsequent storms. Her final enrollment was surrendered on Dec. 10, 1884. This ship's name has been misspelled more than any other vessel's, with variations like Christina, Christine,

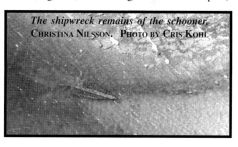

The shipwreck remains of the schooner, CHRISTINA NILSSON. PHOTO BY CRIS KOHL

Nilson, Nilsson, Nelson, Neilson and others being so rampant that even the *Chicago Inter Ocean* once quipped that, "The schooner *Christine Nilsson* has a bad list. The painter has spelled her name this season with one s."

J. E. Bailey (October 8, 1884)

The press, on October 16, 1884, quoted a captain as reporting that "the wrecking tug *Leviathan* was lying at Northport Tuesday, being unable to work on the schooner *J. E. Bailey*, ashore at Gill's Pier, on account of the unfavorable weather," and the next day, "The schooner *J. E. Bailey*, ashore at Gill's Pier, was today abandoned to the underwriters. She was insured for $5,000." A year-end report states that the 196-ton, twin-masted *J. E. Bailey* (130' x 26' x 10', official #75646, built in 1874 at Saugatuck, Michigan) was worth $6,666 at the time of her total loss, while her uninsured cargo of wood was valued at $500.

Ellen Couture **(August 4, 1885)** -- See Chapter 21, pages 169 to 172.

Lilly Hamilton (August 21, 1885)

This Canadian, 320.78-ton, three-masted schooner (137' x 26'2" x 11'1", official #71271, Canadian), built at Port Burwell, Ontario, on Lake Erie, by George Pontine and launched on April 25, 1874, carried 680 tons of salt from Kincardine, Ontario, for Milwaukee when she sprang a leak and foundered in heavy seas 20 miles southeast of Cana Island. The crew escaped in their yawl and were picked up by a passing steamer. The insured ship and cargo were worth $10,000 ($6,000 for the ship, $4,000 for the cargo).

Cecilia (September 8, 1885)

Off Jacksonport, riding out a storm with her anchors slipping, this three-masted, 175.82-ton schooner (118'2" x 25'7" x 8'4") was blown on shore and wrecked. Her rigging and equipment were stripped. She was built originally as a bark in 1868 at White Lake, Michigan.

Emma Leighton (September 8, 1885)

Built in 1867 at Port Huron, Michigan, this 82-ton scow schooner was struck by a storm and blown ashore from her moorings at Rowleys Bay.

Japan (October 19, 1885) -- See Chapter 3, pages 75-78.

F. J. King (September 15, 1886) -- See Chapter 13, pages 135-138.

Quickstep (October 6, 1886)

This 65.7-ton schooner, built in 1868 at Little Bay de Noc, Michigan, hit a rock at the entrance to Washington Island's Detroit Harbor and sank. The rigging was saved.

William L. Brown (October 21, 1886)

Launched in 1872 at Oshkosh, Wisconsin, as the *Neptune* (and receiving its new name in 1880), this 336.10-ton wooden steamer (140' x 28' x 13') sprang a leak and foundered with its 550 tons of iron ore cargo but no lives lost about one mile from Peshtigo Reef in Green Bay. The engine, boiler, anchors and chain were salvaged from the 80-foot depth, and the remains (masts, propeller tips, wooden railings, bilge pumps and other artifacts) attract divers to this site. The wreck of the *William L. Brown* was located in about 1970 by diver Frank Hoffman. Visibility in this orange-colored water is usually only 4 to 8 feet.

Detroit (November 7, 1886)

A Duluth newspaper called the *Detroit* "another instance of a weak, unseaworthy craft foundering..., because having been caught in a heavy sea, her seams opened and she sank, affording her crew barely time enough to get off in the yawl boat." The 319-ton schooner *Detroit* (139'6" x 23' 3" x 11', official #157157) was wrecked in a storm on a reef off Summer Island with an iron ore cargo bound from Escanaba to Cleveland. Built by the famous Canadian shipbuilder, Louis Shickluna, for Mr. John Battle at St. Catharines, Ontario, in 1872 as a bark named the *Mary Battle* (official Canadian #85418), she changed owners and was renamed under unusual circumstances, summarized by the *Detroit Free Press* on Tuesday, November 9, 1886:

> ...In the fall of 1884 she was wrecked on Keewenaw Point, Lake Superior, and abandoned to the insurance companies. Capt. Murphy took the contract to release her but was not successful until the spring of 1885, when the *Battle* was towed to a port of safety. For his trouble and expense the plucky wrecker was given the vessel as compensation. The *Battle* being a total construction loss was rebuilt and enrolled as an American bottom, when she was christened *Detroit*....

Capt. S. A. Murphy, a Detroit salvager, was described by that newspaper as "one vessel owner on the chain of lakes [who] has had more than his share of ill-luck" because "his fleet of tugs and sailing craft have met with more mishaps than usually falls to the lot of one owner." His last schooner, *Detroit,* reportedly sank in 125 feet of water off Summer Island.

Union (November 10, 1886)

Built at Sheboygan, Wisconsin, in 1867, this 52-ton schooner (59' x 15' x 6') sprang a leak and was driven ashore in a storm between Eagle Harbor and Sister Bay.

James Reid (June 12, 1887)

This wooden tug (90' x 17'4" x 8'7"), built as the *General Burnside* at Sandusky, Ohio, in 1867, and renamed in 1882, burned to a total loss on a shoal in Sturgeon Bay. After the engine, shaft and other parts were removed, the hull was scuttled in Green Bay.

Frank D. Barker (September 27, 1887)

Thick weather caused this ship to run aground on Spider Island near Rowleys Bay. Intense salvage efforts for over a year failed to release this cargoless vessel before she was thrown onto her beam ends by heavy seas which tore her decks loose and broke off her cabin. This 290-ton schooner (137' x 26' x 11') was built in Clayton, New York, in 1867.

Blazing Star (November 10, 1887)

In clear weather, this 265-ton schooner (137' x 26' x 10') somehow stranded on Fisherman's Shoal near Washington Island. Jettisoning much of the lumber cargo failed to free the ship. Built by H. Burger at Manitowoc in 1873, she was stripped and abandoned in 1888.

Sophia Lawrence (November 21, 1887)

This small, 20-ton scow, built only five years earlier in Menominee, left Egg Harbor with a cargo of wood, but strong winds forced her ashore where she broke in two.

Fleetwing (September 26, 1888) -- See Chapter 14, pages 139-144.

H. S. Hubbell (November 13, 1888)

A wooden steamer built at Lorain, Ohio, in 1882, this ship (142' x 30' x 11') caught fire at 5:00 A.M. off Poverty Island while enroute from Chicago to Manistique. A kerosene lamp in the cook's galley had exploded. The crew abandoned ship "while the vessel drifted on her way ablaze from end to end." They were later picked up by the steamer, *New Orleans*. The 398.76-ton *Hubbell*, owned in Chicago and valued at $36,000, was insured for $24,000.

Erastus Corning (May 21, 1889) -- See Chapter 15, pages 145-146.

James Garrett (May 30, 1889)

This three-masted, 266-ton schooner (138' x 27' x 9'), built in 1868 by Stokes in Sheboygan, Wisconsin, picked up 200 cords of wood at the Lily Bay pier. Suddenly a strong northeaster arose and stranded the ship; months later, the wreck was swept out into the lake.

Kittie Laurie (August 9, 1889)

This small, uninsured, 13-ton schooner (39' x 12' x 5'6"), built by Robert Laurie at Green Bay in 1872, stranded two miles north of Ephraim and broke up. No lives were lost.

W. C. Tillson (October 30, 1889)

Fire destroyed this 49.44-ton tug (53'6" x 15'7" x 7', official #80599) about one mile from the mouth of Sturgeon Bay as the ship towed two log rafts from Peshtigo to Sturgeon Bay. This vessel had been constructed in 1876 at Sheboygan, Wisconsin, by Charles Huntley.

A. S. Piper (October 14, 1890)

This 21-ton tug (54' x 12') burned to a total loss off Sturgeon Bay's upper mill pier. Built in 1880 in Milwaukee, this tug was reported still visible at the head of the bay in 1904.

Forest (October 28, 1891) -- See Chapter 4, pages 79 to 92.

Myra (October 30, 1891)

The 17-ton tug (52' x 14' x 3'9"), built in 1884 at Menominee, burned at Little Sturgeon.

L. C. Butts (November 1, 1891)

Built at East Saginaw, Michigan, by T. Arnold in 1872, this large, 769-ton, three-masted schooner (173' x 32' x 19') was run aground just off the east side of Washington Island after she sprang a leak in a storm. The vessel was stripped of her canvas and rigging before she broke in half. The *Marine Review* of November 12, 1891, wrote that the ship and her cargo of 1,200 tons of coal were " a total loss... insured for $10,000." Locals recovered some coal.

E. P. Ross (November 15, 1891)

This 28-ton tug, built in 1874 at Buffalo, broke away from her mooring during a storm and stranded in Sawyer Harbor. Settled in eight feet of water, her boiler was later salvaged.

Newsboy (November 17, 1891)

This old three-masted schooner turned into a schooner-barge (152'2" x 31'4" x 12'8") was built in 1862 during the Civil War at Saginaw, Michigan, by Kirby & Hoyt. This ship stranded during a storm on Fisherman's Shoal near Rock Island with 54,000 bushels of corn, all of which was lost. The crew barely escaped. Martin Knudsen, the lighthouse keeper at Pilot Island, wrote a letter to the *Door County Advocate* claiming that the loss of the *Newsboy* showed the desperate need for a lifesaving station at Death's Door. This led to the establishment of the Plum Island Life-Saving Station in 1895.

H. W. Scove (December 5, 1891) -- See Chapter 4, pages 79 to 92.

Ira Chaffee (1892) -- See Chapter 30, pages 235-250.

Laurel (March 12, 1892)

Built in 1852 at Blasten Bend, Ohio, this 62-ton scow schooner (80' x 20' x 5') was blown by strong gales high onto the beach at Washington Island. Her last owner reportedly planned to burn this old, wooden ship to salvage the iron, "of which there are many tons."

James E. Gilmore (October 16, 1892) -- See Chapter 4, pages 79 to 92.

A. P. Nichols (October 28, 1892) -- See Chapter 4, pages 79 to 92.

Petrel (November 5, 1892)

This schooner (79' x 15' x 5'), built in 1864 at Pultneyville, NY, and valued at $1,000 in 1892, was wrecked at Anderson's Pier near Monument Pt. at the mouth of Sturgeon Bay.

Veto (November 5, 1892)

Built 13 years earlier at Egg Harbor, this 56-ton schooner (92' x 16' x 5') dragged her anchor and stranded there to become a total wreck, her crew barely surviving.

J. K. Stack (April 12, 1893)

Ice crushed this very small, 12.26-ton schooner (32'9" x 10'4" x 4'), which was built in 1875 at Escanaba, Michigan, while in winter lay-up at Eagle Harbor in Ephraim.

Sassacus (September 29, 1893)

Stranded near Jacksonport in a wild storm on Sept. 29th, this 109-ton scow schooner (94'7" x 22'3" x 6'7") was pulled off, but capsized on Oct. 8th and came ashore about two miles north of the Ship Canal entrance. This vessel was built in 1867 at Oswego, New York.

Windsor (September 30, 1893) -- See Chapter 16, pages 147-150.

Willard A. Smith (October 14, 1893) -- See Chapter 21, pages 169-172.

A. Travis (November 18, 1893)

Built in 1867 at Pentwater, Michigan, this 101-ton schooner (106' x 20' x 6') stranded at North Point near Cana Island, the Sturgeon Bay Life-Saving team rescuing the crew.

E. P. Royce (November 26, 1893) -- See Chapter 16, pages 147-150.

South Side (December 9, 1893)

This 139-ton scow schooner (101' x 25' x 5'), heading to Milwaukee with a cargo of wooden ties and Christmas trees, sprang a leak and took refuge at Baileys Harbor, where she sank and broke up before she could be recovered. She was built in 1867 at Milwaukee.

L. May Guthrie (September 26, 1894)

Fisherman's Shoal claimed this 137-ton schooner (102' x 24' x 7'; built in 1874 at Conneaut, Ohio), while her crew, with some difficulty, and her cargo of bark were removed.

J. H. Johnson (May 1, 1895)

A dangerous rock just four feet below the surface at Sister Shoals near the Sister Islands impaled this 66-ton tug (98'5" x 16'3" x 4'), which had been built in 1882 at St. Joseph, Michigan. The cabin and hay cargo washed ashore; the engine and boiler were salvaged.

Mariner (July 10, 1895)

This old, 30-ton schooner (52' x 15' x 5'; built in Ohio City, Ohio, in 1854) became waterlogged and was run onto Green Island; the lumber cargo and rigging were salvaged.

E. R. Williams (September 22, 1895) -- See Chapter 17, pages 151-156.

Otter (October 10, 1895) -- See Chapter 18, pages 157-158.

Red, White and Blue (October 12, 1895) -- See Chapter 22, pages 173-178.

Mystic (October 15, 1895) -- See Chapter 4, pages 79 to 92.

Mattie C. Bell (November 27, 1895)

Summer Island is where this large, 769-ton schooner (181' x 35'4" x 11'5", built in 1882 at Saginaw, Michigan) stranded in a snowstorm 200 feet from shore just north of the east point while in tow of the steamer, *Jim Sheriffs*. The tug, *A. J. Wright*, according to the *Detroit Free Press* in September, 1896, "...has been working on the stranded craft since last June, but was finally compelled to give up the job, having stripped her of everything. All the coal was taken off her. She evidently has a large rock through the middle of her bottom...."

Fountain City (May 5, 1896) -- See Chapter 30, pages 235-250.

Emeline (August 8, 1896)

This 170-ton schooner (115' x 22' x 7'), built in 1862 at Vicksburg, Michigan (this town was later renamed Marysville so as not to confuse it with the Vicksburg which lies just south of Kalamazoo), capsized off Baileys Harbor, where the crew landed in their yawl. The schooner was towed to that port, where she eventually sank and broke in two, the bow half remaining in 21 feet of water at Anclam's Pier and the stern settling 600 feet north.

Australasia (October 17, 1896) -- See Chapter 19, pages 159-162.

Alleghany (October 29, 1896)

Often misspelled *Allegheny*, this 402-ton steamer (167' x 29' x 14'), built in 1856 at Milwaukee, stranded in a storm on Summer Island along with the *Transfer*, the barge she was towing. Both vessels, sailing light, ended up near the wreck of the *Mattie C. Bell*. The ship was recovered, but was so badly damaged that she was burned for her iron. The *Alleghany* was reportedly the first propeller-driven steamer built at Milwaukee.

Transfer (October 29, 1896)

This 360-ton schooner-barge (142'8" x 28'4" x 10'6") stranded on Summer Island along with her towing steamer, the *Alleghany*. The *Detroit Free Press* on October 31, 1896, reported that, "...It is a bad spot and the wrecks may stay there." The *Transfer*, which had been built in 1874 at Grand Haven, Michigan, broke up at that site the next year.

Success (November 26, 1896)

A daring rescue by four men in their fishing boat saved the crew of this 151-ton scow schooner (104' x 26' x 7') when it stranded in a storm in shallow water a mile north of the Whitefish Bay pier. The *Success*, built in 1875 at Manitowoc, was a total loss.

Alfred Mosher (May 16, 1897) -- See Chapter 30, pages 235-250.

Agnes Arnold (May 30, 1898)

This 30-ton tug (68'4" x 13' x 5'4"), formerly the *Bob Mills* when built at Buffalo, New York, in 1864, burned to a total loss at Chambers Island. She was valued at $3,000.

Keystone (September 12, 1898)

A northwest gale stranded this large, 722-ton steamer (163'9" x 34'4" x 11'3"; built in 1880 at Buffalo, New York) on Summer Island, where it caught on fire and burned to a complete loss. It was valued at $15,000 and insured, and the coal cargo was salvaged.

Annie Dall (October 18, 1898)

Launched as the *Mary* in 1848 at Milan, Ohio, this two-masted, 149.53-ton schooner (110'9" x 24'6" x 7'7") was renamed the *Annie Dall* after a complete rebuild at Chicago in 1883. She stranded on the beach near Jacksonport on Oct. 18th and was pulled off on Oct. 24th, only to capsize two miles off shore, a total loss. Her remains reportedly washed ashore.

Harry Johnson (October 24, 1898)

This unrigged and undocumented barge broke loose from the tug, *Wright*, in the same gale which wrecked the *Annie Dall*. The barge stranded and broke up in Rock Island Passage.

M. Capron (October 31, 1898)

Built at Conneaut, Ohio, in 1875, this 169-ton schooner (116'4" x 22'5" x 8'9") was blown onto the beach at Baileys Harbor and wrecked, almost taking another ship with her.

C. Harrison (October 31, 1898)

Strong winds at Whitefish Bay stranded and broke up this old, two-masted schooner (93'9" x 23'9" x 8'1"; built in 1854 at Milwaukee). Her last owner had paid $50 for her.

Joys (December 24, 1898) -- See Chapter 30, pages 235-250.

O. M. Nelson (June 4, 1899) -- See Chapter 4, pages 79 to 92.

Emmanuel (December, 1899)

Built at Fish Creek in 1890, this 23-ton scow schooner (65' x13'8" x 4'3") was purposely stranded by her owner and dismantled for her iron components because she sailed poorly.

Sardinia (July 6, 1900) -- See Chapter 3, pages 75-78.

Farrand H. Williams (September 11, 1900) -- See Chapter 21, pages 169-172.

Boaz (November 9, 1900)

This three-masted, 127-ton schooner (118'9" x 22' x 7'), built in 1869 at Sheboygan, Wisconsin, took shelter at North Bay near Baileys Harbor. The crew and the elm lumber cargo were removed before the ship sank. Today she lies broken in 15 feet of water.

Pankratz Barge #2 (November 10, 1900)

This 6-month-old unrigged barge, bult by Rieboldt and Wolter at Sturgeon Bay and owned by the George Pankratz Lumber Company, sank in the Ship Canal. The Life Saving Station Wreck Report provides details (original spelling and grammar retained):

> ...At 5:30 o'clock P.M. the tug *Duncan City* was comming out through the Canal with a flat scow in tow loaded with 150 cords of stones. While almost to the station, the port tow line parted and the current in the Canal was running very swift... the pull came on the starboard quarter of the Scow and she sheerd of in to the rivetment of

the canal by the station, stowed in her bow and sunk at once in the canal, the 3 men on the Scow steped of on to the Dock, it was nothing to do at this time for the Scow was under the water, and had blocked the Navigation altogether, it was then necessary to lookout for other Crafts not to enter the Canal.... On the 24th we assisted in removing part of the stones forward on the Scow which was above the wreck, on the 26th we again assisted the government officials at the wreck with our small boat in running wires and Dynamite for to blow the Scow to pieces and the Dredges did the rest of the work.

This barge was valued at $7,500, and the 150 cords of stone at $850.

William Finch (November 14, 1900)

Built at Grand Haven, Michigan, in 1878, this small, 49-ton, twin-masted schooner (68' x 17'3" x 5'2") was wrecked on the shore at Egg Harbor by a northwest gale.

Mary Mills (December 12, 1900) -- See Chapter 30, pages 235-250.

Peoria (November 10, 1901)

The schooner *Peoria*, having recovered from her stranding at Baileys Harbor during the Big Blow of 1880, stranded for good and broke up there more than two decades later. Built at Black River (Lorain), Ohio, in 1854, this ship measured 112'1" x 24'3" x 8'8".

Pride (November 22, 1901)

This 83-ton, three-masted schooner (87' x 26' x 6'), built in 1849 at Sandusky, Ohio, stranded in Washington Harbor with a cargo of wood and potatoes. The old ship was frozen on the rocks that winter, and later broke up and sank to a depth of 60' in the harbor.

J. S. Williams (May, 1902) -- See Chapter 30, pages 235-250.

Cleveland (June, 1902) -- See Chapter 30, pages 235-250.

The dramatic wreck of the schooner, Pride, in Washington Harbor. Cris Kohl Collection

Thomas C. Wilson (November, 1902)

Strong winds destroyed this 30-ton schooner (58'5" x 15'4" x 5') at Egg Harbor. The remains of this ship (which was built in 1868 at Black River, Ohio) were used as firewood.

Bay State (April, 1903) -- See Chapter 30, pages 235-250.

Kate Hinchman (Spring, 1903) -- See Chapter 30, pages 235-250.

Erie L. Hackley (October 3, 1903) -- See Chapter 20, pages 163-168.

H. W. Sage (October 4, 1903)

Carrying a heavy iron ore cargo from Escanaba while being towed by the steamer, *Samoa*, this huge, 848-ton schooner-barge (202' x 36' x 13') sank off Poverty Island in a storm. The steamer saved the crew. The *Sage* had been built in 1875 at Bangor, Michigan.

Leo (1904) -- See Chapter 30, pages 235-250.

Dan Hayes (1905) -- See Chapter 30, pages 235-250.

Ebenezer (1905)

Built in Ephraim n 1890, this small, 39-ton, three-masted schooner (57' x 15'5" x 5'5") was stripped and abandoned after sitting on the shore at Ephraim for some time.

Iver Lawson **(October 19, 1905)** -- See Chapter 21, pages 169-172.

Foam **(October 26, 1905)**

One of the severe fall storms of 1905 stranded and wrecked this 42-ton scow-schooner (81'4" x 18'6" x 4'6"; built in 1882 at Menekaunee, Wisconsin) at Little Sturgeon Bay.

Charley J. Smith **(October 28, 1905)** -- See Chapter 30, pages 235-250.

R. J. Hackett **(November 12, 1905)** -- See Chapter 22, pages 173-178.

Cecilia Hill **(1906)** -- See Chapter 30, pages 235-250.

George Presley **(June 18, 1906)** -- See Chapter 30, pages 235-250.

Nellie and Annie **(November 21, 1906)**

This one ship named after two ladies was a scow schooner (67'3" x 17'6" x 4'4") built at Chicago in 1872. A storm washed the ship ashore and wrecked it at Sawyer Harbor.

John M. Nichol **(December 13, 1906)**

A blizzard stranded this large, wooden freighter (263' x 41'6" x 15'7") on Summer Island, where the 2,126-ton ship broke in two and became a total loss. The *Toledo Blade* of December 17, 1906, reported on the rescue:

> ...They [the crew] suffered terribly from exposure and several of them had badly frozen hands and feet. Two fishermen in a small gasoline launch made a thrilling and spectacular rescue of the 19 members of the crew Friday when the entire after end of the *Nicol* was torn away and the forward part was threatening to go to pieces any moment. The crew saved nothing but the clothing they wore....

The 2,500 tons of barbed wire cargo were salvaged the following March (during which a hardhat diver nearly lost his life), and "land pirates" stripped the ship clean. This ship was launched on December 31, 1888, at West Bay City, Michigan, by F. W. Wheeler & Company.

Romuldus **(August, 1907)**

This 9-ton schooner (42' x 11'4" x 4'2"), built in 1897 at North Muskegon, Michigan, was abandoned and allowed to sink in the mud at Baileys Harbor.

Kate Williams **(September, 1907)**

This 165-ton tugboat (112'6" x 20'9" x 9'8") sank in Jackson Harbor at Washington Island, and the next year was spent in well-documented and oft-photographed salvage efforts which recovered the machinery and boiler, but the hull was a total loss. The ship was built in 1862 at Cleveland, Ohio.

S. B. Paige **(September 10, 1907)**

Northwest winds stranded this ship on the middle ground in Sturgeon Bay where it became a total loss. This 47-ton schooner (79' x 20' x 4'5") was built in 1863 at Oshkosh.

Anspatch **(February 19, 1908)**

This 15-ton tug (45'3" x 12'3" x 5'3"), built at Detroit in 1879, was blown by a blizzard onto ice, punctured and sunk at the mouth of Sturgeon Bay. Two crew were reported lost.

Seaman **(November 15, 1908)** -- See Chapter 4, pages 79 to 92.

Berwyn **(November 23, 1908)** -- See Chapter 5, pages 93 to 98.

German **(November 28, 1908)** -- See Chapter 30, pages 235-250.

Mary L. **(December 5, 1908)**

This 13-year-old, 28-ton schooner (62' x 17' x 4'7") was punctured by ice and towed into the shallows on Sturgeon Bay's west side equidistant from the bayside Ship Canal entrance and the city. The vessel burned there in July, 1910, the fire accidentally set by local boys using the ship as a clubhouse. The *Mary L.* was built in 1895 at White Lake, Michigan.

The schooner, MADONNA, (left) *at Sheboygan.*
COURTESY OF HENRY BARKHAUSEN

Madonna (January, 1909)

This graceful schooner had seen better days when her captain decided to remove the cabin for use as a workshop and burn the rest of the ship at Washington Island. This 76-ton vessel (79'8" x 24'4" x 6'2") was built in 1871 at Milwaukee.

Lilly Amiot (June 6, 1909)

Ship explosions were rare, but when a vessel was loaded with considerable dynamite and dozens of barrels of gasoline, and her owner lit a match to find a leak, the unimaginable happened. The ship first caught on fire quickly and was cut away from the pier at Ellison Bay. Two hours later, it exploded on the west side of the bay, hurtling a blazing barrel high into the air with a noise heard 15 miles away. Miraculously, no one was injured. This 25-ton gas launch (47'4" x 12'4" x 4'7") was built as a schooner in 1873 at Cheboygan, Michigan.

Elva (July 24, 1911)

Built at Port Huron, Michigan, in 1862, this 69.35-ton schooner (86'9" x 19' x 6') stranded and was wrecked at Sturgeon Bay.

Sanilac (December, 1911) -- See Chapter 30, pages 235-250.

Mishicott (January 26, 1912) -- See Chapter 30, pages 235-250.

Spatula (August 12, 1912)

This wooden gas launch, about 40 feet long, burned to a total loss at the Fish Creek dock. The commodore of the Green Bay Yacht Club owned this $2,000 vessel.

D. F. Rose (September, 1912) -- See Chapter 30, pages 235-250.

Minnie Warren (November, 1912) -- See Chapter 30, pages 235-250.

Iris (March, 1913)

After stranding at Jackson Harbor on Washington Island, this 62-ton, two-masted schooner (74' x 19'2" x 6'6"; built at Port Huron, MI, in 1866) was stripped and abandoned.

Grace (August 22, 1913)

This seven-ton gas screw boat, built in 1901, stranded at North Bay.

C. C. Hand (October 6, 1913) -- See Chapter 23, pages 179-182.

Louisiana (November 8, 1913) -- See Chapter 24, pages 183-196.

Plymouth (November 8, 1913) -- See Chapter 24, pages 183-196.

Pewaukee (November 10, 1913) -- See Chapter 30, pages 235-250.

Joseph L. Hurd (November 10, 1913) -- See Chapter 30, pages 235-250.

Emma Bloeker **(April, 1914)** -- See Chapter 30, pages 235-250.

James H. Martin **(April, 1914)** -- See Chapter 24, pages 183-196, and Chapter 30, pages 235-250.

Oneida **(April, 1914)** -- See Chapter 30, pages 235-250.

Resumption **(November 7, 1914)** -- See Chapter 5, pages 93 to 98.

Myron Butman **(November 19, 1914)** -- See Chapter 30, pages 235-250.

Torrent **(March, 1915)**
This tug, after failing inspection, was stripped and prepared for scuttling in Lake Michigan. The 203-ton ship (115' x 21'2" x 12'3") was built in 1869 at Cleveland by Elihu Peck.

Robert Holland **(May 11, 1915)** -- See Chapter 30, pages 235-250.

Peter Coates **(June 17, 1915)** -- See Chapter 30, pages 235-250.

Pup **(July 19, 1915)**
With her machinery removed and used as a barge, this 13-ton fish tug (45' x 11'8" x 4'6"); built at Saugatuck, Michigan, in 1894) sprang a leak and sank with 20 bags of cement off Washington Island while being towed from Washington Harbor to West Harbor.

Starlight **(November 12, 1915)**
Fire broke out on this gas-powered schooner carrying farm produce from Sister Bay to Menominee. Near Chambers Island, the crew abandoned the sinking ship in their yawl boat. This 31-ton vessel (60' x 15') was built in 1897 at South Haven, Michigan.

City of Glasgow **(October 6, 1917)** -- See Chapter 25, pages 197-200.

Eddie **(April, 1918)** -- See Chapter 30, pages 235-250.

Libby Nau **(June, 1918)** -- See Chapter 30, pages 235-250.

Frank O'Connor **(October 2, 1919)** -- See Chapter 26, pages 201-218.

Coller **(January 19, 1921)**
This fish tug broke away from her dock at Jacksonport and washed ashore, a total loss.

Advance **(October 19, 1921)** -- See Chapter 30, pages 235-250.

W. H. Meyer **(August, 1922)** -- See Chapter 30, pages 235-250.

Vermillion **(August, 1922)** -- See Chapter 30, pages 235-250.

G. M. A. Herrmann **(September, 1922)** -- See Chapter 30, pages 235-250.

Lakeland **(December 3, 1924)** -- See Chapter 27, pages 219-222.

I. N. Foster **(1927)** -- See Chapter 30, pages 235-250.

Frances IV **(August 6, 1927)**
Three people lost their lives when this 65-foot-long, Canadian motor yacht, in a fleet from the Chicago Yacht Club cruising to Georgian Bay, Ontario, suddenly exploded four miles off Horseshoe Bay. The ship burned for two hours prior to sinking.

Cynthie **(September 19, 1928)**
Two of the three men died on this 8-ton, gasoline-powered fish tug (27'5" x 8'8" x 3'3"; built at 1907 at Sturgeon Bay) when it burned and sank five miles off Sherwood Point.

Leila C. **(October 3, 1928)** -- See Chapter 4, pages 79 to 92.

Michael J. Bartelme **(October 4, 1928)** -- See Chapter 28, pages 223-228.

Coila (March 10, 1929)

Stranded at Jacksonport, this six-ton, gas screw boat (29' x 8' x 3'6"), built in 1902 at Manitowoc, Wisconsin, was a total loss. No lives were lost.

Pathfinder (March 10, 1929)

Launched as the *Minnie R.* in 1905 at Manitowoc, Wisconsin, this ten-ton gas screw boat (32'2" x 9' x 3') stranded at Baileys Harbor and became a total loss.

Adriatic (1930) -- See Chapter 30, pages 235-250.

Cabot Brothers (October 25, 1930)

Built at Sturgeon Bay in 1902 as the *Johanna W.*, this 11-ton gas screw boat (30'2" x 9'2" x 3'6") burned to a complete loss at Sawyer, across from Sturgeon Bay.

Oak Leaf (1928) -- See Chapter 30, pages 235-250.

Ida Corning (1928) -- See Chapter 30, pages 235-250.

Empire State (1929) -- See Chapter 30, pages 235-250.

Alice B. Norris (1932)

Abandoned in Sturgeon Bay since 1927, this old schooner was raised and towed to Summer Island by Capt. John Roen and sunk as a breakwater. This large, 692-ton, three-masted ship (194' x 32'4" x 31'2"), built in Milwaukee by Wolf & Davidson in 1872, was named by a Milwaukee ship chandlery and vessel owner after his eldest daughter (1852-1922), who was then in her second year of a 42-year school teaching career.

Georgia (June 13, 1932)

Launched as the *City of Ludington* at Manitowoc, Wisconsin, on September 4, 1880, and renamed *Georgia* in 1898, this 895-ton ship (195'7" x 34'4" x 12') spent nearly five decades conveying excursionists between Chicago and Mackinac Island, with numerous stops at Door County ports along the way. The ship, idle at Sturgeon Bay since 1926, was dismantled in 1930-1931 (for example, her lifeboats were sold to individuals as pleasure craft, and her cabin was cut off and used as a store) and, on June 13, 1932, the hull was raised and towed to Summer Island and sunk for use as a breakwater.

Nyack (1933)

The hulk of this wooden ship was sunk next to the *Georgia* at Summer Island for use as a breakwater and dock. The 1,188-ton *Nyack* (231' x 33' x 14'7"; official #130125), was launched on May 28, 1878, at Buffalo, New York, and worked as a passenger and freight steamer. While at Muskegon, Michigan, being rebuilt, the ship burned on December 30, 1915. The hull, towed to Sturgeon Bay, was partially rebuilt in 1918, but lay idle in the bone yard there for several years before being formally abandoned on February 1, 1933.

Mueller (September, 1933) -- See Chapter 30, pages 235-250.

Captain Lawrence (September 19, 1933) -- See Chapter 29, pages 229-234.

North Shore (1934) -- See Chapter 30, pages 235-250.

Mary Ellen Cook (February 27, 1934) -- See Chapter 30, pages 235-250.

Halsted (1934) -- See Chapter 30, pages 235-250.

Wisconsin (1935)

Launched as the *F. and P. M. No. 1* (Flint and Pere Marquette -- a railroad) in 1882 at Detroit, and renamed the *Wisconsin* in 1906, this wooden steamer was abandoned at Chicago in 1912, but was converted into a barge in 1914 and, in 1918, rigged as a 556-ton schooner-barge (187' x 30'5" x 12'2"). She was burned to her waterline as a spectacle for many paying customers in 1935 just north of Green Island where she sank in 85 feet of water.

Lucia A. Simpson **(December 3, 1935)** -- See Chapter 30, pages 235-250.

E. G. Crosby **(December 3, 1935)** -- See Chapter 30, pages 235-250.

Swift **(December 3, 1935)** -- See Chapter 30, pages 235-250.

Petoskey **(December 3, 1935)** -- See Chapter 30, pages 235-250.

Beaver **(December 3, 1935)** -- See Chapter 30, pages 235-250.

Waukegan **(December 3, 1935)** -- See Chapter 30, pages 235-250.

Kenosha **(December 3, 1935)** -- See Chapter 30, pages 235-250.

Leathem D. Smith **(1942)** -- See Chapter 30, pages 235-250.

Reliance **(December 11, 1943)**
This overloaded fish tug (31'2" x 9'5" x 4') disappeared in a huge storm with all three hands somewhere in Lake Michigan while heading from Death's Door across the lake.

Nauti-Girl **(August 26, 1945)**
This 50-foot power boat began sinking in strong gales a mile off shore south of Cana Island. All on board barely reached land. The ship sank, but washed ashore and broke up.

Pup **(November 25, 1946)**
This 8-ton fish tug sank in 40 to 50 feet of water during strong gales while anchored off the northeast corner of Summer Island after taking hunters to the island.

America **(May 5, 1950)**
A storm reportedly sank this 13-ton boat in the lake five miles off Sturgeon Bay.

Anabel II **(January 12, 1952)**
This 62-ton fish tug (58' 9" x 15' x 6'3"; official #228126), built in 1928 at Manitowoc, Wisconsin, burned to a total loss at the Roen Steamship Company Dock at Sturgeon Bay.

Bridgebuilder X **(December 18, 1959)**
Built in 1911 at Lorain, Ohio, as the steel-hulled fish tug *Pittsburgh*, renamed *Bide-A Wee* in 1939 and used as a Soo Locks tour boat, then renamed *Bridgebuilder X* in 1956 (because the boat was used for the Mackinac Bridge construction), this 46-ton vessel (61' x 16' x 7'2") foundered somewhere in Lake Michigan while enroute from Sturgeon Bay to South Fox Island. Both men on board perished.

Part of the ROEN BARGE *wreck site.*
PHOTO BY KIM BRUNGRABER

Roen Salvage Barge **(October 20, 1969)**
Towed by the tug, *John Purves*, this barge, loaded with 60 tons of construction equipment, was bound for Rogers City, Michigan, when it leaked and sank three miles south of Poverty Island in 110 feet of water just inside the Michigan state line.

Buccaneer **(July 1, 1981)**
This $10,000 catamaran houseboat sank in 100 feet of water four miles off Egg Harbor while heading to Menominee. The two people on board were rescued by the Coast Guard.

Eagle **(September 3, 1984)**
Perhaps as a stroke of supernatural retribution, the boat which diver Frank Hoffman used to locate numerous shipwrecks itself became a shipwreck when strong gales stranded and broke up the 32-foot-long, twin-engined, steel-hulled vessel on St. Martin Island.

Death's Door
Flotsam and Jetsam

News accounts of maritime mishaps and miscellaneous nautical events of the Death's Door region, interesting incidents and amusing anecdotes which did not necessarily result in permanent shipwrecks, would fill hundreds of pages. This random selection of some of those accounts provides a better idea of this region's maritime character:

SHIP BUILDING IN DOOR COUNTY.---

Mr. David Clow, from Chamber's Island, was in town a few days since, and gave us the dimensions of the largest vessel yet built in door county, which he is building at Chamber's Island, measuring 120 ft. keel; 27 ft. breadth of beam; 10 ft. depth of hold. She is to be rigged as a fore and aft schooner, and will be ready to go into the grain or lumber trade in May. We wish the vessel and its worthy builder every success in so commendable an enterprise, and as there is an abundance of all kinds of valuable ship timber in Door county, we hope to see this branch of industry increase, and flourish.

--- *Door County Advocate*, **Sat., March 22, 1862 (this was the very first issue of that newspaper, and the ship in the story was the** *Sarah Clow*; **capitalization and punctuation remain intact, as in all of these articles)**

The sailors on the schooner *J. H. Mead* have quit the vessel at Sturgeon Bay, declaring that they will not risk their lives on the craft.
--- *Cleveland Herald*, **December 2, 1881**

The diminutive schooner *Schlitz Global*, built at the expense of the Milwaukee brewing firm for Capt. Adolphe Fritsche to sail around the world and advertise beer with, got as far as Sturgeon Bay, Wis., and lies there, sunk.
--- *Detroit Free Press*, **May 6, 1899**

The tug *Protection* reached here yesterday morning with the schooner *Mary L. Higgie*, which she succeeded in releasing from Fisherman's Shoal, and is towing to Chicago. Nearly all the vessel's canvas has been used for jackets, which cover her bottom from stem to stern, and yet the constant services of a steampump are required to keep down the water.

--- *Milwaukee Sentinel,* **December 8, 1875**

FOUND.

On the beach, near Little Sturgeon Bay, a Scow; said scow is painted black, is 80 feet long, nineteen feet wide in the centre, and tapering to seventeen feet at the ends. She has a Capstan on one end.

Said scow is in the hands of the undersigned, at Little Sturgeon Bay, and, which will be delivered to the owner, upon proving property and paying charges.   JAS. C. GARDNER.

Little Sturgeon Bay, Door Co., Wis. June 21, 1862.

--- **classified ad in the** *Door County Advocate,* **June 28, 1862**

The crew of the tug *Leathem* captured two deer in the waters of Green Bay while the craft was off Horseshoe Bay one day last week.

--- *Door County Advocate,* **November 13, 1879**

The bottle imp is about again. A bottle was picked up on the shore of Green Bay with a paper inclosed, upon which was written the following: "Steamer *J. D. Martin*, milwaukee, Wis. We are sinking in Lake Michigan. Nine, full crew, all told. Boat cannot stand the weather; heavy northeast wind, and heavy sea running; must drown or swim." [Authors' note: There has never been a steamer named the *J. D. Martin* registered on the Great Lakes, so this was likely a prank.]

--- *Chicago Inter Ocean,* **May 20, 1882**

---The wind was on a regular rampage Thursday night and well calculated to make a sailor rejoice that he wasn't ashore exposed to the danger of falling chimney tops.

--- *Door County Advocate,* **February 9, 1871**

STURGEON BAY, WIS., April 18.--The ice in Green bay began moving last evening and the steamer *Rumbell,* Capt. E. B. Graham, got caught in the floe, and will likely be carried into Lake Michigan. Several "hookers" in Fish creek were also caught and will likely be ground to pieces. The ice is likely to do great damage to wharves and other shipping, as it is very thick and is moving rapidly.

--- *Detroit Free Press,* **April 19, 1899**

---One of the most miraculous escapes from death on record happened to a sailor on the schooner *Mystic Star* on Thursday while the vessel was off the Manitous---opposite Bailey's Harbor.--- The man was out on the jibboom when a tremendous sea washed him off. He was seen to fall, and the alarm given, but before any effort could be made to rescue him, another huge wave washed him so close to the stern of the vessel that he caught the boat tackle fall, which was thrown him, and he was pulled on board by his over-joyed shipmates in a "jiffy." It was a most providential escape.

--- *Door County Advocate,* **October 30, 1879**

Many of the large passenger vessels on the Great Lakes ended their season Tuesday due to the provision of the LaFollette Seamans act. The law provides that after Sept. 15 life boat space must be provided for every passenger and crew member of a lake vessel thus cutting down the passenger capacity.

--- *Door County Advocate,* **September 17, 1920 [This U.S. law came about as a result of the many lives lost due to insufficient lifeboats on board when a ship named *Titanic* sank in the Atlantic Ocean eight years earlier.]**

SCHOONER MAGIC OFF.--Mr. Braasch, the man who purchased the schooner *Magic* from the Underwriters as she laid upon the beach at Bailey's Harbor, got her off in six hours. Her injuries too are reported to be very light. That the insurance on the vessel was paid to the former owner is the wonder of all. We heard it passed around yesterday point blank that the vessel was sold. Mr. Braasch, the lucky purchaser of the wreck, will bring her to this port for repairs.--*Milwaukee Wisconsin*

--- *Detroit Advertiser & Tribune,* **May 27, 1870**

It is announced that the schooner *Nabob* has been released from Cana Island, and that she will soon be in Milwaukee, speedily repaired, and ready for commission again. It may be that she will bring a cargo of wood and posts from North Bay to Milwaukee. But Mr. Peacock, of Chicago, the former owner, refused, up to last night, to believe the vessel had been got off, saying such reports had often been in circulation before, and when the schooner *Alice M. Beers* passed Cana Island at 7 o'clock Tuesday morning, the *Nabob* was still ashore there and the *Leviathan* working at her. "If she is off," says Mr. Peacock, "it doesn't much concern me now. She is in the hands of the underwriters. I abandoned her last fall."

On the other hand, the underwriters say it does concern Mr. Peacock, because the vessel will be repaired and given back to him. Of the justice or equity of this course THE INTER OCEAN cannot speak. It is evident that there is to be more litigation.

--- *Chicago Inter Ocean,* **June 17, 1881**

The steamer *Northwest* came into our bay Saturday afternoon with a load of folks from Pensaukee and Oconto, accompanied by a brass band who blew brass right lustily. After a pic nic dinner at Sawyer's Harbor they steamed up to the town and stayed here long enough for the excursionists to "slop over" all through town. --- Fair women laughed loudly, talked muchly and threw missiles charmingly, while brave men did ditto.

--- *Door County Advocate,* **September 8, 1870**

...On December 5, 1903... *Ann Arbor No. 1,* en route to Menominee, encountered the steamer *J. Emory Owen* ablaze off the Sturgeon Bay ship canal. The ferry helped extinguish the fire and then towed the *Owen* to the canal, where the disabled ship shortly sank from the weight of water in her hold. The *J. Emory Owen* was salvaged and rebuilt as the *F. A. Meyer*.

--- from *The Great Lakes Car Ferries* by George W. Hilton

It will be remembered that in the fall of 1874, two men, Halley and Root, went out in their fishermen's boat and never returned. The oars, net boxes &c. coming ashore made it evident they were drowned during a terrible snow storm which arose soon after they went out. This occurred on Thursday, Nov. 12. Some weeks previous to this, on a Sunday evening, Halley had an altercation with a neighbor, who struck him with a stone on the head, injuring him so severly that he was partially insane at the time he went out in the boat. It is supposed by the people on the island, that had it not have been for Halley's partial insanity, the unfortunate men would have weathered the storm and returned safely to shore.

Soon after this disaster, a mysterious light was seen moving along near the ice on Thursday evening, followed again on Sunday evening. These lights appeared during the whole winter regularly on Thursday and Sunday evening, and occasionally during the summer, and have been seen every Thursday and Sunday night during the present winter. The light usually has the appearance of being at the mouth of the Harbor, about a mile to a mile and one-half away. It usually has the appearance of a lantern moving along, about as a man would carry it, sometimes moving along four or five miles, but usually passing back and forth over a space of about a mile near the bluff at the mouth of the harbor. Sometimes it will appear to flare up and look as large as a bushel basket, and again it will rush along at railroad speed for a mile or two. The light is usually a pure white light with never a halo. Wm. Betts pursued the light one night last winter. He left his house for the purpose, but he was unable to get any nearer than apparently one-half to one-fourth mile of it, when he went fast the light moved faster and as he slacked his pace the light would follow suit. Finally it turned and moved off toward St. Martin's Island, and led him on to such poor ice that he could not follow it further.

Now the mystery about this is; its appearing on Thursday and Sunday nights, the one the day of the week on which Halley was hurt and the other on which he and his companion were drowned, and its being seen in winter mainly when atmospheric lights are not produced by natural causes. Nearly every person on the island has seen it several times, and many have seen it dozens of times, and there is no doubt of its regular appearance as above stated.

--- *The Expositor* (Sturgeon Bay, WI), Vol. 3, No. 16, February 4, 1876, page 1

The shipbuilding, shipwrecks, strandings and all other nautical aspects of Death's Door took place during all four seasons, so any time of the year is a good time to visit this region and experience its intense and extensive maritime history.

BIBLIOGRAPHY

A. Books

Avery, Thomas, and Avery Color Studios. *The Mystery Ship from 19 Fathoms.* AuTrain, Michigan: Avery Color Studios, 1974.

Barcus, Frank. *Freshwater Fury.* Detroit: Wayne State University, 1960.

Barkhausen, Henry. *Great Lakes Sailing Ships.* Milwaukee, Wisconsin: Kalmbach Publishing Co., 1947.

Barry, James P. *Ships of the Great Lakes, 300 Years of Navigation.* Berkeley, California: Howell-North Books, 1973.

Beasley, Norman. *Freighters of Fortune.* New York and London: Harper & Brothers Publishers, 1930.

Bosman, Peter. *Lighthouses & Range Lights of Door County, Wisconsin.* Ellison Bay, Wisconsin: Wm. Caxton Ltd., 2000.

Boyer, Dwight. *True Tales of the Great Lakes.* New York: Dodd, Mead & Company, 1971.

Bowen, Dana Thomas. *Memories of the Lakes.* Daytona Beach, Florida: Dana Thomas Bowen, 1946.

............*Shipwrecks of the Lakes.* Daytona Beach, Florida: Dana Thomas Bowen, 1952.

Burridge, George Nau. *Green Bay Workhorses: The Nau Tug Line.* Manitowoc, Wisconsin: Manitowoc Maritime Museum, 1991.

Burton, Paul and Frances. *Door County Stories and Stories from the Belgian Settlement.* Ephraim, Wisconsin: Stonehill Publishing, 2003.

Christianson, Carl Raymond. *Ship Building and Boat Building in Sturgeon Bay, Wisconsin from the Beginning to 1985.* No place of publication given: Carl Raymond Christianson, 1989.

Clary, James. *Ladies of the Lakes.* Lansing, Michigan: Michigan Department of Natural Resources, 1981.

............*Ladies of the Lakes II.* West Bloomfield, Michigan: Altwerger and Mandel Publishing Co., Inc., 1992.

Cooper, David J. *1986-1987 Archaeological Survey of the Schooner "Fleetwing" Site, Site 47 DR168, Garrett Bay, WI.* ECU Research Report No. 6. Greenville, NC: Progress in Maritime History and Underwater Research, 1988.

............with John O. Jensen. *Davidson's Goliaths, Underwater Archaeological Investigations of the Steamer Frank O'Connor and the Schooner-Barge Pretoria.* Madison, WI: State Historical Society of Wisconsin, 1995.

............*Survey of Submerged Cultural Resources in Northern Door County, 1988 Field Season Report.* Madison, Wisconsin: State Historical Society of Wisconsin, 1989.

............with Bradley A. Rodgers. *Report on Phase I, Marine Magnetometer Survey* in *Death's Door Passage, Door County, Wisconsin, 1989*. Madison, Wisconsin: State Historical Society of Wisconsin, 1990.

Coppess, Margaret. *Island Story, The History of Michigan's St. Martin Island*. Iron Mountain, Michigan: Mid-Peninsula Library Cooperative, 1981.

Creviere, Paul J., Jr. *Wild Gales and Tattered Sails*. Wisconsin: John Paul Creviere, Jr., 1997.

Curtis, Kaye, ed. *Island Tales*. An anthology, 1973?, which includes "A Gleam Across the Water, The Biography of Martin Nicolai Knudsen, Lighthouse Keeper on Lake Michigan" by Arthur and Evelyn Knudsen.

Cuthbertson, George. *Freshwater, A History and a Narrative of the Great Lakes*. New York: The MacMillan Company, 1931.

Cutler, Elizabeth F., and Walter M. Hirthe. *Six Fitzgerald Brothers, Lake Captains All*. Milwaukee, Wisconsin: Wisconsin Marine Historical Society, 1983.

Doner, Mary Frances. *The Salvager, The Life of Captain Tom Reid on the Great Lakes*. Minneapolis, Minnesota: Ross and Haines, Inc., 1958.

Door County Almanak. Bailey's Harbor, Wisconsin: Future Arts, Inc., 1982.

Door County Almanak No. 3. Sister Bay, WI: The Dragonsbreath Press, 1986.

Eaton, Conan Bryant. *Death's Door, The Pursuit of a Legend*. Washington Island, Wisconsin: Conan Bryant Eaton, 1967. Revised editions 1974 and 1980.

.... *Rock Island*. Washington Island, Wisconsin: Conan Bryant Eaton, 1969. Revised edition 1979.

.... *The Naming*. Washington Island, Wisconsin: Conan Bryant Eaton, 1966.

.... *Washington Island: 1836-1876*. Washington Island, Wisconsin: Conan Bryant Eaton, 1972. Revised edition 1980.

Erickson, James Arnold. *North Bay, Door County, Wisconsin, From Pristine Wilderness to Viable Community*. Freeman, SD: Pine Hill Press, Inc., 1998.

Frederickson, Arthur C. and Lucy F. *Ships and Shipwrecks in Door County, Wisconsin, Volume One.* Frankfort, Michigan: Arthur C. and Lucy F. Frederickson, 1961.

.... *Ships and Shipwrecks in Door County, Wisconsin, Volume Two.* Frankfort, Michigan: Arthur C. and Lucy F. Frederickson, 1963.

Greenwood, John O. *Namesakes 1900-1909*. Cleveland, Ohio: Freshwater Press, Inc., 1987.

.... *Namesakes 1910-1919*. Cleveland, Ohio: Freshwater Press, Inc., 1986.

.... *Namesakes 1920-1929*. Cleveland, Ohio: Freshwater Press, Inc., 1984.

.... *Namesakes 1930-1955*. Cleveland, Ohio: Freshwater Press, Inc., 1978; rev. edition, 1995.

Harrington, Steve, with David J. Cooper. *Divers Guide to Wisconsin, including Minnesota's North Shore*. Mason, Michigan: Maritime Press, 1991.

Heden, Karl E. *Directory of Shipwrecks of the Great Lakes*. Boston: Bruce Humphries, Publishers, 1966.

Hennepin, Father Louis. *A New Discovery of a Vast Country in America, In Two Volumes*. Toronto, Ontario: Coles Publishing Company Limited, 1974 (Originally published by A. C. McClurg and Company, Chicago, 1903, reprinted from the second London issue of 1698).

Hilton, George W. *The Great Lakes Car Ferries.* Berkeley, California: Howell-North, 1962.

Hirthe, Walter M. and Mary K. *Schooner Days in Door County.* Minneapolis: Voyageur Press, Inc., 1986.

Holand, Hjalmar R. *History of Door County: The County Beautiful.* Chicago: S. J. Clarke Publishing Co., 1917.

.... *My First Eighty Years.* New York: Twayne Publishers, Inc., 1957.

.... *Old Peninsula Days, Tales and Sketches of the Door Peninsula.* Fifth Revised Edition. Ephraim, Wisconsin: Pioneer Publishing Company, 1934.

Jackson, John N., and Fred A. Addis. *The Welland Canals, A Comprehensive Guide.* St. Catharines, Ontario: Welland Canals Foundation, 1982.

Jinkins, Ann, and Maggie Weir. *Sturgeon Bay.* Charleston SC, Chicago IL, Portsmouth NH, San Francisco CA: Arcadia Publishing, 2006.

Kinsey, Virginia, and Edward Schreiber, eds. *Fish Creek Echoes, A Century of Life in a Door County Village.* John & Nancy Sargent: Fish Creek, WI, 2000

Kohl, Cris. *The 100 Best Great Lakes Shipwrecks, Volume I.* West Chicago, Illinois: Seawolf Communications, Inc., 1998; second edition, 2005.

.... *The 100 Best Great Lakes Shipwrecks, Volume II.* West Chicago, Illinois: Seawolf Communications, Inc., 1998; second edition, 2005.

.... *The Great Lakes Diving Guide.* West Chicago, Illinois: Seawolf Communications, Inc., 2001.

.... *Shipwreck Tales: The St. Clair River (to 1900).* Chatham, Ontario: Cris Kohl, 1987.

.... *Shipwreck Tales of the Great Lakes.* West Chicago, Illinois: Seawolf Communications, Inc., 2004.

.... *Titanic, The Great Lakes Connections.* West Chicago, Illinois: Seawolf Communications, Inc., 2000.

.... *Treacherous Waters: Kingston's Shipwrecks.* Chatham, Ontario: Cris Kohl, 1997.

MacLean, Harrison John. *The Fate of the Griffon.* Chicago: Sage Books/The Swallow Press, 1974.

Mills, James Cooke. *Our Inland Seas, Their Shipping & Commerce for Three Centuries.* Chicago: A. C. McClurg & Co., 1910.

Mansfield, J. B., ed. *History of the Great Lakes, Volumes I and II,* Chicago: J. H. Beers & Company, 1899.

Martin, Charles I. *History of Door County, Wisconsin.* Sturgeon Bay, Wisconsin: Expositor Job Printing, 1881.

Osler, E. B. *La Salle.* Don Mills, Ontario: Longmans Canada, Ltd., 1967.

Parkman, Francis. *La Salle and the Discovery of the Great West.* Williamstown, Massachusetts: Corner House Publishers, 1968 (reprint edition; originally published in 1897).

Peterson, Charles L. *Charles L. Peterson: Of Time and Place.* New London, Minnesota: White Door Publishing Company, 1994.

.... *Charles L. Peterson: Reflections.* New London, Minnesota: White Door Publishing Company, 2001.

Purinton, Dick. *Over and Back, A Picture History of Transportation to Washington Island.* Detroit Harbor, Washington Island, Wisconsin: Washington Island Ferry Line, Inc., 1990.

Quaife, Milo M. *Lake Michigan* (The American Lakes Series). Indianapolis and New York: Bobbs-Merrill Company, 1944.

Ratigan, William. *Great Lakes Shipwrecks and Survivals.* Grand Rapids, Michigan: Wm. B. Eerdmans Publishing Company, 1960.

Rowe, Alan. *Hollow Pits, Sunken Ships.* Milwaukee, WI: Rowe Publications, 1979.

Sapulski, Wayne. *Lighthouses of Lake Michigan, Past and Present.* Manchester, Mchigan: Wilderness Adventure Books, 2001.

Sholem, Stanford H. *Horseshoe Island, The Folda Years.* Ephraim, Wisconsin: The Ephraim Foundation, Inc., 1998.

Snider, C. H. J. *The Griffon.* Toronto: Rous & Mann Press Limited, 1956.

.... *Tarry Breeks & Velvet Garters, Sail on the Great Lakes of America, in War, Discovery, and the Fur Trade, under the Fleur-de-Lys* (First Book of Schooner Days). Toronto, Ontario: Ryerson Press, 1958.

Stabelfeldt, Kimm A. *Explore Great Lakes Shipwrecks, Volume II Covering Wrecks on the Upper Part of Lake Michigan and Green Bay off the Coasts of Wisconsin and Michigan.* Wauwatosa, Wisconsin: Stabelfeldt & Associates, Inc., 1993 (fourth edition, 1996).

Thomas, Stacy and Virginia. *Guarding Door County, Lighthouses and Life-Saving Stations.* Charleston SC, Chicago IL, Portsmouth NH, San Francisco CA: Arcadia Publishing, 2005.

Treasure Ships of the Great Lakes. Detroit: Maritime Research & Publishing Company, 1981.

Vail, Malcolm. *Tales of Ephraim Waters.* Ephraim, Wisconsin: Ephraim Foundation, Inc., 1956. Published for the 50th anniversary of the Ephraim Yacht Club.

Van der Linden, Rev. Peter J., ed., and the Marine Historical Society of Detroit. *Great Lakes Ships We Remember.* Cleveland, Ohio: Freshwater Press, Inc., 1979; revised 1984.

.... *Great Lakes Ships We Remember II.* Cleveland, Ohio: Freshwater Press, Inc., 1984.

.... *Great Lakes Ships We Remember III.* Cleveland, Ohio: Freshwater Press, Inc., 1994.

Van Harpen, Jon Paul. *Door Peninsula Shipwrecks.* Charleston SC, Chicago IL, Portsmouth NH, San Francisco CA: Arcadia Publishing, 2006.

.... *Jacksonport Historical and Archaeological Findings of the Door County Maritime Heritage Society for the 1990 Field Work.* Door County, Wisconsin: J. P. Van Harpen, 1991.

Wiley, Charles Frederick. *Did the Eagle Get You, Dr. Moss?: A Memoir of Ephraim Summers.* Sister Bay, Wisconsin: William Caxton, Ltd., 1990.

Zurawski, Joseph W. *Door County.* Chicago: Arcadia Publishing, 1998.

.... *Sister Bay, Wisconsin.* Chicago: Arcadia Publishing, 2000.

.... *Sturgeon Bay Shipbuilding.* Chicago: Arcadia Publishing, 2001.

B. Periodical Literature

Barada, Bill. "The Treasure of Poverty Island." *Skin Diver* Magazine. Vol. 18, No. 3 (March, 1969), 22-25, 75.

Bowen, Dana Thomas. "The Green Bay Mystery Schooner." *Inland Seas.* Vol. 25, No. 4 (Winter, 1969), 267-278, 308-309.

Boyd, Richard J., Mike J. Burda and Greg Sutter. "The *Hackley* Tragedy Revisited." *Anchor News* (January/February, 1983), 4-13.

Caravello, Joe. "The Raising of the *Alvin Clark*...and the Fall of Frank Hoffman." *Reader* (*Chicago's Free Weekly*). Vol. 8, No. 27 (April 6, 1979), 1, 28-31.

Chabek, Dan. "Quest of the *Griffon*, Cleveland divers search for ancient wreck." *Skin Diver* Magazine, Vol. 11, No. 12 (December, 1962), 10-11, 48.

Hill, Lee. "Menominee's 'Mystery' Ship, Capsized by Violent Storm, Lay on Lake Bottom 105 Years; Now It's Yours to Explore." *Wisconsin Week-End.* Vol. 16, No. 21 (August 20, 1970), 1,3,4.

Johnston, Joseph E. "Schooner *Alvin Clark.*" *Telescope.* (March, 1959), 3-5.

Kohl, Cris. "10 Great Wrecks of the Great Lakes." *Rodale's Scuba Diving Magazine.* Vol. 13, No. 3, Issue 115 (April, 2004), 43-50, 105.

.... "Flames on Lake Michigan (the *Frank O'Connor*)." *Wreck Diving Magazine.* Vol. 2, No. 2 (Spring Issue, 2005), 30-35.

.... "Great Lakes Schooners." *Scuba Diving Magazine.* Vol. 14, No. 9, Issue 132 (October, 2005), 33-38, 96.

.... "Great Wrecks! Great Lakes!" *Skin Diver Magazine.* Vol. 51, No. 6 (June, 2002), 52-55.

.... "The *Ocean Wave,* Old Shipwreck, New Controversy." *Wreck Diving Magazine.* Vol. 2, No. 4 (Winter Issue, 2005), 46-53.

McCutcheon, C. T., Jr. "*Alvin Clark:* An Unfinished Voyage." *Wooden Boat.* No. 52 (May/June, 1983), 52-58.

Murphy, Rowley. "Ghosts of the Great Lakes." *Inland Seas.* Vol 17, No. 3 (Fall, 1961), 195-201.

Quimby, George I. "The Voyage of the *Griffin*: 1679." *Michigan History*, Vol. 49, No. 2 (June, 1965), 97-107.

Shastal, Eugene D. "Midwest Dive Inn, Wisconsin's Door County Turns on Inland Dive Scene." *Skin Diver* Magazine, Vol. 17,No. 7 (July, 1968), 26-27, 62.

Spectre, Peter H. "The *Alvin Clark:* The Challenge of the Challenge." *Wooden Boat.* No. 52 (May/June, 1983), 59-68.

Van Harpen, Jon Paul. "Shipwreck Surveying Has Big Year." *Door County Magazine*, Vol. 10, Issue 2 (Summer, 2006), 8-9.

Watterson, John S. "The Gilchrist Transportation Company." *Inland Sea*s, Vol. 15, No. 3 (Fall, 1959), 215-221

Whipple, Hank. "The Shipwrecked Schooner *Emeline* 'Makes the Charts.'" Inland Seas, Vol. 61, No. 4 (Winter, 2005), 324-330.

C. Newspapers

The *Door County Advocate*, publishing continuously since early 1862 (thus making it the oldest business in Door County today), proved to be extremely helpful in our quest for detailed shipwreck facts and maritime information in general, particularly from that period between 1901 and 1918 when this newspaper printed the maritime news on page one, giving it deserved prominence.

Various issues of the following newspapers were utilized:

Algoma (Wisconsin) *Record - Herald*
Chicago American
Chicago Daily News
Chicago Evening Post
Chicago Free Weekly
Chicago Herald and Examiner
Chicago Inter-Ocean
Chicago Journal
Chicago Times
Chicago Tribune
Cleveland Herald
Cleveland Leader
Cleveland News and Herald
Cleveland Plain Dealer
Detroit Free Press
Detroit News
Detroit Times
Door County (Wisconsin) *Advocate*
Door County (Wisconsin) *Democrat*

Duluth Evening Herald
Duluth Herald
Duluth News Tribune
Escanaba (Michigan) *Daily Press*
Escanaba (Michigan) *Daily Mirror*
Escanaba (Michigan) *Iron Port*
Escanaba (Michigan) *Tribune*
Expositor, The (Sturgeon Bay, WI)
Fond du Lac (Wisconsin) *Daily Reporter*
Gladstone (Michigan) *Delta*
Green Bay (Wisconsin) *Advocate*
Green Bay (Wisconsin) *Gazette*
Green Bay (Wisconsin) *Press Gazette*
Green Bay (Wisconsin) *Republican*
Labor World (Duluth)
Manistique (Michigan) *Pioneer-Tribune*
Manitowoc (Wisconsin) *Citizen*
Manitowoc (Wisconsin) *Daily Herald*
Manitowoc (Wisconsin) *Herald-Times*

Manitowoc (Wisconsin) *Pilot*
Manitowoc (Wisconsin) *Tribune*
Marinette (Wisconsin) *Eagle*
Marinette (Wisconsin) *Eagle-Star*
Marquette (MI) *Daily Mining Journal*
Menominee (Michigan) *Herald*
Menominee (Michigan) *Herald-Leader*
Milwaukee Journal
Milwaukee Sentinel
New York Times
New York Tribune
North Tonawanda (NY) *Evening News*
Port Huron Daily Times
Port Huron Times Herald
Sturgeon Bay (Door County, WI) *Advocate*
Toledo Blade
Tonawanda (New York) *News*

D. Miscellaneous

Collections of archival materials available at: the Center for Archival Collections, Bowling Green State University, Bowling Green, Ohio (this collection includes the material which formerly comprised the Institute for Great Lakes Research); the Door County Historical Society, Sturgeon Bay, Wisconsin; the Door County Maritime Museum and Lighthouse Restoration Society, Inc., Sturgeon Bay, Wisconsin; the Great Lakes Historical Society, Vermilion, Ohio; the Cris Kohl Collection of Great Lakes Shipwrecks and Maritime History; the Marine Historical Collection of the Milwaukee Public Library/Wisconsin Marine Historical Society, Milwaukee, Wisconsin, particularly the Collection of the late Herman Runge.

Guide to Door County Shore Dives. Green Bay, Wisconsin: Green Bay Scuba Shop, 2001.

Hucek, Tom. "Old Door" County Coastal Settlements. Poster of 19th Century Door County History. 1991.

Illustrated Atlas of Door County. Oshkosh, Wisconsin: Randall and Williams, 1899.

Interviews/Communications with: Jim Baye, Gary Cihlar, Clive Cussler, Dr. John Halsey, Steve Radovan, Jim Robinson, Jon Paul Van Harpen, Randy Wallender.

Janda, Rosie, Editor. *Journal of Light-house Station at Cana Island, Lake Michigan.* 2004.

List of Merchant Vessels of the United States (various years of this annual report).

Marine Review (various issues).

U.S. Dept. of the Treasury, Records of the Bureau of Customs, National Archives, Great Lakes Branch, Chicago, Illinois. Various Wreck Reports, Enrollments and other documents.

INDEX

Words in *italics* denote a ship's name.
A number in **bold** denotes a photograph or a drawing on that page.

ABOUT THE AUTHORS

CRIS KOHL and JOAN FORSBERG are a husband-and-wife team who are Great Lakes Maritime historians, authors and active shipwreck divers.

Cris, a prize-winning land and underwater photographer, has been a diver for over 30 years and has explored shipwrecks in several oceans and all of the Great Lakes. His specialty training includes Full Cave Diving certification. He has English degrees and a Master of Arts degree in History from the University of Windsor, Ontario. Cris has written over 250 magazine and newsletter articles, his work being published in newspapers like the *Washington Post* and the *Toronto Globe and Mail,* and in magazines such as *Wreck Diving, Sport Diver, Scuba Diving, Rodale's Scuba Diving, Skin Diver, Discover Diving, Immersed,* and Canada's *Diver* and *Cottage Life,* and maritime journals such as *Inland Seas.* Cris Kohl has taken part in many Great Lakes shipwreck searches, discoveries, identifications and surveys. His numerous television appearances include being on the History Channel, the Discovery Channel and Chicago's CBS-2. A Past President of the Underwater Archaeological Society of Chicago, Cris was inducted into the prestigious Boston Sea Rovers organization in 2004.

Joan, a native New Yorker who has a History degree, studied at Wells College, Hofstra University and Elmhurst College, and owned and managed the healthcare software firm, Wheaton Systems Corporation. She has been on the staff of Chicago's annual "Our World--Underwater" Show since 1993, and the Chairman of its "Shipwrecks and Our Marine Heritage" branch since 1996. She has written shipwreck articles for *Wreck Diving Magazine* (for which she now works as Copy Editor) and *Immersed,* and she is the author of the celebrity "cook-and-tell" book, *Diver's Guide to the Kitchen.* Joan is a fitness instructor and personal trainer. She is also an underwater model, most often appearing in Cris' photographs.

Together, Cris and Joan love to research shipwrecks and explore them underwater. They give multimedia presentations about maritime history, and they are popular presenters at major scuba shows throughout North America, such as "Our World -- Underwater" in Chicago, "Beneath The Sea" in New York City, and the annual Boston Sea Rovers' Show.

They also produce a quarterly newsletter called "Shipwrecks!"

Cris and Joan live in Chicago, but spend as much time as possible every year in the Door County area of Wisconsin and upper Michigan.

Shipwrecks at Death's Door is their twelfth published book.

284

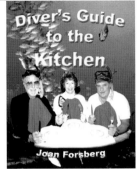

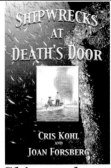

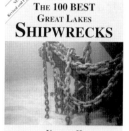

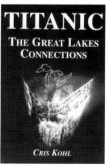

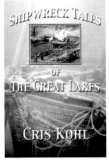
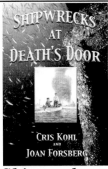